Royal Authority in Anglo-Saxon England

Edited by

Gale R. Owen-Crocker
Brian W. Schneider

BAR British Series 584
2013

Published in 2016 by
BAR Publishing, Oxford

BAR British Series 584

Royal Authority in Anglo-Saxon England

ISBN 978 1 4073 1158 6

BAR Publishing is the trading name of British Archaeological Reports (Oxford) Ltd.
British Archaeological Reports was first incorporated in 1974 to publish the BAR
Series, International and British. In 1992 Hadrian Books Ltd became part of the BAR
group. This volume was originally published by Archaeopress in conjunction with
British Archaeological Reports (Oxford) Ltd / Hadrian Books Ltd, the Series principal
publisher, in 2013. This present volume is published by BAR Publishing, 2016.

Printed in England

BAR
PUBLISHING

BAR titles are available from:

BAR Publishing
122 Banbury Rd, Oxford, OX2 7BP, UK
EMAIL   info@barpublishing.com
PHONE   +44 (0)1865 310431
FAX   +44 (0)1865 316916
www.barpublishing.com

Contents

List of Figures

Contributors

Mark Atherton studied Modern Languages, Medieval Studies and English Language and Literature at Oxford and York and now teaches English medieval literature and language at Oxford University, where he is a lecturer at Regent's Park College and Mansfield College. He has taught at universities in Brussels and Cologne, and he worked for two years on the literary sources project *Fontes Anglo-Saxonici* at Manchester University. He is the author of *There and Back Again: J.R.R. Tolkien and the Origins of the Hobbit* (I.B. Tauris, 2012), *Complete Old English (Anglo-Saxon)* (Hodder, 2010), and *Hildegard of Bingen: Selected Writings* (Penguin Classics, 2001). He has published articles on the cultural background to philology in the nineteenth century and at present is working on word and image in late Old English literature.

Nicholas Brooks was Professor of Medieval History in the University of Birmingham from 1984 until his retirement in 2004; he is the author of *The Early History of the Church of Canterbury: Christ Church from 597-1066* (Leicester, 1984) and of numerous articles and of volumes of edited studies and of collected works. He was General Editor of Leicester University Press's *Studies in the Early History of Britain* from 1978 to 1998 and of Ashgate Publishers' *Studies in Early Medieval Britain* from 1999 to 2009. He is chairman of the British Academy and Royal Historical Society's joint Research Project on 'Anglo-Saxon Charters' and is currently seeing the massive two-volume edition of the *Charters of Christ Church Canterbury* [Anglo-Saxon Charters, 17, 18 (2013), jointly edited with Dr Susan Kelly] through the press.

Marilina Cesario is lecturer in the Earliest English Writings and Historical Linguistics at Queen's University, Belfast. She has published articles on the Latin and English traditions of the *Revelatio Esdrae*, on wind and sun prognostications, natural phenomena in the *Anglo-Saxon Chronicle* and on manuscripts. She has edited with K. Prietzel a special issue on *Holy and Unholy Appetites in Anglo-Saxon England. A Collection of Studies in Honour of Hugh Magennis* (*English Studies*, 2012). She is currently working on a monograph on the Signs of the Weather in Anglo-Saxon England which is funded by the Leverhulme Trust.

Nick Higham is Professor Emeritus at the University of Manchester, since his retirement in 2011. He is best known for his work on early Anglo-Saxon England and King Arthur, including *King Arthur: Myth-Making and History* (2002), *(Re-) Reading Bede: The Ecclesiastical History in Context* (2006), and the Jarrow Lecture in 2011, *Bede as an Oral Historian*. He has recently edited *Wilfrid: Abbot, Bishop and Saint,* to be published in 2013, and with Martin Ryan will publish *The Anglo-Saxon World* with Yale U. P. in 2013.

Christopher Grocock read Latin and French at Royal Holloway College, University of London, and then studied medieval Latin epic for his PhD at Bedford College, University of London, before spending some time in sales and marketing. From 1993 to 1996 he was Project Director of the Bede's World Museum, Jarrow. After working as a museums consultant and freelance lecturer he has gradually been absorbed by teaching, and now works in the Classics Department of Bedales School, Steep, a post which allows him time to continue research writing. He is the editor of *Ruodlieb* (Aris and Philips, 1985), Gilo of Paris' *Historia Vie Hierosolimitane* (Oxford, OMT, 1997; with Elisabeth Siberry); *Apicius* (Prospect Books, 2006; with Sally Grainger), and *Abbots of Wearmouth and Jarrow* (Oxford: OMT, forthcoming July 2013, with Ian Wood). This last volume contains editions, translations and commentary on Bede's *Homily i. 13 on Benedict Biscop, Historia Abbatum, Epistola ad Ecgbertum Episcopum,* and the anonymous *Vita Ceolfridi*. He has also written several articles on the history and Latinity of the medieval period, and has been a regular contributor to MANCASS conferences since 2006. He is Chairman of the Friends of Butser Ancient Farm and a Principal Examiner for the OCR examination board.

Ian Howard read History at Liverpool University. He is a Fellow of the Institute of Chartered Accountants in England and Wales. After a career in industry and commerce, he returned to academic studies and was awarded a PhD by Manchester University. He has drawn on his professional knowledge to explain the fiscal and economic implications of the English coinage evidence from the reign of King Edgar to the reign of King Cnut and he has researched source documentation to improve knowledge of the chronology of events in this period: there is a précis of this work in appendices to his book about *Æthelred II*. Dr Howard's published work includes books about the reigns of *Swein Forkbeard* (Boydell), *Harthacnut* (The History Press) and *Æthelred II* (BAR) and contributions to other books, including *The Oxford Encyclopedia of Medieval Warfare and Military Technology* (OUP) and *King Harold II and the Bayeux Tapestry* (Boydell).

Charles Insley took up an appointment as Senior Lecturer in Medieval History at the University of Manchester in 2012, having previously been at Canterbury Christ Church University. He is Deputy Director of MANCASS. He is co-editor of *Cathedrals, Communities and Conflict in the Anglo-Norman World* (2011) and the author of numerous papers on Anglo-Saxon documentary history. His edition of *Charters of Crediton and Exeter* in the British Academy series 'Anglo-Saxon Charters' is in preparation.

Gale R. Owen-Crocker (editor) is Professor of Anglo-Saxon Culture at The University of Manchester, UK and Director of the Manchester Centre for Anglo-Saxon Studies. She co-founded and co-edits the interdisciplinary journal *Medieval Clothing and Textiles*, and is a general editor of the series Medieval and Renaissance Dress and Textiles. Her books include *The Bayeux Tapestry: Collected Papers*, Variorum Collected Studies Series (2012), *An Encyclopaedia of Dress and Textiles of the British Isles, c.450-1450* (with Elizabeth Coatsworth and Maria Hayward, 2012); *The Material Culture of Daily Living in Anglo-Saxon England* (with Maren Clegg Hyer, 2011); *Working with Anglo-Saxon Manuscripts* (2009); *An Annotated Bibliography of Medieval Textiles of the British Isles, c. 450-1100* (with Elizabeth Coatsworth, 2007); *King Harold II and the Bayeux Tapestry* (2005); *Dress in Anglo-Saxon England: revised and enlarged edition* (2004); *The Four Funerals in Beowulf and the Structure of the Poem* (2000).

Brian Schneider (editor) is the author of *The Framing Text in Early Modern English Drama* (2011) and a number of articles. Entering academic life after retiring from a business career, he was awarded a John Bright Fellowship in 2003, was runner-up in the Louis Martz Essay Competition in the same year, and has been part-time research/administrative assistant on three grant-funded, Anglo-Saxon-related research projects at the University of Manchester and Manchester Metropolitan Universities, including the five-year Lexis Project due to end in 2013. He also took on a management role in three MANCASS conferences, including the conference that led to this volume.

Gareth Williams studied history at the Universities of St Andrews and Bergen, and since 1996 has been Curator of Early Medieval Coins at the British Museum. Within that role, he specialises in Anglo-Saxon and Viking coins, and in other forms of quasi-monetary and social exchange in the period. He has a particular interest in the study of coins in their wider historical and archaeological contexts, and lectures on the subject for several universities. Recent areas of research include the use of coinage in England in the 5th-7th centuries, Viking hoards of the tenth century, the character of precious-metal economies in the Viking age, and the relationship between coinage, Viking camps, and the emerging Anglo-Saxon and Viking towns of the late 9th and 10th centuries. He has published extensively on both history and numismatics, and won the 2008 Lhotka Memorial Prize for his book *Early Anglo-Saxon Coins.*

Preface

Since its establishment in 1985 the Manchester Centre for Anglo-Saxon Studies has regularly hosted international, interdisciplinary conferences, especially an annual Easter Conference. Any academic conference, despite its unified theme, produces different kinds of papers and the 2006 MANCASS Easter conference titled 'Royal Authority: Kingship and Power in Anglo-Saxon England' was not unusual in this. There were straightforward historical pieces, some based on charter evidence, analysing sources of knowledge about royal power; and others which pinpointed loss of power or insecure pretensions to the crown. There were also offerings which teased material relevant to the conference theme out of artefactual and literary sources. For the purposes of publication the material has been divided into two books.[1] This volume includes one long essay, a survey of Anglo-Saxon coins in relation to kingly authority, which developed from Gareth Williams's Guest Lecture at the conference. There are six shorter essays, two on text (Cesario on prognostication embedded in the *Anglo-Saxon Chronicle* and Atherton on the significance of coins in relation to rulership in the Old English legend of the *Seven Sleepers*); and one on parchment production as an indicator of monastic economy and royal patronage (Grocock). Others have been grouped together here because they all present counter arguments to the conference's enquiry into the nature of royal power, showing royal weakness: retirement into a monastery as not simply for piety but as a voluntary or otherwise renunciation of power by an aged or vulnerable king chosen in preference to exile or death (Higham); failure of a king to lead his people against an invading enemy leading to disloyalty among secular subjects and exploitation by the ecclesiastical (Brooks); and the manipulation of the reputation of a man to turn him into a heroic king, when he was no more than a faction leader of doubtful morality (Howard).

The editors are grateful to Dr Charles Insley who kindly agreed to write the Introduction to this volume, which usefully contextualises and summarises the essays.

Gale R. Owen-Crocker

Director, Manchester Centre for Anglo-Saxon Studies

---

[1] The other is *Kingship, Legislation and Power*, ed. Gale R. Owen-Crocker and Brian Schneider (Woodbridge, forthcoming 2013).

Abbreviations

ASC Anglo-Saxon Chronicle

ASE Anglo-Saxon England

BAR British Archaeological Reports

BCS Walter de Gray Birch, *Cartularium Saxonicum: a collection of charters relating to Anglo-Saxon history*, 3 vols. (London, 1885–93)

BL British Library

BNJ British Numismatic Journal

EETS Early English Text Society os original series ss suplementary series

HA Bede's *History of the Abbots of Wearmouth and Jarrow*

HE Bede's Ecclesiastical History of the English People, ed. B. Colgrave and R. A. B. Mynors (Oxford, 1999)

KCD J. M. Kemble, *Codex Diplomaticus Aevi Saxonici*, 6 vols (London, 1839-48)

S or Sawyer followed by the number of the document P.H. Sawyer, *Anglo-Saxon Charters: an Annotated List and Bibliography*, Royal Historical Society Guides and Handbooks 8 (London, 1968), revised version at http://www.esawyer. org.uk

TRHS Transactions of the Royal Historical Society

Chapter 1 Introduction

Charles Insley

The *Chronicon* of John of Worcester rather gleefully records in February 1014 the death, in great pain, of Swein Forkbeard, king of the English, who had forced King Æthelred II into exile the previous year.[1] Although the C text of the *Anglo-Saxon Chronicle* records Swein's death very briefly, without any elaboration, according to the *Worcester Chronicle* the tyrant Swein (*Suanus tirannus*) was felled by the spirit of St Edmund, who caused Swein to fall from the stallion on which he was sitting, fatally injuring him.[2] Swein, 'tormented with great pain until twilight', left this life 'with a wretched death'on 3 February.[3] Leaving aside the parallels between Swein's equestrian death and that of another eleventh-century tyrant, William the Conqueror, Swein's demise caused a political crisis. His recent seizure of the English kingship left his son Cnut, then based in Gainsborough, extremely exposed, and the English political establishment, who had so recently sworn oaths to Swein, instead negotiated with the exiled Æthelred through his young son Edward and agreed to his return, in the words of the compiler of the *Anglo-Saxon Chronicle*, 'if only he would govern them more justly than before'.[4] What followed is well known, and for the next eighteen months English politics was dominated by a vicious and messy three-way struggle between factions which backed Æthelred, his son Edmund, and Cnut, until finally, by the end of 1016, Cnut was left the last man standing.[5]

Quite why Edmund turned on his father is unclear, although the complexities of his family could not have helped and it may be that Edmund, the eldest surviving son of Æthelred's first marriage, felt in danger of being eclipsed by Æthelred's sons of his subsequent marriage to Emma, daughter of Duke Richard II of Normandy; it was, after all, one of these boys who was involved in the negotiations that restored their father.[6] It is possible that Æthelred was in poor health by this point, since he would have been approaching fifty years of age in 1014 and had comfortably outlived all of his predecessors since Alfred. Given all of the above, it is perhaps unfortunate for Æthelred that, unlike the seventh- and early eight-century kings discussed by Nick Higham in this collection of essays, he could not therefore simply retire from the kingship and enter the cloister. Such action might have precluded the

mess of 1015-16 and is perhaps a salutary reminder that in some respects, earlier Anglo-Saxon modes of kingship may have been more flexible and adaptable than those of the tenth and early eleventh century, supposedly the height of the Old English state.[7]

It is appropriate, therefore, to begin an introduction to this collection of essays, which originated in a conference held by the Manchester Centre for Anglo-Saxon Studies in April 2006 entitled 'Royal Authority: Kingship and Power in Anglo-Saxon England', with Æthelred II, for a number of reasons.[8] First, two of the essays in this collection, those of Nicholas Brooks and Ian Howard, directly concern Æthelred. Second, Æthelred has long been regarded as the quintessential bad king, the 'worst king' in English, if not British history. Since the late 1970s, and David Hill's ground-breaking edited volume marking the millennial anniversary of Æthelred's controversial accession in 978, there has been a lively and successful Æthelred rehabilitation industry.[9] Simon Keynes, Pauline Stafford and the late Patrick Wormald all argued in that volume that Æthelred was a horribly misunderstood figure, whose reign encompassed important achievements in the compilation of English law, and who faced political and military problems that were not of his making and that would have taxed any ruler in his position.[10] All this is true, but one inevitably comes to the conclusion that, notwithstanding these many caveats, Æthelred was just not very good at being king: he lacked the personal skills

---

[1] *The Chronicle of John of Worcester: vol. II 840-1100*, ed. R. R. Darlington and P. McGurk (Oxford, 1995), 476-7.

[2] *ASC* C, *s.a.* 1014; *John of Worcester II*, 476-7.

[3] *John of Worcester II*, 476-7.

[4] *ASC* C, *s.a.* 1014.

[5] See below, pp. 29-35 Howard, 'The making of Edmund Ironside' and Charles Insley, 'Politics, conflict and kinship in early eleventh-century Mercia', *Midland History* 25 (2000), 28-42.

[6] *ASC* C, *s.a. 1014.*

[7] For discussions of the nature, power and sophistication of the late Old English state see: Sarah Foot, 'The historiography of the Anglo-Saxon "nation-state" in *Power and the Nation in European History*, ed. Len Scales and Oliver Zimmer (Cambridge, 2005), pp. 125-2; Sarah Foot, 'The making of *Angelcynn*: English identity before the Norman Conquest', *TRHS*, 6th Ser. 6 (1996), pp. 25-49; James Campbell, 'The united kingdom of England: the Anglo-Saxon achievement', in *Uniting the Kingdom: the making of English history*, ed. Alexander Grant and Keith J. Stringer (London, 1995), pp. 31-47; James Campbell, 'The late Anglo-Saxon state: a maximum view', *Proceedings of the British Academy* 87 (1994), 39-65; James Campbell, 'Some agents and agencies of the late Anglo-Saxon state', in *Domesday Studies*, ed. J. C. Holt (Woodbridge, 1987), 201-18; James Campbell, 'Observations on English government from the tenth to the twelfth century', *TRHS*, 5th Ser. 25 (1975), 39-54; Patrick Wormald, '*Engla Lond*: the making of an allegiance', *Journal of Historical Sociology* 7 (1994), 1-24; Patrick Wormald, 'Germanic power structures: the early English experience', in Scales and Zimmer, *Power and the Nation*, pp. 105-24.

[8] A further selection of papers from this conference, focussing on the origins, development and manifestations of Anglo-Saxon kingship can be found in *Kingship, Legislation and Power*, ed. Gale R. Owen-Crocker and Brian W. Schneider, (Woodbridge, forthcoming 2013).

[9] *Ethelred the Unready: papers from the millenary conference*, ed. David Hill, BAR, British Series 59 (Oxford, 1978).

[10] Pauline Stafford, 'The reign of Æthelred II: a study in the limitations on royal policy and action' in Hill, *Ethelred*, pp. 15-46; Simon Keynes, 'The declining reputation of King Æthelred the Unready' in Hill, *Ethelred*, pp. 227-53; Patrick Wormald, 'Æthelred the lawmaker', in Hill, *Ethelred*, pp. 47-80.

and charisma that were an essential part of the make-up of an early medieval ruler.[11] The king that emerges from the sources (in themselves fraught with problems) was capricious, vindictive and fundamentally pusillanimous, an unfortunate combination in early medieval context.[12] This, in turn, leads to the third reason for starting with Æthelred; the study of kingship itself, as an institution and as a political system.

Much of the historiography of kingship as a political system tends to see it in a positive light, especially in England, where the development of monarchy is ineluctably tied up with the development of the English kingdom during the later Anglo-Saxon period.[13] Past historians have identified particular kings whose kingships were instrumental in the process of 'making' England, so attention focuses on Alfred the Great, Athelstan and Edgar, who are classically cast as 'strong' or 'good' kings, whose rule strengthened and consolidated the nascent English kingdom. In this light, Æthelred is seen as an anomaly, a king whose reign indicates some of the fundamental weaknesses of kingship in the early medieval world: its implicit and explicit reliance on the character and personal qualities of the king himself, for instance, or its lack of coercive power. More recent scholarship has moved away – although not entirely – from the 'state'-centred narrative approach, and explored some of these limitations on early medieval kingship, above all the processes by which the exercise of kingship was negotiated between ruler and ruled and, in particular, the role political elites played in the functioning of kingship as an institution.[14]

Though attention naturally remains drawn to successful or effective kings the essays which follow here take a different course, and explore some of the issues of royal weakness and royal failure; the loss of political power, whether voluntary or not. Two of the essays here also

explore some of the material dimensions of kingship. Much study of Anglo-Saxon monarchy leans heavily on documentary evidence: it is to the narrative sources, along with charters, laws and other pseudo-legal memoranda that historians tend to turn when seeking to describe the shape and texture of Anglo-Saxon kingship. There are, of course, exceptions to this; one thinks of the recent 'Landscapes of Governance' project led by Andrew Reynolds and Stuart Brookes on the physical, landscape history dimension to Anglo-Saxon government, while numismatists such as Michael Dolley, Michael Metcalf, Christopher Blunt, Mark Blackburn and most recently Gareth Williams have demonstrated the vital importance of coins as a source for the study of English kingship.[15]

The conventions of English kingship, as they seem to have existed at the end of the tenth century and the start of the eleventh, mean that Æthelred had to soldier on until the bitter end – in his case his death in April 1016. In the first essay in this collection, Nick Higham explores one of the more remarkable aspects of early Anglo-Saxon kingship: the number of kings who resigned their kingships and retired to some sort of ecclesiastical setting, either to a monastery or to Rome.[16] Higham identifies ten kings who either entered a monastery or went to Rome between the early seventh century and c. 760 and identifies some of the possible contexts. The use of tonsure as a form of political marginalisation was well established within the Merovingian kingdoms by the sixth century and the slow, piecemeal conversion of the southern English beginning in the early seventh century seems to have exported it across the Channel and the North Sea;[17] it is therefore significant, as Higham points out, that the earliest recorded English kings to enter monasteries were kings on the southern and eastern seaboards, whose kingdoms seem to have had close connections with the Merovingian world.[18]

Kingship itself, as a political system, may only have been a couple of generations old by the time the Augustinian mission landed in Kent, and this lack of deeply entrenched conventions may have allowed its norms to be malleable and shaped by the new religious environment in which these seventh-century kings found themselves. There were strong connections between the early English religious houses and the dynasties that ruled and competed for rule in the English kingdoms and it is likely that monastic 'exile' offered a very useful alternative to real, physical exile, or death, as the consequences of loss of political

---

[11] There is a significant body of literature that deals with the reign of Æthelred. For an introduction, see the following: S. D. Keynes, *The Diplomas of King Æthelred 'the Unready', 978-1016* (Cambridge, 1980), pp. 84-231; S. D. Keynes. 'A tale of two kings: Alfred the Great and Æthelred the Unready', *TRHS*, 5th Ser. 36 (1986), pp. 195-217; S. D. Keynes, 'Re-reading King Æthelred the Unready' in *Writing Medieval Biography, 750-1250: Essays in Honour of Frank Barlow*, ed. David Bates, Julia Crick and Sarah Hamilton (Woodbridge, 2006), pp. 77-97; Ann Williams, *Æthelred the Unready: the ill-counselled king* (London, 2003); Ryan Lavelle, *Æthelred II, King of the English 878-1016* (Stroud, 2003).

[12] The main account of Æthelred's reign is to be found in the C version of the *Anglo-Saxon Chronicle*; for the likelihood that the annals for most of Æthelred's reign were composed after the king's death see Keynes, 'Declining reputation', pp. 230-1.

[13] See above, n. 7; in particular, Foot, 'The historiography of the Anglo-Saxon "nation-state"'.

[14] Stafford, 'Limitations'; Pauline Stafford, 'Political ideas in late tenth-century England: charters as evidence', in *Law, Laity and Solidarities: essays in honour of Susan Reynolds*, ed. Pauline Stafford, Janet Nelson, and Jane Martindale (Manchester, 2001), pp. 68-82; Keynes, *Diplomas*, pp. 163-231; Ann Williams, '*Princeps Merciorum Gentis*: the family, career and connections of Ælfhere, ealdorman of Mercia', *ASE* 10 (1981), pp. 143-72; Charles Insley, 'Assemblies and charters in late Anglo-Saxon England', in *Political Assemblies in the Earlier Middle Ages*, ed. P. S. Barnwell and Marco Mostert (Turnhout, 2003), pp. 47-60; Charles Insley, 'The family of Wulfric Spott: a Mercian marcher dynasty', in *The English and their legacy: essays in honour of Ann Williams*, ed. David Roffe (Woodbridge, 2012), pp. 115-28.

[15] There is a vast body of scholarship dealing with Anglo-Saxon numismatic history. For an introduction see M. A. S. Blackburn, *Viking Coinage and Currency in the British Isles* (London, 2011); *Anglo-Saxon monetary history: essays in memory of Michael Dolley*, ed. M. A. S. Blackburn (Leicester, 1986); *Coinage in Tenth-Century England: from Edward the Elder to Edgar's Reform*, ed. C. E. Blunt, B. H. I. H. Stewart and C. S. S. Lyon (Oxford, 1989); see also the collection of essays in *Anglo-Saxon Coins: studies presented to F. M. Stenton on the occasion of his 80th birthday 17th May 1960*, ed. R. H. M. Dolley and D. M. Metcalf (London, 1961).

[16] Nicholas. J. Higham, 'The shaved head that shall not wear the crown', pp. 7-16.

[17] Below, p. 12

[18] Below, pp. 9-11.

power. The motivations of these early monastic retirees is, of course, difficult to recover; a difficulty exacerbated by the ecclesiastical – especially monastic – preoccupations of our main source for this period, Bede's *Ecclesiastical History*. Despite this, only in the case of the East Anglian king Sigeberht can we be remotely confident that piety might have been a major factor in his decision to retire. Bede describes Sigeberht as both 'learned' and 'religious' and it is likely that Sigeberht received both conversion and education in Frankia.[19]

Quite when Sigeberht resigned the East Anglian kingship and retired is unclear, although the likelihood is in the second half of the 630s. At this point he may only have been king for a few years and is unlikely to have been elderly. Piety may certainly have played its part in Sigeberht's decision but, as Higham argues, the complex web of dynastic politics within the early seventh-century English kingdoms also played a major role. Sigeberht seems to have benefited in his early years from association with the domination of the southern English by the Deiran king Edwin; Edwin's death and the resulting reconfiguration of alliances and political hierarchies within the southern English kingdoms – in particular the emergence of the Mercian king Penda as a major actor on the political stage – seems to have made things much less propitious for Sigeberht and it may be that his resignation was related to this, as well as the nascent power of Edwin's Northumbrian rival, Oswald.[20] Sigeberht's retirement may have been a way to defuse hostility towards the East Anglian kingdom by the new Northumbrian regime. If this was the case, it seems to have worked; however, when Penda turned his attention to East Anglia, Sigeberht's aristocracy dragged him from his monastic seclusion and forced him to lead the East Anglian army in battle against the Mercians. The outcome was, perhaps, as tragic as it was predictable: Sigeberht, armed only with a stick, was cut down during the rout of the East Anglians by Penda's army.

Beyond individual piety, attention seems to focus on either advancing years or political circumstance as the main reasons for a king entering the cloister. Old age or, at least, an awareness of illness or impending death accounts, according to Higham, for half of the ten kings he identifies. A factor that is often overlooked in this sort of retirement is the ability it gave the retiree to have some sort of involvement of the choice of successor. In this context, retirement can be seen as a mechanism for managing the smooth transition of power in an often unstable political environment and where principles of succession were still highly fluid. Of course, as in Frankia, it seems likely that not all those who were tonsured were subjected to it voluntarily, although only in the case of the Northumbrian king Ceolwulf, in 731, is there clear evidence of a king being tonsured against his will, albeit temporarily in Ceolwulf's case.[21]

The next two essays move the focus of this collection forward three centuries from the early days of Christian kingship among the Anglo-Saxons; Nicholas Brooks's essay concerns the deeply troubled reign of Æthelred II,[22] while Ian Howard's takes as its context the messy aftermath of Æthelred's death in 1016 and the factional wrangle that ensued.[23] The centrepiece of Brooks's contribution is the will of an Essex thegn called Æthelric of Bocking, and the wrangle over whether the provisions of the will should stand in the light of Æthelric's treasons.[24] Brooks uses this dispute to highlight some of the weaknesses of Æthelred's kingship: its military incompetence and lack of leadership and the king's inability to stand up to his ecclesiastics.

What is striking about Brooks's contribution is what it reveals about the relationship between a king and his senior ecclesiastics. Much of the accepted wisdom about the tenth-century English kingdom stresses the very close and harmonious relationship between kings and senior churchmen as a critical ingredient in the function of the kingdom. Episodes where kings had poor relationships with senior clerics seem to have been few and far between. Athelstan seems to have enjoyed a cool relationship with Bishop Frithestan of Winchester (d.931) and, more generally, the Old and New Minster Winchester communities, while Eadwig notoriously fell out with St Dunstan, who spent time in exile as a result.[25] The apogee of church-state harmony seems to have been during the quasi-monastic kingship of Æthelred's father Edgar, a relationship admirably demonstrated by the frontispiece to the *Regularis Concordia*, showing Edgar flanked by Saints Dunstan and Æthelwold, jointly issuing the revised English rule.[26]

The case of Æthelric's will, however, shows the subversion of this relationship.[27] Æthelric died at some point in *c.* 995 or 996, having earlier incurred the king's wrath for his treasonable dealings with the Danes; Æthelric was accused of having plotted to receive Swein Forkbeard in Essex.[28] Brooks argues that this treachery was part of the same sequence of events that saw an East Saxon army under Ealdorman Byrhtnoth wiped out at Maldon in the summer of 991. Æthelric's will now proved to be a bone of contention. No formal charges had been brought

[19] Bede, *Historia Ecclesiastica*, II.15; III.18; below, pp. 00-00.
[20] Below, pp. 9-10.
[21] Below, p. 16.

[22] N. P. Brooks, 'Treachery in Essex in the 990s: the case of Æthelric of Bocking', pp. 17-27.
[23] I. Howard, 'Promoting royal authority in Anglo-Saxon England: the making of Edmund Ironside', pp. 29-35.
[24] S 1501 (will), S 939 (confirmation).
[25] *The Liber Vitae of the New Minster and Hyde Abbey, Winchester*, ed. S. Keynes (Copenhagen, 1996), pp. 19-22; The *Life of St. Dunstan*, in *EHD* I, pp. 900-1; Pauline Stafford, *Unification and Conquest: a political and social history of England in the tenth and eleventh centuries* (London, 1989), pp. 45-9.
[26] London, British Library, MS. Cotton Tiberius A. iii, fol. 2v; Catherine E. Karkov, *The Ruler Portraits of Anglo-Saxon England* (Woodbridge, 2004), pp. 86-7, 95; R. Deshman, '*Benedictus monarcha et monarchos*: early medieval ruler theology and the Anglo-Saxon reform', *Frühmittelalterliche Studien* 22 (1988), pp. 204-40 at p. 207.
[27] S 939; *The Charters of Christ Church Canterbury*, ed. N. P. Brooks and S. E. Kelly, Anglo-Saxon Charters 18 (Oxford, forthcoming 2013), nos. 136-7.
[28] Below, p. 20.

against Æthelric during his lifetime; although his treasons were widely known, Æthelric and his wife Leofwynn had enlisted powerful advocates in the form of Archbishop Sigeric and Bishop Ælfstan of London. After his death, however, it was likely that Æthelric's lands would be forfeit. His will made bequest of Bocking to Canterbury Christ Church and his widow Leofwynn now promised her 'morning gift' (land in her own possession) in addition to the monks of Christ Church if the king would withdraw the charge. In this Archbishop Sigeric's successor, Ælfric, seems to have acted as Leofwynn's patron. This strategy clearly worked; at a well-attended meeting of the royal council at Cookham in Berkshire, Æthelric's will and its provisions were allowed to stand.

This episode tends to attract relatively little comment and what comment it does attract tends to focus on the treachery of Æthelric as indicative of the wider problems of aristocratic loyalty faced by Æthelred. Such comment is fair; Æthelric's actions fall into a wider pattern of elite ambivalence towards Æthelred in the face of renewed Scandinavian attack.[29] However, the significance of the Cookham meeting, as Brooks clearly demonstrates, goes far beyond this. Æthelred had, in effect, allowed himself, at a large-scale gathering ('*ealle ða ðegnas þær widan gegæderode wæron ægðer ge of Westsexan ge of Myrcenan, ge of Denon ge of Englon*' ['all the thegns were gathered there from far and wide, both West Saxons and Mercians, Danes and English'])[30] to be browbeaten by Ælfric and forced to back down over the exercise of royal power. Forfeiture was a powerful tool in the king's armoury for securing loyalty and obedience, but in the case of Æthelric's will, the Church, acting on behalf of Æthelric's widow, but also in its own interests, had subverted Æthelred's exercise of royal power.[31] Effectively, he had been made to look weak in the most public of political settings.[32]

Brooks also delves into the possible motivations for Æthelric's 'treachery', highlighting the divisions that may have occurred in local society in the absence of effective royal leadership. There is no record of Æthelred ever having led an army in battle and, as Brooks argues, this may have caused a crisis of leadership. The poem that memorialises the Battle of Maldon of 991 also celebrates the idea of fighting for one's lord and kingdom; but in the absence of effective military leadership from the king himself, dealing with the Danes and making agreements may have seemed a much more logical course of action.

Æthelred's sons seem to have been far more willing to involve themselves in fighting, none more so than Edmund Ironside. Again, historical narratives construct Edmund as a hero in rather bleak circumstances. Ian Howard reassesses the evidence for the construction of Edmund's heroic image and argues that Edmund's image was consciously

manipulated in three eleventh-century sources: the *Anglo-Saxon Chronicle*, the *Encomium* of Queen Emma, and a lost text concerning Edmund embedded in the twelfth-century chronicle of John of Worcester.[33] The reality of the events that took place during 1015 and 1016 is difficult to recover with any certainty, but the evidence points to a highly factionalised political environment, where Edmund seems to have allied himself to powerful midlands and northern lords, such as Ealdorman Uhtred, against his ailing father.[34] Another faction seems to have been headed by Eadric *Streona*, the ealdorman of Mercia since 1007, a man constructed by the Worcester sources – Hemming's late eleventh-century cartulary-chronicle and John of Worcester's *Chronicon* – as the villain of the last years of Æthelred's reign.[35]

Howard suggests that the Chronicle annals for 1015 and 1016 deliberately presented Edmund in terms that emphasised his personal bravery and decisiveness, while the *Encomium*, probably written in the early 1040s, also emphasises his bravery, along with the treachery and guile of Ealdorman Eadric.[36] Howard then turns to the account of Edmund and the closing years of Æthelred's reign contained in the Worcester *Chronicon* and suggests that this was based on a mid-eleventh century account of Edmund's deeds.[37] This account may have been composed during the later 1050s as part of the process that saw the return from Hungary of Edward the Exile, Edmund's son. As Howard suggests, what better way to secure the succession of the son than to praise the father's warlike and kingly qualities?[38]

Underpinning Howard's contribution is the role texts might play in the contemporary and posthumous shaping of a king's reputation. It is also clear that in the later Anglo-Saxon world material objects might also serve a similar function: to represent the king and act as a witness to his power. Above all, coin, with the portrait of the king – crowned from the coins of Athelstan onwards – served to function not just as a store of value or a means of exchange, but as a tangible manifestation of royal power. Gareth Williams's essay underscores the strength of this relationship between royal power and coinage. Although historians tend to see the tenth- and eleventh-century coinage as one of the key manifestations of the Anglo-Saxon state, it is also the case, as Williams points out, that coinage could also highlight the weakness of kings, or fluctuations in royal power. This is especially true in the middle years of the tenth century, when the same moneyers who had minted coin in York and the north for Athelstan now minted coin for the revived Scandinavian kingdom in York; moreover these coins were minted in a distinctively

---

[29] E.g. see Keynes, *Diplomas*, p. 208.

[30] S 939.

[31] Patrick Wormald, *The Making of English Law: King Alfred to the twelfth century* (Oxford, 1999), pp. 306-7.

[32] Insley, 'Assemblies and charters in late Anglo-Saxon England', p. 52

[33] Below, pp. 30-33.

[34] See Insley, 'Politics, conflict and kinship', p. 37.

[35] *Hemmingi Chartularium Ecclesie Wigorniensis*, ed. T. Hearne, 2 vols (Oxford, 1723), I, pp. 280-1; *The Chronicle of John of Worcester* II, p. 504.

[36] Below, pp. 31-32.

[37] Below, p. 33.

[38] Below, p. 33.

different style from the earlier issues, substituting a form (*CVNVNC*) of the Old Norse word for king, *konungr*, rather than the standard form of *REX*.[39]

Williams also offers an interesting reassessment of numismatic assumptions about the *renovatae monetae* generally attributed to Edgar. While there was an impressive level of royal control over coinage in England during the later tenth century, as witnessed by a high degree of standardisation across issues, there is a tendency to over-systematize this and suggest a series of rigid recoinage cycles. Such recoinages do seem to have taken place, but it is far from clear, as Williams outlines, that these recoinages conformed to a set pattern, or even began in Edgar's reign. Nevertheless, as Williams concludes, the level of control English kings of the tenth and eleventh centuries appear to have enjoyed over coinage stands in stark contrast to the highly decentralised systems of other northern European kingdoms of the same date.

Deep royal interest in coin and monetary policy during the late Anglo-Saxon period also features, as Mark Atherton shows, in the Old English *Legend of the Seven Sleepers of Ephesus*.[40] This text, dating from the later tenth century, has received little attention until recently, although it is full of interesting period information.[41] The story is based around the experiences of a group of early Christians, who are walled up by the Emperor Decius (249-51) in a cave near Ephesus, only to wake several hundred years later. When one of their number, Malchus, is sent into Ephesus to buy provisions, his use of antiquated coin is rapidly picked up by the mercantile population of Ephesus, who accuse him of attempting to pass off forged coin. At this point, the real story comes out and serves as a reminder of divine providence. As Mark Atherton elaborates below, the Old English version is really a reinterpretation of the story, rather than a strict translation, and should, in Atherton's words, be seen as 'essentially a document of its time'. Katy Cubitt, in a recent article, has used the story to suggest that the strictures in the legislation of Alfred the Great, Edward the Elder and Athelstan that reeves should be able to read the law that they dispensed were more than just rhetoric, given that the story makes great play of the reeve who deals with Malchus's case referring to lawbooks.[42]

In this collection, Atherton takes a different approach to the text and uses it to explore the culture of urban communities in the late Anglo-Saxon period, and the role played in those communities by royal officials. In the Old English story it is the town reeve (*portgerefa*) who examines the coins and declares them to be out of circulation. If, as Atherton argues, the text is witness to conditions in English towns,

then it is clear that people, especially royal officials, were very aware of issues of currency and antiquity in relation to coin, and that there was a great preoccupation with counterfeiting. Also highly revealing about conditions are the attitudes of the '*cypemen*' ('merchants') of Ephesus, who are suspicious of Malchus's coins but willing to keep quiet if he will share what they assume is a treasure hoard with them. When Malchus refuses, the merchants hand him over to the authorities, and here we also glean some interesting insights into Anglo-Saxon judicial procedure; the role of advocates or warrantors (*midspreca*) and the use of sworn oaths and declarations, all of which are borne out by contemporary late tenth-century lawcodes.

Christopher Grocock's essay takes a different tack, and examines the relationship between monastic book production and royal patronage.[43] In particular, Grocock explores the resource implications of book production for monastic communities, both in relation to the physical plant required for the preparing of the skins, but also the number of animals and thus the amount of land needed to support book production. This in turn leads to the question of what sort of animal skin was used, since the same amount of land would support larger numbers of sheep and goats than cattle. Given the small number of unfolded sheets – two, or at most three – of parchment/vellum that could be made from a single animal, the production of large codices implies very large quantities of animals; Grocock suggests that the Moore Bede alone would have required the output of ten acres of pasturage. The large quantity of animals required for the production of books, especially if those books were produced quickly, suggests a level of landed resources that would have made the major centres of manuscript production exceptionally wealthy. This wealth and the essential need, therefore, for royal support and sponsorship, are underlined by the production of the *Codex Amiatinus*. That the *Codex* and its sister manuscripts required the use of 1,500 calfskins is well known; the implications of this, however, need more consideration. Grocock calculates that were the codices produced in one year, this would have required the output of 1,100 acres, a significant landed estate by any standards.[44] Again, calculations about the Wearmouth-Jarrow scriptorium tend to focus on the number of scribes required, but even the preparation of the skins for use by those scribes would have required significant labour and facilities. All in all, Grocock argues, only royal support could support this level of book production by minsters.

Those Anglo-Saxons who sat 'upon the ground' and told 'sad stories of the death of kings'[45] will have spent much of their time looking at the sky. In the final essay in this collection, Marilina Cesario examines the relationship

[39] Below, p. 57.

[40] Mark Atherton, 'Coins, merchants and the reeve: royal authority in the anonymous Old English *Legend of the Seven Sleepers*', pp. 63-70.

[41] *The Anonymous Old English Legend of the Seven Sleepers*, ed. Hugh Magennis (Durham, 1994).

[42] Catherine Cubitt, '"As the Lawbook Teaches": reeves, lawbooks and urban life in the Old English Legend of the Seven Sleepers', *English Historical Review* 124 (2009), 1023-49.

[43] C. W. Grocock, 'Books and kings: some thoughts on the economic demands on the medieval economy made by the provision of parchment for scriptoria in the Anglo-Saxon world in early medieval Northumbria', pp. 71-85.

[44] Below, p. 83.

[45] William Shakespeare, *Richard II*, III.ii, lines 155-6; *The Riverside Shakespeare*, 2nd ed., gen.ed. G. Blakemore Evans (Boston, MA, 1997).

between natural phenomena and earthly events in the *Anglo-Saxon Chronicle*.[46] The recording of phenomena such as solar and lunar eclipses, comets and other celestial events is a marked feature of the *Chronicle* from its beginnings through to the twelfth century, although, as Cesario points out, Bede also recorded natural phenomena in the *Ecclesiastical History*. For both Bede and the *Chronicle* compilers, these celestial events were directly related to earthly affairs. Cesario catalogues the recording of such phenomena and notes that only in the case of lunar eclipses were such phenomena not generally linked to traumatic or otherwise problematic events. Solar eclipses were often recorded in the same annal as the death of a king or bishop, while comets seem to have been uniformly regarded with horror and portending the worst kind of trouble, most famously the sighting of Halley's Comet in 1066. What is most striking about the recording of these events in the *Chronicle* is the willingness of its compilers to tinker with their chronologies to align celestial happenings with earthly events in an explicitly causal way.[47]

The contents of this volume remind us that the exercise of kingship was rarely a straightforward or unproblematic affair. Anglo-Saxon kings, from the seventh century to the eleventh, operated in highly unstable political environments where the price of failure might well be death, whether at the hands of their own nobility or at the hands of enemies. Nor should we necessarily assume that,

for all the developments in royal ideology and representation between the seventh and the tenth century, the latter period was somehow more stable than the earlier. At first glance, the English kingdom created by the successors of Alfred the Great in the tenth and eleventh centuries seems an impressive organism – and in many ways it was – but it is very easy to overstate its stability. There seem to have been divisions of the kingdom between brothers or half-brothers in 924 and in 957, and between rivals in 1016. In the first two cases, dynastic accident ensured that such divisions would be short-lived, while in the latter, given the silence of the contemporary sources, we can only conclude that the death in October 1016 of Edmund 'Ironside' was immensely convenient for Cnut. We should not forget that two English kings of the tenth century were murdered: Edmund I in 946 and Edward 'the Martyr' in 978. The former's death in a drunken brawl seems to have been an unfortunate accident, whereas there is the strong whiff of factional politics around the latter royal death.[48] Life could be equally tough for royal sons and brothers: even Athelstan, arguably the architect of the kingdom of the English and by most accounts a good/strong king, was implicated in the untimely and watery demise of his half-brother Eadwine in 933.[49] The essays that follow this introduction illuminate some of these darker nooks and crannies of English kingship, as well as using literary texts and artefacts to ask new questions about Anglo-Saxon kings and kingship.

[46] Marilina Cesario, 'Kingship and prognostication', pp. 86-95.
[47] Below, p. 95.

[48] Barbara Yorke, 'St Edward, king and martyr: an Anglo-Saxon murder mystery', in *Studies in the Early History of Shaftesbury Abbey*, ed. Laurence Keen (London, 1999), 99-116.
[49] William of Malmesbury, *Gesta Regum Anglorum*, ed. R. A. B. Mynors, R. M. Thompson and M. Winterbottom (Oxford, 1998), II.139, pp. 226-7; Folcuin, *Gesta Abbatum Sithiensium*, ed. Oswald Holder-Egger, Monumenta Germaniae Historica, Scriptores, xiii (Hanover, 1881), ch. 107, pp. 628-9.

Chapter 2 The Shaved Head that shall not wear the Crown

Nicholas J. Higham

Anglo-Saxon kings who retired into monasteries or to Rome (or both, of course) attracted little attention in modern scholarship until they became the subject of a seminal paper published in 1983.[1] Clare Stancliffe surveyed the practice in pre-Viking England and identified a number of occurrences which she compared with a similar incidence in Ireland but relatively few in continental Europe. She focused particularly on kings in their prime, as opposed to those in failing health or of advanced years, suggesting that candidates who laid down their status while still fit to carry out the various roles of a king may have been motivated primarily by religious conviction. Instances of varying types are commonest in Anglo-Saxon England for the period 685-710, which Stancliffe characterised as one infused with a monastic 'craze', shared by much of the Anglo-Saxon elite. She suggested that Wilfrid and perhaps Benedict Biscop were largely responsible for the notion of retiring to Rome spreading in England, but viewed Anglo-Saxon royals opting for a religious life in part as a consequence of contact with Ireland and in part of the particular nature of the English conversion, in which monk-bishops played such a prominent role in both the Roman and Irish or Scottish traditions.

In this context it is perhaps important to note that kingship is widely thought to have begun among the Anglo-Saxons only a couple of decades earlier than the conversion to Christianity itself. So according to Bede, the East Anglian royal family descended from an ancestor-figure called Wuffa,[2] the grandfather of Rædwald, king in the first quarter of the seventh century, who was therefore unlikely to have ruled much earlier than the 550s. Ida, the founding figure of the Bernician royal house, is of similar date (547-59, according to Bede's recapitulation),[3] and Oisc, titular founder of the Kentish kingship, arguably no more than a generation earlier.[4] It may well be that there were very few kings, if any, before about 550, although Bede does seem to have envisaged *imperium*-wielding kings, so kings who had a degree of authority over other kings (here generally termed 'over-kings') already established significantly before 600,[5] which seems difficult to imagine without at least a scatter of dependent rulers. 'Over-kingship' and kingship may well have developed virtually at the same time but the former obviously cannot have pre-dated the latter. The upsurge in 'princely graves' in various parts of south-east England between about 570 and 630 may well provide a chronology of sorts for the establishment of kingly power but this is by no means as visible in other regions. This may imply that the inception of kingship was elsewhere less clearly marked in funeral practice (in Northumbria, for example). It may also be that the date at which kingship surfaced was somewhat variable across the regions of Anglo-Saxon England, arguably arriving first in territories bordering the North Sea and Channel, from Kent in the south to Bernicia in the north. But the overall point I am making is that Anglo-Saxon kingship seems to have been comparatively new when the conversion to Christianity began in the years around 600, and was still very much finding its way as a social and political strategy in the 620s and '30s. This novel form of social organisation is likely, therefore, to have been highly experimental as regards mechanisms for managing crises or impending crises affecting any particular individual; likewise the problems inherent in the transmission of 'ruler-ship' from one individual or generation to another.

Before the conversion to Christianity, flight into exile, with all its inherent risks, was arguably the principal means by which members of the elite, including members of these newly emerging royal families, might hope to retain life and limb in the face of hostility at home or a successful challenge from a rival. Stray hints in the literature imply that Anglo-Saxon courts and those of near neighbours were fairly well awash with members of the elite currently in exile from their own particular homeland. In practice, of course, many early seventh-century kings — such as Ælle of the *Deiri* around 600, or his nemesis, Æthelfrith of the *Bernicii*, c. 616 — perished violently, either in battle or as victims of dynastic coups. It was often their younger male relatives and prospective heirs rather than they themselves who sought safety in exile outside the family's kingship, as did Ælle's son Edwin and grandson Hereric, and Æthelfrith's sons Eanfrith, Oswald and Oswiu. But there were certainly pagan kings who sought refuge in flight, as Cenwalh of the West Saxons did among the East Angles for three years (where he was then either converted or reconverted) when attacked by his erstwhile brother-in-law, Penda of the Mercians, in the late 640s.[6]

[1] Clare Stancliffe, 'Kings who opted out', in *Ideal and Reality in Frankish and Anglo-Saxon Society*, ed. Patrick Wormald with Donald Bullough and Roger Collins (Oxford, 1983), pp. 154-76.

[2] *HE* II.15: hence the 'Wuffingas'.

[3] *HE* V.24.

[4] *HE* II. 15. V. 24 II.5 has Æthelberht (died 616-18) as great-grandson of Oeric Oisc, from whom the dynasty took the name: 'Oiscingas'.

[5] See *HE* II.5, which has two 'over-kings' before Æthelberht in the late sixth century, which arguably pushes kingship back towards the mid-century. The first, Ælle of the South Saxons, is dated in the *Anglo-Saxon Chronicle* to the late fifth century, but this is a far from contemporary source which should probably be discounted. Ceawlin of the West Saxons, the second in Bede's list, is more appropriately dated to the later sixth century in the *Chronicle*. For the chronology of Æthelberht himself, which remains somewhat doubtful, see Nicholas Brooks, 'The creation and early structure of the kingdom of Kent', in *The Origins of Anglo-Saxon Kingdoms*, ed. Stephen Bassett (London, 1989), pp. 54-74, at 67.

[6] *HE* III.7.

The spread of Christianity offered, however, an alternative form of political and dynastic absenteeism, by which a leading figure, including a king, might opt out of both familial and political life, and therefore from kingship, by entry to the priesthood or to a monastery. Irish adoption of this strategy was ably demonstrated by Stancliffe. It does, however, need to be viewed very much within a contemporary social, political and dynastic setting. Both Ireland and conversion-period England had a plenitude of kingships so it should not surprise us that the practice is more visible in these arenas than in neighbouring Merovingian Frankia, where a single dynasty had established exclusive claim to kingship across a vast area from around 500. That similar notions were, however, alive in sixth-century Gaul can be shown by reference to Gregory of Tours' *Historiarum Libri X*, which offers a pertinent story of dynastic in-fighting in the aftermath of the death of Clovis's son and co-heir, Chlodomer, *c.* 524.[7] Chlodomer's brothers rid themselves of the threat posed by Chlodomer's sons, whom they considered their mother, Clovis's widow Chlotild, to have particularly favoured, by offering her two options: her grandsons should either have their hair cut, so lose the distinguishing feature of the Merovingian dynasty, or be killed. She reportedly preferred their death and two, Theudolad and Gunthar, were despatched, but a third prince, one Chlodoald, was saved, only later to cut off his own hair and become a priest. This story centres largely, of course, on the long hair which the Merovingians sported as a symbol of royal status, but Chlodoald's choice of a clerical career following a visit to the barber's suggests that he was pursuing an alternative path in the hope of avoiding the terrible end met by his brothers. Although the relationship between royal birth and hair length here is rather different from that implicit in Anglo-Saxon royals entering a monastery and opting for tonsure, Chlodoald's choice, and Gregory's telling of this story, does provide an early Frankish analogy to the practice of royal tonsure in England across the next century and a half.

It is interesting to notice that the notion of tonsure was picked up in later Frankia, with Ebroin, mayor of the palace in Neustria, being forcibly tonsured by his enemies and despatched to the monastery of Luxeuil in Burgundy in 673, apparently on the assumption that this would effectively disbar him from office, although he did recover power just two years later and reinstate his young protégé King Theuderic, who had in the interim similarly had his hair cut off.[8] Parallels between this incident and the forcible tonsure of King Ceolwulf of the Northumbrians in 731 are self-evident, and the later incident was perhaps even informed to some extent by the earlier, both in terms of the initial perpetrators and of course also of the victims, both of whom subsequently recovered power.

Why enter a monastery rather than merely accept ordination, as Chlodoald did in the 520s? One advantage of tonsure was that it was a far simpler and quicker process, removing an individual from lay society virtually overnight but bringing with it far less requirement to then take a leading role in the complex ritual life of the Church, and the detailed training which that required. Some Merovingian princes may well have received an education, of sorts, as their Carolingians equivalents certainly did; with a very few exceptions seventh-century Anglo-Saxon æthelings were almost certainly illiterate and without any knowledge of Latin.[9] Tonsure was both the more accessible and the less demanding, therefore, of these two means of acquiring religious as opposed to secular and dynastic credentials. In early England, there are comparatively few royals who seem to have become priests without entering monasteries first,[10] and significantly more who merely became monks, although even their numbers should not be over-exaggerated.

Both tonsure and ordination seem to have been regarded in important respects as oppositional to kingship, so viewed as rendering a particular royal ineligible to rule, because they cut across key characteristics of what was considered to be behaviour appropriate to the kingly role. A king was expected to protect his people, so play a leading role in warfare, but the religious at this date seem to have been excused active military service, let alone responsibility for leadership in war; there is at any rate a noticeable dearth of stories concerning Anglo-Saxon religious engaged in battle, although some did on occasion accompany armies on campaign. Kings were expected to marry and father sons by whom to perpetuate the dynasty and so the kingship, whilst clerical unions were generally frowned upon (although some presumably occurred). Clergy and monks, in contrast, were expected to opt out of familial relationships and switch their allegiance instead to the 'family' represented by their religious community. No children of clergy are known to us from seventh-century England, although such may well, of course, have existed, and clergy and monks were expected to be celibate. Finally, the lay/religious dichotomy to an extent replicated the division of roles between men and women in contemporary society. Men represented the household away from the home, in the assembly or law-court, for example, in relations with patrons or clients, in negotiating marriage or other social alliance, or on the field of battle. Burial with weapons in traditional sixth- and early seventh-century

---

[7] Gregory of Tours, *Historiarum libri X*, in *Monumenta Germaniae Historica, Scriptorum Rerum Merovingicarum*, I, part 1, ed. W. Arndt and Bruno Krusch (Hanover, 1884), III, 18. For a translation, see *The History of the Franks by Gregory of Tours*, II, trans. O. M. Dalton (Oxford, 1927), pp. 101-3.

[8] *Liber Historiae Francorum*, ed. B. Krusch, *Monumenta Historiae Germanica, SSRM*, II (Hanover, 1888), pp. 215-328: chapter 45.

[9] The obvious exception is King Aldfrith, the Northumbrian king who died in 705, but he had been raised in Ireland with no expectation of the succession and was apparently educated for the priesthood before becoming king comparatively late in life. His later reputation in Ireland for wisdom arguably reflects this early trajectory. Generally, see Nicholas J. Higham, *(Re-)Reading Bede: the* Ecclesiastical History *in Context* (London, 2006), pp. 42-3.

[10] Trumhere, who was distantly related to Oswiu, became bishop of the Mercians and Middle Angles in the reign of Wulfhere (658-75), having previously been abbot of Gilling from 655: *HE* III.21, 14; Eorcenwold, bishop of London in the late seventh century, may have been of royal birth and is not known to have been a monk, although he founded both a monastery and a nunnery. Egberht, bishop then archbishop of York, is the next example, although Bede referred to his monastery in his letter of 734.

cemeteries arguably reflects the emblems considered appropriate to those performing such roles at the upper end of a hierarchically organised society.[11] The female role on the other hand lay predominantly inside the household. It was women who were sometimes buried with latch-lifters or what are termed 'girdle-hangers', many of which were arguably keys of one sort or another, or with a variety of implements associated with weaving and activities around the hearth.[12] By accepting either tonsure or ordination, men were laying aside aspects of their masculinity and adopting instead a role which was in important respects closer to female norms. Women, of course, were considered ineligible in their own right as candidates for kingship in early England and rarely seem to have been killed or ill-treated by dynastic rivals, as royal males often were, being seen instead rather as agents through whom the legitimacy of the royal pretensions of one kin group might be transferred to or shared with another. Æthelfrith of Bernicia, for example, apparently despatched the king of Deira then married his daughter and ruled in his place, and his youngest son, Oswiu, later exploited his maternal connections to a large extent throughout his reign (642-70), marrying his mother's niece (Eanflæd) and reuniting the Northumbrian Church with the Catholic world first patronised in the north by the Deiran Edwin, his maternal uncle but his father's enemy.

The first known instance of an Anglo-Saxon royal retirement into a monastery occurred in the second generation of the English conversion, with a king whose contacts with the near-Continent were uniquely close. This was Sigeberht of the East Angles. It is unfortunate that we have not better information regarding Sigeberht, whose activities on the Continent are unrecorded in any Frankish source. Only a generation later, the Merovingian queen Balthild was almost certainly English in origin and quite possibly East Anglian, and her early owner (given that she was a slave) and then sponsor, the mayor of the palace, Erchinoald, seems to have had close links with East Anglia. All in all it is quite possible that Balthild and Sigeberht were in some way related but he goes unmentioned in the *Vita Domnae Balthildis* as in other near-contemporary continental works.[13] We are dependent therefore on a single insular source; Bede alludes to Sigeberht in three passages of his *Historia Ecclesiastica,* (II.15; III.18; III.19) but in insufficient detail to allow us as clear a vision of his career as we might have wished.

Bede depicted Sigeberht as having been in exile in Frankia before attaining the throne, during the reign of his brother, King Eorpwald, and perhaps also that of his father,[14] the

'over-king' Rædwald of the East Angles.[15] Eorpwald's conversion to Christianity was secured sometime in or very soon after 627 by the then *imperium*-wielding 'over-king', King Edwin of the Northumbrians, much as his father's baptism had been a consequence of Æthelberht's 'over-kingship' a generation earlier. However, Eorpwald was killed by pagan rivals among the East Angles and replaced by the otherwise unknown Ricberht for three years (627/8-730/1).[16]

What Sigeberht had been doing in Gaul is not clear, but Bede's description of him as *doctissimus* ('most learned') in *HE* II.15, then *bonus ac religiosus* ('good and religious') in *HE* III.18, if it has any substance, may imply that he had taken refuge in a monastery or similar and received a Christian education while in exile. If he was in exile from before 624, he clearly had time to achieve this. Given the apparently close relations at this date between the East Anglian royal family and members of the western Frankish elite, one might perhaps suppose that he was taken in and supported while in exile by his family's *amici* on the Continent,[17] and a monastic billet might well have been the obvious means. However, following three years of Ricberht's rule, the exiled prince returned (perhaps with Frankish support?) and claimed the throne. Bede makes no comment on the mechanics of this event but this may well have been in the nature of a coup or even civil war.

One might, perhaps, surmise that Sigeberht's cause also had the support of King Edwin of the Northumbrians, the current 'over-king' of all southern Britain (from the mid 620s to *c.* 633), who had earlier been in exile in East Anglia at Rædwald's court and had already interested himself in the religion of the latter's son and heir (as above). Given his own religious affiliation, Edwin might be expected to have favoured a Catholic candidate. There is some evidence to suggest that he shared something of the same Merovingian connections as the East Angles, which might perhaps have given him further reason to support Sigeberht. During the period *c.* 616-25, Edwin married Æthelburh, the daughter of Æthelberht of Kent (died *c.* 616-18) and his wife Bertha, the daughter of the Merovingian king Charibert of Paris, thereby forming an alliance with Æthelburh's brother, the half-Frankish

[11] As Heinrich Härke, '"Warrior Graves"? The back-ground of the Anglo-Saxon weapon burial rite', *Past and Present* 126 (1990), 22-43.
[12] Sonia C. Hawkes, 'The dating and social significance of the burials in the Polhill cemetery', in *Excavations in West Kent 1960-1970*, ed. Brian Philp (Dover, 1973), pp. 186-201, at 195.
[13] Paul Fouracre and Richard A. Gerberding, *Late Merovingian France: History and Hagiography 640-720* (Manchester, 1996), pp. 97-102.
[14] For Sigeberht's relationship with Rædwald, see Nicholas J. Higham, *An English Empire: Bede and the early Anglo-Saxon kings* (Manchester, 1995), p. 191. That Sigeberht may have been Eorpwald's half-brother

derives from twelfth-century interpretations of Bede and should arguably be set aside as a highly non-contemporary gloss on the earlier work. Although one cannot be sure, I prefer the explanation that Bede preferred to define Sigeberht's status by reference to his Christian brother rather than to his apostate father owing to his focus on the exemplary Christianity of this early ruler.
[15] In *HE* III.18, Bede claimed that Sigeberht had taken refuge in Gaul from Rædwald, suggesting that he may have been abroad even earlier than Eorpwald's succession. Writing over a century later, Bede is unlikely to have had reliable information on such details and his comments may imply that he had rather different information from Canterbury via Nothhelm and the otherwise obscure Abbot Esi, to whom he attributed information regarding the East Angles in his Preface, which he was here attempting to reconcile.
[16] *HE* II. 15: whether Ricberht was a member of a rival dynasty or from the Wuffingas is unclear.
[17] The closeness of this relationship, which is admittedly best evidenced in the next generation, is discussed by Fouracre and Gerberding, *Late Merovingian France*, p. 102.

Eadbald, then king of Kent, and in addition establishing significant links with the Merovingian world. That the Frankish end of this connection was still live at the close of Edwin's reign is confirmed by the actions of his widow, who Bede remarked initially retired with Bishop Paulinus and the survivors of her family to Kent but thence sent her son Uscfrea and step-grandson Yffi to Frankia to the protection of King Dagobert, her great-nephew, who ruled all Frankia until he died in 638, because she distrusted Eadbald and Oswald, the new Northumbrian 'over-king'.[18] Edwin's niece, Hereswith, mother of the later King Ealdwulf (663-713), was married into the East Anglian royal family, presumably as a matter of policy by Edwin himself, and after Edwin's death her sister Hild retired there, proposing thence to enter a nunnery in Frankia, only to be summoned home and established at the head of a succession of Northumbrian religious houses by Bishop Aidan.[19] Erchinoald, the Neustrian mayor of the palace from 640, was a member of King Dagobert's maternal family and served as protector of his young son, Clovis II (638-57) in the aftermath of Dagobert's death, and Edwin's brother-in-law King Eadbald of Kent (died 640) may well have married Emma, Erchinoald's daughter,[20] once he had accepted Christianity. Erchinoald's protégé, the apparently Anglo-Saxon and possibly East Anglian royal slave-girl, Balthild (above), married Clovis II in the late 640s, and bore him several sons.[21]

In the background to Sigeberht's seizure of the East Anglian throne, therefore, one can dimly distinguish an active network of political and familial connections between powerful circles at the Neustrian court and the royal families of Kent, East Anglia and Deira, which is likely to have supported and sustained Sigeberht's successful attempt on the throne of the East Angles and influenced the direction that his religious policies then took.

Having established himself, Sigeberht began what Bede describes as a highly fruitful alliance of mutual interest in the Christian cause with a Burgundian cleric named Felix. It seems likely that the same familial connections were working here: Bede informs us that Felix had travelled to England and approached Archbishop Honorius in Eadbald's Kent, who appointed him as the first bishop of Dunwich, to aid Sigeberht.[22] This is unlikely to have been an entirely political appointment. The syncretism of the careers of Felix and Sigeberht, both launched from Frankia, may even imply a degree of co-ordination between them and some degree of support for both from powerful connections both within Frankia and Anglo-Saxon England. It would not be wildly speculative to imagine that they had come across one another previously

in Frankia and had agreed their future co-operation should Sigeberht's bid for power meet with success. The coastal location of the new see on the very periphery of East Anglia emphasises its dependence on maritime connections, with north-west France, Kent and Edwin's territories, which at this date arguably stretched down through Lindsey to the northern edge of the Wash.

Bede's chronology seems to imply that Sigeberht's reign began no earlier than 630 and no later than the summer of 631, although this can be no more than inference. What Bede considered particularly significant was their joint initiative to establish a school, the 'teachers and masters' of which were provided by Felix,[23] primarily one suspects by recruiting from his own homeland, again one might suppose with assistance from associates there. In addition, the Irish nobleman Fursa arrived in East Anglia later in the reign and was given land by Sigeberht on which to found a monastery, at *Cnobhere* (generally but not certainly identified as Burgh Castle), once again, like Dunwich, right on the coast. When Fursa in turn removed to Frankia, probably in the 640s, he was initially given generous patronage and support by Erchinoald, which again reinforces the view that this powerful mayor of the Neustrian palace had an interest in East Anglian royal circles and had perhaps even been an ally of Sigeberht.

It is of course difficult to differentiate Irish from Gaulish and Burgundian Christianity at this date and there seems little point in making the attempt. Sigeberht's own connections and his clerical establishment were clearly a mix of Gaulish/Burgundian and Irish, albeit, perhaps, with an emphasis on the former. Indeed, his connections mirror those of Erchinoald himself. His own name was, of course, one well-known in Merovingian circles in the sixth century, from which it was later borrowed by two Anglo-Saxon dynasties in close proximity, the East Angles and East Saxons.[24] There is something particularly 'Merovingian' about Sigeberht's kingship, therefore, just as there is about elements of the Sutton Hoo treasure,[25] such as the coins from numerous different Frankish mints, which has generally been dated to the 620s, only marginally before his reign. Similarly, the name Erchinoald crops up in south-east England over the next few decades, perhaps reflecting his influence in the 640 and '50s.[26]

Sigeberht is unlikely to have been any great age when he became a monk. If, as Bede claims, he was in a monastery 'for some considerable time' before his death,[27] in the early 640s (certainly before 645), his retirement probably

[18] *HE* II.20. Oswald had every reason to wish to eliminate Edwin's immediate descendants, who might grow up to become potential rivals for the throne of Northumbria, so Æthelburh's decision is entirely explicable.
[19] *HE* IV.23.
[20] Karl Werner, 'Les Rouages de l'administration', in *La Neustrie. Les pays au nord de la Loire de Dagobert à Charles le Chauve*, ed. P. Perin and L-C. Feffer (Rouen, 1985), pp. 41-46, at 42.
[21] Fouracre and Gerberding, *Late Merovingian France*, pp. 97-104.
[22] *HE* II.15.

[23] *HE* III.18.
[24] The name occurs twice within the East Saxon royal house: Sigeberht '*Parvus*' and Sigeberht '*Sanctus*', the latter of whom Oswiu persuaded to accept Christianity in the early 650s: *HE* III.22.
[25] The classic study remains that by Rupert Bruce-Mitford, *The Sutton Hoo Ship-Burial*, 3 vols (London, 1975-83).
[26] Most explicitly as the name of the bishop of London from 675 but several members of the Kentish royal line derive elements of their names from his and may well be his descendants: see Fouracre and Gerberding, *Late Merovingian France*, p. 104.
[27] *HE* III.18.

occurred in the second half of the 630s, after being king for only a few years. This is unlikely, therefore, to be an instance of a king retiring into a monastery owing to the expectation that he was close to death. One might suspect more political motives, to do with shifting patterns of power. As already established, his reign began against the backdrop of Edwin's 'over-kingship', and his kingship is likely to have found favour with Edwin himself, his brother-in-law Eadbald of Kent, whose archbishop collaborated in Felix's appointment, and their Frankish connections in Neustria, which Sigeberht may well have shared. The lengthy crisis precipitated by Edwin's fall, however, *c.* 633, eventually brought to power a very different northern king, Oswald (*c.* 635-42), who established himself as the 'over-king' of all southern England and set about promulgating the alternative of Ionan Christianity, which was in important respects out of step with Catholic Europe. Oswald was necessarily unsympathetic towards various of Edwin's familial connections, despite being related to him quite closely, having apparently inherited his father's feud with the latter's father and having himself been in exile abroad during Edwin's reign, presumably in fear for his life. He aligned himself politically with Dalriada to the north, where he had found support while in exile, and the *Gewissae* or West Saxons of the upper Thames valley, to the south, whose King Ceawlin had putatively preceded the Kentish Æthelberht (whose daughter Edwin had married) as 'over-king' of southern England. While visiting the West Saxons, Oswald served as god-father to King Cynegisl then married his daughter.[28] It is presumably relevant that this tight dynastic alliance was with a family who had in the mid 620s attempted to assassinate King Edwin.[29] This looks very much like the drawing together of those who opposed Edwin's legacy, his memory and his surviving associates, on the one hand, and also Penda of the Mercians on the other (who was emerging as a serious threat to all parties during this same period). Despite Bede's care to write up Oswald in the most honourable terms, this warrior-king was sufficiently feared in Kent for Edwin's surviving family to be despatched to safety in Merovingian Gaul (above). Given that Edwin had earlier intervened in the religious policy of East Anglia, Sigeberht perhaps had good reason to be nervous regarding Oswald's attitude towards his own tenure of the East Anglian throne, particularly since like Edwin he also controlled Lindsey, on East Anglia's northern borders.

Sigeberht may well, therefore, have felt vulnerable to the changing patterns of power in the second half of the 630s and the death or political eclipse of his own *amici*. It is likely to have been with Oswald in power (*c.* 635-42) and allied to the West Saxon royal family that Sigeberht retired to a monastery and received the tonsure. We do not know which house he selected since Bede merely stated that it was one which he had himself founded: it may have been

Cnobhere; one at Dunwich seems equally plausible; but it was much later believed to be Bury St. Edmunds.[30]

There seems to have been a combination of factors influencing Sigeberht, therefore. His apparent learning, his lengthy exile in Frankia and his conversion there are all compatible with the assumption that his behaviour was conditioned by personal piety and by his earlier experiences abroad, but it is also appropriate to view Sigeberht's early retirement as a response to changing dynastic politics and shifts in the fragile balance of power between major families in Anglo-Saxon England and nearer Frankia. The death of Edwin in battle at the hands of the British Cædwallon and the Mercian Penda arguably created difficult political circumstances for both Sigeberht in East Anglia and Eadbald in Kent. Oswald of Bernicia's rise to pre-eminence by his triumph over Cædwallon then alliance with the West Saxon royal house implies the transfer of power to a new network of familial connections spanning Anglo-Saxon England, very different from that which had pertained during Sigeberht's own seizure of the East Anglian throne and development there of a continental-style Church. There is some logic therefore in Sigeberht's making way for a relative on the East Anglian throne who was perhaps less closely identified with this particular circle of powerful families, both within England and the near-Continent; his action achieved a measure of success in that East Anglia seems to have survived Oswald's 'over-kingship' intact and without experiencing active military intervention.

Seventh- and eighth-century monasteries could be very comfortable places indeed, to which retirement might seem attractive at times when political risks seemed particularly high. One has only to recall Bede's king, Ceolwulf's reputation as a retiree who both enriched his chosen house with lands and treasure and popularised the consumption of beer at Lindisfarne to appreciate the point. Entry to a monastery may well have offered considerable advantages to Sigeberht. Firstly he was able to manage the succession in favour of Ecgric, who Bede described as already his *sub-regulus* and his kinsman.[31] He seems, therefore, to have been a close associate and Sigeberht's preferred candidate. The presence of elaborate graves within the Sutton Hoo and Snape cemeteries, the royal palace of Rendlesham, the see of Dunwich and the *wic* at Ipswich all in the coastal area of south-east Suffolk has long been read to imply that the Wuffingas dynasty were centred here,[32] so Ecgric may hitherto have been the sub-ruler of the more northerly 'folk' into which the kingship divided, centred on Norfolk. Secondly he was able to achieve this while preserving his own life and, quite possibly but less certainly, aspects of his own aristocratic lifestyle.

[28] *HE* III.7.
[29] *HE* II.9.

[30] Barbara Yorke, *Kings and Kingdoms of Early Anglo-Saxon England* (London, 1990), p. 71.
[31] *HE* III.18.
[32] Yorke, *Kings and Kingdoms*, p. 70.

The manner of his eventual death, however, reveals that contemporary society was far from accepting of the retirement of a king. Sigeberht may well have out-lived Oswald but succumbed to his nemesis, Penda, who invaded East Anglia probably soon after having defeated and killed Oswald in 642. In the face of invasion by Penda's triumphant army, Sigeberht was dragged out of his monastery by the East Angles, so Bede tells us, in the hope that the presence of so experienced a leader might inspire their forces with confidence.[33] Sigeberht, however, refused to arm himself with anything more than a stick and was cut down in the rout, along with Ecgric and most of the East Anglian warriors.

There is a dichotomy here, therefore, between the understanding of monasticism by Sigeberht, who was presumably attempting to fulfil the expectation of monastic retirement as conceptualised in either or both of Frankia and Ireland, and very different understandings of the same on the part of an only partially converted regional elite, which had difficulty accepting the notion of royal retirement and expected the man who they still felt to be their king to be available for active service on the battle field at a time of crisis. It should be added that the clergy may also have viewed royal retirement with some distrust and even misgiving, supposing that they were then seeking to develop among the converted English an ideology of kingship as an institution rooted in the power of God, not lightly to be set aside by man.[34] Such doubts may well have limited efforts to commemorate such figures as Sigeberht in later Anglo-Saxon England, who might otherwise have seemed ripe to become the focus of a cult.

The deaths of Sigeberht and Ecgric seem to have brought their immediate lineages as kings to at least a temporary end, since Anna, who is the next known king of the East Angles (by 645), was termed by Bede 'the son of Eni'.[35] That said, Anna invested heavily in Sigeberht's monastery of *Cnobhere*,[36] which may imply sympathy for his predecessor, and he certainly continued both Sigeberht's Christianising policies and his familial connections, marrying one of his daughters, Seaxburh, to King Eorcenberht of Kent (Eadbald's son and heir). Another, Æthelthryth, later to become a saint, initially married Tondberht *princeps* of the South Gyrwe, which suggests that Anna was seeking to extend his influence in the fens. Æthelthryth's second marriage, to Ecgfrith of the Northumbrians (Edwin's grandson in his maternal line), occurred after her father's death (*c.* 655), but still continued the same group of familial interests to a new generation. Anna's stepdaughter, Sæthryth, and daughter, Æthelburh, both became abbesses of the Neustrian nunnery at Brie,[37] which perhaps implies continuing connections with important families on the Continent. Anna likewise

maintained his predecessor's opposition to Penda, whose invasions eventually ended his reign and his life.

Unsurprisingly, perhaps, given his grisly end, Sigeberht's tonsure was not followed by a spate of imitators among Anglo-Saxon rulers, although some family members did begin to seek the monastic life (as Anna's several daughters and stepdaughter). It is noticeable that none of the kings converted by Irish missionaries or their English acolytes entered monasteries, which might encourage us to downplay this source of inspiration among the English. There were, however, several prominent retirements in Gaul in the intervening years, which may well have influenced Anglo-Saxon perceptions of the suitability of such strategies for themselves. Firstly the dowager queen Balthild, widow of Clovis II (died 657), having acted as regent for her son Chlothar III during his minority, was forced into retirement at her own foundation of Chelles in 664, which was one of the small number of religious houses which women connected with kings Edwin and/ or Eadbald chose to enter.[38] Then her son Theuderic III was forced to accept the tonsure at St Denis in 673 as a consequence of political failure, but later regained the throne on his brother's death in 675. Other instances were distinctly later, with the emergence of the monk Daniel to accept the throne as Chilperic II *c.* 714, apparently having himself been consigned to a monastery as a child in the 670s. Chilperic was certainly known to the English, being named in the anonymous *Life of Ceolfrith* as the king who welcomed the abbot of Wearmouth/Jarrow to Gaul and aided him on his way to Rome, in 716.[39] Finally, the last Merovingian king, Childeric III (743-51), was 'retired' to a monastery in 751 by Pippin III, bringing the Merovingian dynasty to a final conclusion.

Unsurprisingly, perhaps, we have to wait until the 680s for anything comparable in Anglo-Saxon England, where two instances of royal retirement occurred in swift succession among the West Saxons: first King Centwine (*c.* 676-85/6) was identified as a monk in a poem written by Aldhelm to celebrate a church built by abbess Bugga, his daughter, which implies that he had entered a monastery at the end of his reign;[40] then Bede noted that the as yet un-baptised West Saxon king Cædwalla journeyed to Rome (but not to a monastery) after a reign of a mere two years (*c.* 685/6-8), then died very soon thereafter.[41] Both lived in a region of England where continental influence on the conversion process was particularly active in the mid-century, in part through a series of overseas bishops ministering to the *Gewissae* (as Birinus in the 630s and '40s, Agilbert in the late 650s then his nephew Leuthere in the 670s) and again where there seems to have been a fruitful interchange of Irish and continental Christianity.[42]

[33] *HE* III.18.
[34] Susan J. Ridyard, 'Monk-kings and the Anglo-Saxon hagiographical tradition', *Haskins Society Journal* 6 (1994), 13-27, at 21.
[35] *HE* III.18.
[36] *HE* III.19.
[37] *HE* III. 8.

[38] *HE* III.8; IV.23.
[39] *Historia Abbatum, auctore Anonymo*, 32; Charles Plummer, *Baedae Opera Historica* (Oxford, 1896), I, 388-404, at 400.
[40] *Aldhelm: The Poetic Works*, ed. and trans. Michael Lapidge and J. Rosier (Cambridge, 1985), pp. 47-9.
[41] *HE* V.7, 24.
[42] Agilbert had spent time in Ireland and both Malmesbury and Bosham

Centwine's kingship is entirely omitted from his *Historia Ecclesiastica* by Bede, who portrayed Cenwalh's reign as giving way to rule of the kingdom by *subreguli* ('sub-kings') for around ten years.[43] This omission may have been due to Bede's dependence for his knowledge of West Saxon affairs on the current bishop of Winchester, Felix, who seems to have reported at some length concerning the reigns of both Cædwalla (686-8) and Ine (688-726), under whom he was himself appointed and with whose government he was clearly associated, but who omitted reference to Cædwalla's immediate predecessors, Æscwine (*c.* 674-6) and Centwine, perhaps because they represented very different branches of the royal family from that of his own patron. Bede also omitted reference to the West Saxon king current at the time of writing, Æthelheard, who was clearly known in Northumbria since his obit (739) was recorded in the 'Continuation' Chronicle arguably written at York in or shortly after 766,[44] and again one might suspect the same reason given that reference to his kingship might have fitted naturally into the closing chapters of this work. Indeed, this king remains so obscure today that it is quite unclear even how he fits into the royal family tree.

If Bede's information regarding *subreguli* was to an extent at least correct, then we should perhaps view Centwine's kingship as something of a chairmanship over more localised sub-kings, many of whom will have been related to him in varying degrees, some of whom he eventually suppressed or at least reduced in status in favour of his own kingship.[45] Aldhelm referred to three significant victories by Centwine,[46] one of which, specifically over the western Britons, is mentioned in the *Anglo-Saxon Chronicle*,[47] which implies that at some point at least he was an effective warrior king.

There is no way of knowing precisely how old Centwine was when he retired *c.* 685, but he was probably quite old: his brother King Cenwalh (*c.* 642-73) had been a particularly long-lived ruler (then his sister-in-law had briefly been queen regnant) so he may well have come to kingship comparatively late in life, and he was apparently old enough to have adult children when he gave up the kingship. This might therefore be an instance of retirement due in part to advancing age. However, it may also be relevant that the West Saxon throne was frequently contested by several rival lineages within the dynasty. Centwine had himself replaced a distant cousin on the throne following only a very brief reign and it is very likely that this was a less than harmonious process.

Centwine's retirement should therefore be viewed in the context of the rise to prominence of the exiled Cædwalla. Cædwalla's father, Cenberht, whose death the *Chronicle* dated to 661, seems to have been a sub-king under the overall rule of Centwine's brother, Cenwalh, so Cædwalla had perhaps been forced into exile as a consequence of Centwine's suppression of his family's sub-kingdom. He had apparently taken refuge initially in the Chilterns and then the Weald,[48] where he gathered warriors around him then suddenly invaded Sussex, *c.* 685, and killed the South Saxon king, Æthelwealh, 'wasting the kingdom with fierce slaughter and devastation'.[49] This gained him a military reputation, filled his war-chest and provided for his followers but he was rapidly expelled by the South Saxons. However, it was among the South Saxons that he came across and forged an alliance with the émigré Northumbrian bishop, Wilfrid, who had been employing his time since his expulsion from Northumbria *c.* 681 by converting the South Saxons to Christianity. Æthelwealh had himself been a close associate of Wulfhere of the Mercians (658-75), at whose court he had accepted baptism, who had acted as his god-father and then rewarded him by the gift of the provinces of the Isle of Wight and *Meonware*.[50] Even his marriage to a princess from the royal house of the *Hwicce* is likely to have been due to Mercian policy, given that this was another of their client kingships. Cædwalla's killing of Æthelwealh looks, therefore, like an attempt to exploit his comparative isolation since Wulfhere's death, to challenge the tenure of key local provinces in the deep south by an associate of a section of the Mercian royal family currently suffering an eclipse in its fortunes and at the same time signal his seriousness as a warrior prince and contender for the West Saxon throne.

685 was also, of course, the year in which Ecgfrith of the Northumbrians was slain in battle when invading Pictland. Centwine and Ecgfrith had married sisters (for Ecgfrith this was his second marriage), most likely from the Kentish royal family.[51] Centwine had certainly followed Ecgfrith's recent example in excluding Wilfrid,[52] so they do seem to have been acting in concert, to a degree at least. There was by then a long history of friendship and alliance between these two families, in particular between Centwine's brother, Cenwalh,[53] and Ecgfrith's half-brother, Alhfrith, formerly sub-king of the *Deiri*. One can perhaps detect in these links a political alliance aimed at containing the threat to both posed by the Mercians between them.[54] Assuming that these familial

(in Sussex) had Irish connections, the latter clearly being a small Irish foundation.
[43] *HE* IV.12.
[44] *Bede's Ecclesiastical History of the English People*, ed. Bertram Colgrave and R. A. B. Mynors (Oxford, 1969), pp. 572-7, at 572.
[45] Barbara Yorke, *Wessex in the Early Middle Ages* (London, 1995), pp. 79-84.
[46] Lapidge and Rossier, *Aldhelm: The Poetic Works*, pp. 40-1, 47-9.
[47] *MS A*, ed. Janet M. Bately (Cambridge, 1986), *The Anglo-Saxon Chronicle, a Collaborative Edition*, ed. David Dumville and Simon Keynes. The entry for 682, p. 32, translates: 'In this year Centwine drove the Britons as far as the sea'.
[48] *Vita Wilfridi*, XLII; *The Life of Bishop Wilfrid by Eddius Stephanus*, ed. Bertram Colgrave (Cambridge, 1927).
[49] *HE* IV.15.
[50] *HE* IV.13.
[51] Centwine's very name, meaning 'friend of Kent', arguably points to pre-existing alliances between his branch of the West Saxon royal family and the Kentish kings.
[52] *Vita Wilfridi*, XL.
[53] The *Vita Wilfridi*, VII, refers to Cenwalh as the *fidelis amicus* of Alhfrith and the latter was described by Bede (*HE* III.25) as the *amicus* of Agilbert, Cenwalh's bishop.
[54] Nicholas J. Higham, *The Convert Kings: power and religious affiliation in early Anglo-Saxon England* (Manchester, 1997), pp. 253-4.

connections represented dynastic alliances, the death in battle of Ecgfrith, who had only recently (before 679) been the dominant force in southern England, was arguably a severe blow to Centwine's position, as it was to the Kentish court, and could only encourage his enemies. Cædwalla's alliance with Wilfrid,[55] who both Ecgfrith and Centwine had excluded, should therefore be seen as aimed in part at their respective enemies in Wessex and Northumbria. Centwine's retirement to a monastery occurred, therefore, against the backdrop of a sudden decline in the influence of his familial connections, consequent upon Ecgfrith's death in battle, and the very threatening re-appearance of Cædwalla on the political horizon, now a successful warrior at the head of a vigorous body of men at a point when he was himself aging. We cannot today know just what motivated Centwine, of course, but such circumstances must at least command our attention.

With the influence of both the Northumbrians and Mercians in temporary retreat, therefore, and Centwine taking refuge in monastic retirement, Cædwalla rapidly secured the West Saxon kingship. From this base he then invaded and secured Kent for his brother Mul (although he was murdered there in 687), apparently in alliance with a section of the East Saxon royal family, who temporarily secured east Kent, and himself conquered the South Saxons and the Isle of Wight, all within a year or so, making himself supreme south of the Thames by c. 686/7. His sudden resignation and departure for Rome in 688, then baptism there, was perhaps occasioned by injuries received in the assault on the Isle of Wight, which seems to have been a particularly bloody affair.[56] Bede claimed that Oswiu had hoped to depart on pilgrimage to Rome with Wilfrid as his guide, should he survive what actually proved to be his terminal illness in the winter of 669/70.[57] Wilfrid was presumably aware of this and he provides the obvious link to Cædwalla and may have suggested this plan to him. This smacks, therefore, of the search for a miracle cure for life-threatening injuries, rather than a type of monastic withdrawal.

Sebbi of the East Saxons was the next Anglo-Saxon king who we know to have received the tonsure, but this was at the close of a reign of around thirty years (c. 664-693/4) and in the face of what proved to be a terminal illness.[58] Bede claimed that he had long yearned for the monastic life but had been held back by his wife, only eventually retiring with the aid of Waldhere, recently elevated to the bishopric of London (from 693). Given that Sebbi's death was associated with miracles at St. Paul's, this was perhaps a story which Bede had from his friend and informant Nothhelm, a priest of London who would become the next archbishop of Canterbury. Sebbi was succeeded by his sons, who apparently retained his dominant position among the East Saxons, and the whole episode seems to have made little impact on contemporary politics.

We are dependent very largely on Bede for our knowledge of several other royals receiving the tonsure or retiring to Rome during the late seventh and early eighth centuries. The problem is that all we have is his interpretation of such events, which he offered in terms of his own religious convictions. So Sigeberht, for example, had retired to a monastery owing to his 'love for the kingdom of heaven',[59] and Coenred ruled the Mercians 'for some time and very nobly', but renounced his throne 'with still greater nobility' to retire to Rome in 709.[60] As Bede made clear in his Preface, it was his purpose to lay examples of both good and bad behaviour by Englishmen before his audience, and these are examples of what he proposed to present as exemplary behaviour by royals which he was promoting for present consumption, offered very much outside the political contexts in which such decisions were actually made. Bede is reticent, for example, concerning compulsion to accept tonsure — the sole example that we have, that of Ceolwulf of the Northumbrians in 731, comes from the first continuation of his work, written not before 734 and not necessarily by Bede himself.

It must be suspected, however, that several of the retirements to which Bede referred were to an extent at least, involuntary. Let us take as examples Æthelræd of the Mercians c. 704, then his successor Coenred c. 709, in company with Offa of the East Saxons. Æthelræd had succeeded his brother, Wulfhere, in 675. Wulfhere's seventeen-year reign had promised much in terms of a growing political dominance over southern England during the 660s but ended in 675 following ignominious defeat at the hands of Ecgfrith and the Northumbrians, which forced him to pay tribute and cede Lindsey.[61] Æthelræd initially stabilised his regime by marrying Ecgfrith's sister and asserted himself militarily by invading Kent, but then defeated Ecgfrith near the Trent in 679, thereby regaining Lindsey. His reign likewise promised much, therefore. He and his Northumbrian wife championed the cult of her uncle, St. Oswald, who seems to have been out of favour at the Northumbrian court (where Edwin's cult seems to have been being fostered); they recovered his reputed body from the vicinity of the battlefield where he had been slain by Æthelræd's father, Penda, in 642 and translated it to the monastery of Bardney, in Lindsey, which they enriched, so commemorating the recovery of the province.[62] Despite his success against the northerners in 679, however, and the diminution of Northumbrian power following Ecgfrith's death in battle in 685, Æthelræd's reign coincided with the rise of West Saxon hegemony across southern England, from Devon and Somerset to Sussex, Surrey, Kent, London and even Essex, under Cædwalla (685/6-88) then, albeit to a slightly lesser extent, under Ine (688-726). The marriage between Ine's sister, Cuthburg and Ecgfrith's successor, King Aldfrith of the Northumbrians (685-705), arguably cemented a long-lived alliance between the

[55] As described in the *Vita Wilfridi*, XLII; *HE* IV.15 (14), 16 (14).
[56] Yorke, *Kings and Kingdoms*, p. 137.
[57] *HE* IV.5.
[58] *HE* IV.11.
[59] *HE* III.18.
[60] *HE* V.19.
[61] *Vita Wilfridi*, XX.
[62] *HE* III.11.

two kings to keep Mercian ambitions in check. The long peace between Northumbria and Mercia on which Bede commented perhaps owed more to this strategy than any particular commitment on either side to the peace treaty which Archbishop Theodore had negotiated between them in 680.[63] Cædwalla's successful conquests, therefore, Ine's long-term dominance and West Saxon control of London and its diocese for a generation, marked a decline of Mercian influence in southern England. While Æthelræd does seem to have successfully regained a degree of influence among the East Saxons, attempts to re-establish control of eastern Kent had failed by 691, when King Wihtred regained control, much to Bede's approval.[64] Eorcenwold, bishop of London from 675 and founder of Chertsey and Barking, was perhaps a member of the Kentish royal house;[65] that he was named as 'my bishop' in the preface to Ine's Law Code implies a close association with the West Saxon king. The West Saxon Queen Cuthburg's retirement from Northumbria to the nunnery at Barking and the rule there of Eorcenwold's sister even before her husband Aldfrith's death in 705 affirms this shadowy alliance between the royal families of Wessex, Northumbria and Kent at this date, and is witness too to their collective influence in western Essex. Æthelræd was therefore confronted throughout the bulk of his long kingship by a network of familial connections between the courts of Northumbria, Wessex and Kent which constrained his room for manoeuvre and much reduced his influence outside Mercia, most noticeably in parts of south-east England where his brother and predecessor, Wulfhere, had previously exercised considerable authority.

In 697, Æthelræd suffered the loss of his wife, Osthryth, murdered by Mercians unspecified,[66] and eventually himself retired to Bardney in 704,[67] closing a reign of thirty-one years at the one place which symbolised his only lasting achievement, the recovery of Lindsey. A military reputation was arguably the surest way of maintaining an individual in power, but Æthelræd had achieved few if any successes over the last two decades of his reign, despite his best efforts to support Bishop Wilfrid in his struggle against the Northumbrian court to regain his position and assets.[68] The queen's murder and the subsequent accession of his nephew, Wulfhere's son, when he himself had at least one son living, suggests that his retirement occurred against a backdrop of discord within the Mercian royal house, from which he stepped aside by accepting tonsure. By so doing, he seems to have been enabled to live out the rest of his life in peace and comfort, as abbot of Bardney, where he seems

to have retained a degree of political influence for some years.[69] Transition with little pause from king to abbot at the monastic house which he had earlier enriched and where he and his wife had established the cult of a relative of hers does not encourage the view that his tonsure was motivated primarily by religious zeal.

Wulfhere's son, Coenred then acquired power c. 704, but not surprisingly seems to have made little impact on contemporary politics. The *Life of Guthlac* contextualised his reign in terms of British raids against the English nations,[70] which implies that he was little feared on the western marches. We know of no significant achievements on the battle field and he resigned the kingship in 709 to retire to a monastery at Rome, being succeeded by his cousin, Ceolred (705-16), who likewise made little impact on history. Æthelbald, from a rival branch of the royal dynasty, then seized the throne, having lived for much at least of the previous reign in exile on the eastern fringes of the realm, where his associate St Guthlac had established himself at Crowland in the fens.[71] This smacks of a very difficult dynastic situation, with both Æthelræd and Coenred under pressure from rivals from other sections of the royal family. While the evidence is simply not there to be categorical,[72] both perhaps made a virtue of necessity and used tonsure as a mechanism by which to remove themselves from difficult political circumstances, as had Guthlac, of course, who was also a member of the Mercian royal house and had retired from the active life of a warrior to become a hermit.

The case of Offa of the East Saxons is somewhat different. This was a young man sprung from one of the regional dynasties which had never attained 'over-kingship' across the seventh and early eighth centuries. Essex was also a kingdom where there was generally more than one king, either sharing a unitary kingship or dividing the territory between them. In the late seventh century, both Mercian and West Saxon kings were courting the East Saxons and struggling to extend their own influence into the area via local associates and alliances. Offa's father, Sigehere (c. 664-88), whose apostasy Bede noted in the late 660s,[73] seems to have allied himself to the West Saxon pagan king Cædwalla, and shared with him in the conquest of Kent,[74] but Cædwalla's retirement to Rome in 688 enabled the Mercians and Sigehere's cousin, Sebbi (above), to regain

[63] *HE* IV.19 (21).
[64] *HE* IV.26 (24), which arguably implies that he was viewed in Northumbria as a potential ally (as his father and grandfather had been).
[65] And perhaps even a descendant of Eorchinoald, mayor of the Neustrian palace, whose name he had in an anglicised form; Fouracre and Gerberding, *Late Merovingian France*, 104.
[66] *HE* V.24.
[67] *HE* V.24.
[68] See, for example, the *Vita Wilfridi*, XLVIII, LVII. Æthelræd was generally Wilfrid's most reliable ally but seems to have resigned and entered Bardney while Wilfrid was still abroad appealing to the Pope for support primarily against Aldfrith and the Northumbrian episcopacy of the day. He spoke up on his behalf when he returned.

[69] Bede remarks that he was made abbot: *HE* V.19. He was later believed to have died in 716; for discussion of the reign, see Yorke, *Kings and Kingdoms*, pp. 105-11.
[70] *Vita Guthlaci*, XXXIV, in B. Colgrave, *Felix's Life of St. Guthlac* (Cambridge, 1956).
[71] *Vita Guthlaci*, XXIV-XXVII.
[72] Yorke, *Kings and Kingdoms*, p. 111.
[73] *HE* III.30. Bede depicted the revival of paganism as rapidly suppressed by Wulfhere's bishop, Jaruman, bringing Sigehere and his followers back to Christianity. This is likely, however, to have had a political context, since Sigehere's ally, Cædwalla, was also pagan, while his rival within the East Saxon dynasty, the Christian Sebbi, was apparently an associate of Wulfhere. Cædwalla's departure overseas and Wulfhere's suppression of paganism at Sigehere's court arguably represent a revival of Mercian interest among the East Saxons.
[74] Yorke, *Kings and Kingdoms*, p. 49, interpreting S 233.

influence across most of the region. Until 693/4, Sebbi ruled the East Saxons and his son Swæfheard western Kent and Middlesex,[75] then the old king was succeeded by his sons, Sigeheard and Swæfred, under the overall 'over-kingship' of Æthelræd of the Mercians. We know very little of Offa's career: he appears as *rex* in S 64, but this was a grant of land in Warwickshire to the church at Worcester, which might suggest that he had interests among the *Hwicce*, perhaps by gift of a Mercian benefactor; closer to home, S 1784 had him granting land in Hertfordshire to the bishop of London. However, although Bede termed him *rex* in the table of contents preceding book V, in the actual narrative he represented him as only an heir to the East Saxon throne, rather than an actual king,[76] which suggests that he was no more than a junior partner to Sigeheard and Swæfred and highly dependent on external patronage such as only the current Mercian or West Saxon kings might provide. Given the long-reigning Sebbi having finally received the tonsure as he approached death, there was a local precedent for Offa's becoming a monk, although Offa was clearly a much younger man. If his own career depended heavily on his association with Coenred, Wulfhere's son, and was likely to be set back severely by Æthelræd's son now gaining the throne of Mercia, then Coenred's abandonment of kingship and departure overseas may well have seemed the point of no return for Offa's own ambitions, hence the decision to travel south in his company.

Our final three examples require little comment. Given that Ine ruled the West Saxons for some thirty-seven years before he retired to the monastic life at Rome (in 726), it seems reasonable to suppose that he was an old man attempting to put his affairs in order in preparation for death, as Bede supposed.[77] Then King Ceolwulf of the Northumbrians survived forcible tonsure in 731,[78] apparently as the victim of a dynastic coup,[79] but himself opted to enter a monastery (later reputed to be Lindisfarne) in 737, resigning the kingdom to his cousin Eadberht. Given that his brother had contested the throne in 718 and then himself in 729, Ceolwulf is unlikely to have been any great age in 737 and certainly seems to have lived on a good while thereafter, but his reign was seen by Bede as highly problematic, so his decision to take the tonsure is very likely to have been influenced by political and dynastic pressures. The final example is that same Eadberht, who according to the continuation of Bede written in the 660s took the tonsure in 758, twenty years after securing the throne, leaving it to his own son Oswulf. Like Sigeberht, therefore, Eadberht seems to have made use of this strategy as a means of managing the succession, although again like Sigeberht this was only successful in the short term; Oswulf was murdered in the following year and the throne passed outside Eadberht's lineage.

Conclusions

Between *c.* 635 and 760, some ten Anglo-Saxon kings either took the tonsure or left England for Rome. Little short of half (Centwine, Sebbi, Æthelræd, Ine, Eadberht) seem to have been of advancing years or even elderly by the time they took this action, most of whom had reigned for several decades (Centwine being the exception but his brother had been king for three decades before him). An awareness of growing age and the onset of infirmity arguably encouraged this form of resignation as a means both to secure their own final days while putting their lives in order in expectation of a Christian afterlife and at the same time determine their own choice of successor. In particular instances, at the same time it is possible to suggest that they were reacting to shifting or adverse political and/or familial realities (as Sigeberht, Centwine, Æthelræd, Coenred, Offa, Ceolwulf). It is impossible to rule out personal piety as a motive but it is unnecessary to view this as a particularly significant factor, except perhaps in the case of Sigeberht, whom Bede seems to have considered exceptionally well-educated. Some chose the monastic life as a means of escaping from an unpleasant and even dangerous situation, but in 731 Ceolwulf briefly had it thrust upon him, apparently as the victim of an attempted coup.

Tonsure seems to have been thought of as capable of providing a form of internal exile, which ruled out the individual as a candidate for kingship while allowing him a form of honourable and even comfortable retirement, in some instances for comparatively long periods. This notion was circulating widely in the early medieval world, including Merovingian Gaul where several royals and numerous other leading figures retired from politics to become religious, again in a wide variety of circumstances, including both freely and forced. The proliferation of this practice in England, and Ireland, was probably due in part to the relatively large number of regional dynasties and the fast shifting interactions between neighbouring kingships played out in the context of both internal and external competition for the roles of both king and 'over-king'. Royal tonsure should also, however, be viewed in the context of numerous other connections between royals and monasteries, both in life and death, and the popularity of tonsure among the upper sections of society as a whole from around 670. One is reminded of such figures as Dryhthelm,[80] whom Bede depicted as entering Melrose with King Aldfrith's help, or the nunneries or double-houses of Barking, Whitby and Coldingham, all of which numbered royal women among their inmates. While exile or death had long been the likely fates of members of royalty who had lost power, the conversion to Christianity provided a novel mechanism by which to escape into a new life in which risks were much reduced. It is not, perhaps, surprising, therefore, to find Anglo-Saxon royals experimenting with tonsure across the conversion period, exploring its potential as a political and cultural mechanism and seeking to turn it to their needs in a variety of different circumstances across several generations.

[75] S 65, in 704, records a grant of land at Twickenham as king of the East Saxons, with confirmation by Ceonred and Ceolred, kings of the Mercians. By this date, his rule was arguably restricted to West Kent and areas south of London.
[76] *HE* V.19.
[77] *HE* V.7.
[78] Colgrave and Mynors, *Bede*, p. 572.
[79] Higham, *(Re-)Reading Bede*, pp. 188-204.

[80] *HE* V.12.

Chapter 3 Treason in Essex in the 990s: the case of Æthelric of Bocking

Nicholas Brooks

The theme of this, and its companion volume and of the conference that gave rise to them cannot be said to have been neglected by historians. Indeed some might consider that English historians of all periods have devoted rather too much of their attention to kingship and to royal authority. The development of the English monarchy and of the English state has long been the dominant concern of political histories. This preoccupation reflects the concentration of the surviving narrative sources upon the deeds of kings and on their relations with their greatest aristocrats – whether laymen or ecclesiastics.[1] In consequence those historians of the early Middle Ages who might prefer to devote more attention to the lives and conditions of those less fortunate in early medieval society – that is to focus upon the ruled rather than the rulers – face severe difficulties . I hope that I may therefore be permitted some modest subversion of this book's theme by examining the breakdown of royal power and authority through treason or treachery during a reign that was a byword for royal incompetence and weakness, namely that of Æthelred the Unready (978-1016). Such at least was Æthelred's appalling reputation until Professor Keynes began his sustained salvage operation to convince us that Æthelred has been much misunderstood.[2]

This essay examines that reputation by focussing upon an Essex man, indeed a man associated with the manor of Bocking – a place that is indelibly associated in the later Middle Ages with heroes of the under-class, first in the petition of the Bocking tenants to Prior Henry of Eastry (1285-1331) against the exactions of the local Christ Church steward and then in the vital role of men of the manor in the organisation of the early stages of the Peasants Revolt of 1381.[3] It is, however, less easy for historians of the early Middle Ages than for later medievalists to study

history from below. Here we may only avoid royalist spectacles by a very modest excursion down the social scale — that is by reconstructing the point of view of an Essex nobleman, known to us as Æthelric of Bocking. This essay takes the form of an extended commentary on two documents that were preserved as title-deeds in the medieval archives of Christ Church, Canterbury, because the estate of Bocking and related properties in Essex passed into the monks' possession. The first is Æthelric's will, perhaps to be dated in or soon after 991;[4] the second is King Æthelred the Unready's confirmation, perhaps in 995 or 996, of Æthelric's bequest of Bocking to Christ Church.[5] The text of both documents and my translations of them are found in the *Appendix*.

The background to these two documents is provided by the campaign which culminated in the battle of Maldon in 991. Our knowledge of that epic struggle derives primarily from two well-known sources: firstly there is an account of the battle under the year 991 in the C, D and E manuscripts of the so-called *Anglo-Saxon Chronicle* or (as now seems more helpful to call it) the *Old English Royal Annals*.[6] Secondly the extant fragment of the renowned Old English poem, simply known as *The Battle of Maldon*, describes the heroic fight of Ealdorman Byrhtnoth and his companions, who chose to fight an invading Viking force by the river Blackwater near Maldon (Essex) rather than buying them off with tribute and who then stood by their commander, even when that fight became hopeless.

The continuation of the *Old English Royal Annals* covering the years 984–1016 in the C, D and E manuscripts has the following annal for 991:

> In this year Ipswich was ravaged and very soon afterwards Ealdorman Byrhtnoth was killed at Maldon. And in that year it was decided that for the first time tribute (*gafol*) should be paid to the Danish men, because of the great terror they were causing along the coast (*be ðam særiman*) The first payment was £10,000. Archbishop Sigeric first advised that course.[7]

---

[1] For an attempt to explain the pre-occupation of the so-called 'Anglo-Saxon Chronicle' with the kings' deeds, see Nicholas Brooks, 'Why is the *Anglo-Saxon Chronicle* about Kings?', *ASE* 39 (2011), 43-70, and '"Anglo-Saxon Chronicle(s)" or "Old English Royal Annals"?', in *Gender and Historiography: studies in the earlier Middle Ages in honour of Pauline Stafford*, ed. Janet L. Nelson, Susan Reynolds and Susan Johns (London, 2012), pp. 35-48.

[2] S. D. Keynes, 'The declining reputation of King Æthelred the Unready', in *Ethelred the Unready*, ed. David Hill, BAR, Brit ser., 59 (1978), 227-53; Simon Keynes, *The Diplomas of King Æthelred 'the Unready' 978-1016* (Cambridge, 1980), esp. pp. 84–231; *id.*, 'Æthelred the Unready', in *Oxford Dictionary of National Biography* (2004), 1, 409–19; *id.*, 'Re-reading King Æthelred the Unready', in *Writing Medieval Biography, 750–1250: Essays in honour of Frank Barlow*, ed. David Bates *et al.* (Woodbridge,2006), pp. 77–97.

[3] J. F. Nichols, 'An early 14th-century petition of the tenants of Bocking to their manorial lord', *Economic History Review* 2 (1929-30), 300–7; for the role of the men of Bocking in 1381, see Nicholas Brooks, 'The organisation and achievements of the peasants of Kent and Essex in 1381', in *Studies in Medieval History presented to R.H.C. Davis*, ed. Henry Mayr-Harting and Robert Moore (London, 1985), pp. 247–70, at 250–5.

[4] *Anglo-Saxon Wills*, ed. Dorothy Whitelock (Cambridge, 1930), no. 16(i) (S 1501); to be re-edited in *Charters of Christ Church Canterbury*, ed. N. P. Brooks and S. E. Kelly, AS Charters 18 (forthcoming), no. 136. For the date of the will, see below, pp.20, 22-23.

[5] *AS Wills*, ed. Whitelock, no. 16(ii) (= S 939), which will be *Charters of Christ Church*, ed. Brooks and Kelly, no.137.

[6] For the need to rename the 'Chronicle' see Brooks, 'Chronicle and Kings?', and Brooks, '"Anglo-Saxon Chronicle(s)" or "Old English Royal Annals"?'.

[7] This translation and all subsequent ones in this chapter are my own. For the Old English texts of this annal, see the relevant volumes in The Anglo-Saxon Chronicle: a collaborative edition, ed. David Dumville

In its present form this annal is not a contemporary record, since the whole detailed account of the years 983-1016, which is so remarkably critical of the king, seems to have been written (or at least extensively edited) in *c.* 1022,[8] perhaps by a clerk who had entered King Cnut's household. It is instructive that the heroism of Byrhtnoth's companions was of no concern to this annalist; the essential matters for him to record were rather the slaying of the Ealdorman himself and the consequent decision to make the first payment of Danegeld — a decision associated with Archbishop Sigeric. The annalist's focus was therefore directed towards the greatest magnates and the decisions of strategic policy made at the royal court. There is clearly an element of retrospective writing (or editing) here. By identifying the first payment of tribute, the author shows his knowledge that later Danegeld payments were to follow. Indeed three themes dominate the account in the *Royal Annals* of Æthelred's reign from 984 until his death in 1016: the activities of the Viking armies, the failure of English defensive efforts to counter them effectively, and the recurrent and growing payment of tribute (or Danegeld) in an attempt to buy peace. Though this account reflects the viewpoint of an annalist writing in 1022 or very soon thereafter, it certainly utilized information that had been recorded previously — very probably already in the form of annals composed by clerks or priests of Æthelred's household. In the assignment of events to successive years and in the detailed order of events within years this account is therefore likely to be reliable, though its interpretation of those events may have been modified with the advantage or pressures of hindsight.

The brief account in the *Royal Annals* might be supplemented by an annal only found in the A manuscript and entered under the year 993, in script of *s.x/xi*, in a space that had originally been intended to receive only very brief single-line entries for each of the years 991–4:[9]

> 993 Here in this year Olaf came with 93 ships to Folkestone, and ravaged the vicinity and then thence to Sandwich and so thence to Ipswich and overran it all, and so [came] to Maldon. And against them [him] came there Ealdorman Byrhtnoth with his army (*fyrde*) and fought against them [him]; and they slew the ealdorman there and had possession of the field of slaughter. Afterwards peace was made, and the king afterwards received him [Olaf] from the bishop's hand.[10]

This annal seems to conflate, retrospectively, events of the years 991 and 994 into one misdated annal.[11] It is therefore uncertain what authority we should allow A's naming of the Viking leader at Maldon as Olaf and its assigning a fleet of 93 ships to him. In the more detailed account found in the C, D and E manuscripts Olaf Tryggvason, the later king of Norway, is first named as a Viking leader in 994, when with the Danish king, Swein (Forkbeard) he jointly commanded an attack on London with a fleet, there said to be of 94 ships. Moreover, that account goes on to assign both Olaf's peace treaty with Æthelred and Olaf's subsequent episcopal confirmation as an adult Christian to that later year. It seems inherently unlikely that exactly 93 ships had arrived in 993 (for 991?) and exactly 94 in 994. In the copying of one or both these figures we might therefore suppose that the scribal error of 'eye-skip' has occurred, resulting in miscopying the figure of ships from the year-number. But it is also possible that essentially the same army and fleet, under the same overall command and with very much the same number of ships, had been involved both in 991 and 994.[12]

That this is a plausible interpretation is suggested by the fact that the early twelfth-century chronicler, John of Worcester (who knew a version of the *Old English Royal Annals* distinct from that of any extant manuscript) uniquely names the Viking commanders at Maldon; he identifies them as Justin (ON Jósteinn) and Guthmund, son of Steita.[13] These same men are also named (after Olaf) as the leaders of the army or host (*here*), with which King Æthelred and his witan negotiated a peace treaty, seemingly in 994, whose text survives as the lawcode, known to legal historians as II Æthelred.[14] This truce sought to establish secure trading arrangements in English ports between the men of the two leaders, and Olaf's army was also to provide Æthelred with military support against other Viking raiders in return for the payment of tribute (*feoh*) and, in the future, of provisions (*fultum*). Though it is conceivable that John of Worcester derived the names Justin and Guthmund from this undated treaty and wrongly supposed it to belong to 991, it is difficult to explain why he should have named these two men as the Viking commanders at Maldon but have omitted the chief commander, Olaf. He may therefore have had evidence that Olaf was absent from that battle. Byrhtnoth and the

---

and Simon Keynes, namely: vol. 5, *ASC MS. C*, ed Katherine O'Brien O'Keeffe (Cambridge, 2001), p. 86; vol. 6, *ASC MS. D*, ed. G. P. Cubbin (Cambridge, 1996), p. 48; vol . 7, *ASC MS. E*, ed. Susan Irvine (Cambridge, 2004), p. 61.

[8] For the date of the annals 983-1016 in C, D and E, see Keynes, 'Declining reputation', pp. 230–1.

[9] For the text see *Anglo-Saxon Chronicle: MS A*, ed. Janet M. Bately, The AS Chronicle: a Collaborative Edition, ed. Dumville and Keynes, 3 (Cambridge, 1986), 79. Note the ambiguity whether OE *him* is here singular, referring to Olaf, or plural referring to the ships and men that he commanded; and therefore whether Olaf is clearly located at Maldon or not.

[10] I.e. he served as godfather at his confirmation.

[11] For the complex deconstruction of this annal and of the apparent 'caret' mark assigning some of its text to 991, see *ASC MS A*, ed. Bately, pp. lix–lxii, and her refinement of the argument in 'The Anglo-Saxon Chronicle', in *The Battle of Maldon, AD 991*, ed. D. Scragg (Oxford, 1991), pp. 37–50, at 37–8 and 43–7.

[12] See Niels Lund, 'The Danish perspective', in Scragg, *The Battle of Maldon, AD 991*, pp. 114–43, at 130–8, and Ian Howard, *Swein Forkbeard and the Danish Conquest of England 991–1017* (Woodbridge, 2003), pp. 32–7.

[13] *The Chronicle of John of Worcester, s.a.* 991, ed. R. R. Darlington and P. McGurk, Oxford Medieval Texts (Oxford, 1996), II, p. 438: '*Eodem anno Gipesuuic Dani depopulate sunt , quorum duces fuerunt Justin et Guthmund filius Steitan, cum quibus non multo post strenuous dux Orientalium Saxonum Byrhtnothus iuxta Mældunum proelium commisit.*'

[14] II Æthelred, prologue, in *Die Gesetze der Angelschsen*, ed. Felix Liebermann (Halle, 1902), I, p. 220 and A. J. Robertson, *The Laws of the Kings of England from Edmund to Henry I* (Cambridge, 1925), p. 56. Robertson (p. 314) identifies Josteinn as Olaf Tryggvason's uncle.

East Saxon *fyrd* may have encountered just a portion of the Viking army, without its principal commanders, at Maldon and have therefore judged the chances of battle to be favourable. But given the uncertainties inherent in the evidence, it would be wise not to put much weight either upon John of Worcester or the misdated entry in A for the identity of the Viking commanders at Maldon or for the size of their fleet.[15] We are left with the only secure information derived from the *Old English Royal Annals* being the ravaging of Ipswich, the battle of Maldon in which Byrhtnoth was killed and the consequent fateful decision, advised by the Archbishop, to attempt a policy of paying tribute to this army.

Turning next to the poem, *The Battle of Maldon*, we find that the theme of the payment of tribute — or protection-money, as we might describe such 'Danegelds' — was also fundamental for the poet. Professor Donald Scragg, who has devoted much of his prodigious energy to the interpretation of the poem, is inclined on balance to place its composition 'within a few years of the battle'.[16] What is particularly evident is that the poem that we have is primarily a celebration of the bravery of named warriors; there is therefore every reason to suppose that it was composed for an aristocratic East Saxon audience — in particular for the benefit of the kinsmen and descendants of those who are named as fighting and dying so bravely.[17]

From line 42 Byrhtnoth rejects the invitation to buy off the Viking host with a payment of tribute:

> *Byrhtnoð maþelode, bord hafenode,*
> *wand wacne æsc, wordum mælde,*
> *yrre and anræd ageaf him andsware:*
> *'Gehyrst þu, sælida, hwæt þis folc segeð?*
> *Hi willað eow to gafole garas syllan,*
> *ættryne ord and ealde swurd,*
> *þa heregeatu þe eow æt hilde ne deah.*
> *Brimmanna boda, abeod eft ongean!*
> *Sege þinum leodum miccle laþre spell,*
> *þæt her stynt unforcuð eorl mid his werode,*
> *þe wile gealgean eþel þysne,*

> *Æþelredes eard, ealdres mines*
> *folc and foldan. Feallan sceolon*
> *hæþene æt hilde. To heanlic me þinceð*
> *þæt ge mid urum sceattum to scype gangon*
> *unbefohtene, nu ge þus feor hider*
> *on urne eard in becomon.*
> *Nu sceole ge swa softe sinc gegangan:*
> *us sceal ord and ecg ær geseman,*
> *grim guðplega, ær we gofol syllon'.*[18]

Byrhtnoth spoke out; he grasped his shield,
brandished his slender ash-spear, declared his words,
angry and resolute, he gave him answer:
'Sea-raider, do you hear what this army (*folc*) 45
is saying?
They intend your tribute to be a gift of spears,
deadly points and trusty swords,
war-gear (*heregeatu*) that will not benefit you
in the battle.
Messenger of the sea-farers, take the message back again;
tell your people (*leodum*) a much harder tale: 50
that here stands untainted, an earl with his retinue,
who intends to defend this native land (*eþel*),
the country (*eard*) of Æthelred, of my lord,
people and land (*folc and foldan*).
The heathens shall fall in battle. Too shameful 55
I deem it,
that you should board your ships with our money without a fight, now that you thus far here have entered our homeland (*on urne eard*).
You will not get treasure so easily;
[spear's] point and [sword's] edge must first 60
settle between us
the grim game of battle, before we pay tribute (*gofol*)'.

Later, after battle had been joined and the aged ealdorman slain, and after the poet has denounced those who fled, we are given a famous litany of speeches by successive heroic English nobles and the names of many others who fought on before they too were slain beside the body of their dead lord, Byrhtnoth . Among these was Edward the Tall (*Eadweard se langa*):

> *He bræc þone bordweall and wið þa beornas feaht,*
> *oðþæt he his sincgyfan on þam sæmannum*
> *wurðlice wrec, ær he on wæle lege.*
> *Swa dyde Æþeric, æþele gefera,*
> *fus and forðgeorn, feaht eornoste,*
> *Sibyrhtes broðor; and swiðe mænig oþer*
> *clufon cellod bord, cene hi weredon.*[19]

[15] Simon Keynes, 'The historical context of the battle of Maldon', in Scragg, *The Battle of Maldon, AD 991*, pp. 81–113, at 88–90 inclines to be positive about Olaf's participation. Alan Kennedy, 'Byrhtnoth's obits and twelfth-century accounts of the Battle of Maldon', in *ibid.*, pp. 59–80, at 71–2 is more cautious.

[16] Scragg, *The Battle of Maldon, AD 991*, p. 6; for the argument that the poem's account of the arms and armour imply concern for the deficiencies of English equipment *before c.* 1008, see Nicholas Brooks, 'Weapons and armour', in Scragg, *The Battle of Maldon, AD 991*, pp. 208–19, at 215–17. For Professor Scragg's earlier contributions to the study of the poem, see his 'Supplement' (Manchester, 1976) to E. V. Gordon, *The Battle of Maldon* (London, 1937) and his own *The Battle of Maldon* (Manchester, 1981). An attempt to date the poem's composition as late as the reign of Cnut on the basis of the poem's use of *eorl* in styling *Ealdorman* Byrhtnoth was propounded by John McKinnell, 'On the date of *The Battle of Maldon*', *Medium Ævum* 44 (1975), 121–36, but effectively countered in Scragg, *Maldon*, pp. 26–7 and Cecily Clark, 'On dating *The Battle of Maldon*: certain evidence reviewed', *Nottingham Medieval Studies* 27 (1983), 1–22.

[17] For the identity of the named warriors, see Margaret A. L. Locherbie-Cameron, 'The men named in the poem', in Scragg *The Battle of Maldon, AD 991*, pp. 238–52.

[18] Scragg, *The Battle of Maldon, AD 991*, pp. 18–21, lines 42–61.
[19] Scragg, *The Battle of Maldon, AD 991*, pp. 28–30, lines 277–85.

> He broke through the shield wall and fought
> against the warriors,
> until on those seamen he nobly avenged
> his treasure-giving lord, before he [too] lay
> amongst the slain.
> 280 Æthelric did likewise, the noble companion
> (æþele gefera),
> brave and eager to be at the front, he fought
> courageously,
> Sibryht's brother; and very many others clove
> the decorated shield; defended themselves
> keenly.

In her edition of the will of Æthelric of Bocking (and subsequently in *English Historical Documents*) Dorothy Whitelock admitted to being tempted to identify the poem's Æthelric with the similarly named Essex nobleman who bequeathed his estate at Bocking to the community at Christ Church, Canterbury. Moreover, both in the will and in the poem the personal name is spelt in the contracted form *Æþeric*. But as Whitelock conceded, the name is much too common, even in this contracted form, to place any weight upon the coincidence of its occurrence in Essex in the poem.[20]

Moreover, the identification seems highly improbable. The Æthelric of the poem had a brother named Sibryht, is described as *æþele* — that is noble, either in behaviour or in blood — and as *fus and forðgeorn* 'brave and eager for the front'. Since he is explicitly compared with the previously mentioned Edward the Tall, the clear implication is that Æthelric shared Edward's honourable death in the battle. The Æthelric who inherited Bocking from his father does not fit that pattern. His will mentions no siblings at all — though there may have been special reasons for that, as we shall see. More crucially King Æthelred's confirmation in 995x6 of Æthelric's bequest of Bocking to the Christ Church community (*Appendix*, II) specifies that many years before Æthelric's death the king had been informed of his involvement 'in the plot that Swein should be received in Essex, when he first came thither with a fleet' and that the king had informed Archbishop Sigeric.[21] We cannot be certain to which year this charge relates. In the *Royal Annals* the first mention of Swein is when he and Olaf Tryggvason are described as leading a fleet to London on 8 September 994; when repulsed there, they are said to have subsequently ravaged along the coasts of Essex, Kent, Sussex and Hampshire.[22] But that cannot have been the campaign in question, since notorious dealings with Swein in that year would have been very recent events, and there would scarcely

have been time for the news to pass to the king and for him to inform Æthelric's advocate, Archbishop Sigeric, before the latter's death on 28 October 994.[23] Given our uncertainty about the Viking commanders and their strategy in 991, it seems much more likely that Swein had also been involved in some capacity in the Maldon campaign and that Æthelric, the owner of Bocking, was charged with having treated with him at some stage before the battle at Maldon. It is also conceivable that the charge related to an earlier campaign of Swein, which happens not to be mentioned in any extant source, either in 989 or 990 (since Æthelric's involvement would need to have come to light within Sigeric's pontificate, 990–4). But had Swein first brought a fleet to Essex in 989 or 990, it still seems highly improbable that the *Maldon* poet could have referred to Æthelric, brother of Sibryht, so favourably had he been a man suspected of recent treacherous liaison with the Danish king. We may surely conclude that Æthelric of Bocking had not been killed among the heroes of the battle of Maldon.

In company with all extant Old English wills, Æthelric's will (*Appendix*, no. I) bears no date and has to be dated from internal evidence. The mention of Bishop Ælfstan of London, to whom Æthelric bequeaths land at Copford and at Glazen (both in Essex) provides a *terminus post quem* for the will between 959 (when Dunstan last attests as bishop of London)[24] and 963, the first attestation of Ælfstan as bishop.[25] The will must also be dated before Ælfstan's death, which occurred in 995 or 996.[26] If the lord, to whom Æthelric makes a formal payment of weapons and gold at the start of the will, was King Æthelred II, then the will could be dated after that king's accession in 979. It is argued below not only that Æthelred was that lord, but that the will should probably be dated soon after the battle of Maldon, certainly between 991 and 995x6; but to establish that we must first understand the will's content more fully.

As is customary, the will begins by specifying a payment of weapons, arms and moneys, due to the testator's lord — a payment which in other wills is termed 'heriot' (*heregeatu*), i.e. 'war-gear'. Such payments seem to have involved the return to the lord of equipment and resources that the man had received on entering the lord's service.[27] Such payments of heriot were understood to be necessary to ensure that the lord for his part oversaw the carrying out of his man's wishes for the disposal of his property. Æthelric's heriot comprised a payment of 60 mancuses of

[20] Whitelock, *Wills*, p. 147; *English Historical Documents*, I, *c. 550–1042*, ed. D. Whitelock, 2nd ed. (London, 1979), p.579. Scragg, *Maldon*, p.108 and J. McKinnell, 'Date', p.128 both accepted the identification, but it is decisively rejected by Margaret Lockerbie-Cameron, 'The men named in the poem', pp. 242–3, who also lists several known contemporary Æthelrics.

[21] Archbishop Sigeric's pontificate — from 990 (after 13 February) until his death on 28 October 994 — provides the only guide to the date of the king's knowledge of the charge against Æthelric.

[22] *ASC*, 994 CDE.

[23] For the date of Sigeric's death, see Nicholas Brooks, *The Early History of the Church of Canterbury* (Leicester, 1984), pp. 278–9 and p. 383 nn. 58, 63.

[24] BCS 1052 (S 681).

[25] BCS 1101 (S 717). Ælfstan's consecration to the see of London is likely to have occurred after Dunstan's receipt of the *pallium* in Rome in September 960 and his return to England.

[26] He attests KCD 689, 690 and 691 (S 882, 1378, 1379) of 995; his successor, Wulfstan II attests KCD 1291 (S 889) in 996.

[27] N. P. Brooks, 'Arms, status and warfare in late-Saxon England', in *Ethelred the Unready: Papers to the Millennium Conference*, BAR, Brit. ser. 69 (Oxford, 1979), pp.81–103, repr. in id., *Communities and Warfare 700–1400* (London, 2000), pp. 138–61.

gold,[28] and of 1 sword with belt-harness (*fetels*), 2 horses, 2 'targes' (or round shields) and 2 spears (*francan*).[29] If we compare this payment with the rates later laid down in Cnut's secular ordinance we find that Æthelric pays rather less arms and armour than is there specified for a king's thegn — for his payment is short of 2 unsaddled horses, 2 spears and 2 shields — but he does pay an additional 10 mancuses.[30] Surprisingly Æthelric's heriot relates much more closely to the amount specified by Cnut as being due from the king's thegn in the Danelaw who was 'closest to the king'. Though most of Æthelric's bequests lay in Essex (and not, therefore, within the Danelaw), he also left property at the unidentified *Norðho* to two Suffolk churches, St Gregory's Sudbury and Bury St Edmunds. It is indeed conceivable that his legal standing derived from a Suffolk estate, within the East Anglian Danelaw, rather than from Bocking; for the will tells us that Bocking had been an acquisition of his father, rather than an inheritance. His father may therefore have been a Danelaw noble who had made himself useful to English monarchs and had thus earned properties in Essex. Be that as it may, it would seem certain from his heriot that Æthelric had ranked among the king's thegns. It is therefore noteworthy that he does not attest any of the extant royal diplomas of King Æthelred. A certain *Æðelric minister* is indeed found regularly witnessing that king's charters from *c.* 986 until 1013, but that is long after Æthelric of Bocking's death and that thegn has been convincingly identified as the father of Eadric Streona.[31] We may conclude that our Æthelric was indeed a nobleman in Essex and Suffolk with the rank of a king's thegn, but apparently one who seldom attended the royal court.

Æthelric's bequests, as detailed in his will, are mapped in Fig. 3.1. In the first instance all the properties there mentioned were intended to be used to support his wife for as long as she lived. Thereafter they were bequeathed as follows:

i) his estate at Bocking (Essex) was to go to the community at Christ Church (Canterbury), both for Æthelric's soul and that of his father, who 'had first acquired' the property; Æthelric reserved, however, one hide of this estate to be used as a notably generous support for a priest at Bocking.[32]

ii) a nearby estate in the west of Rayne,[33] which is the adjacent parish lying south-west of Bocking, was granted to St Paul's (London), for the bishop to use for lighting (presumably for candles or lamps at St Paul's) but also for 'spreading Christendom to God's people there'. It is unclear whether Æthelric was here also intending his bequest to the diocesan bishop to help to endow a local church at Rayne. The bishop was also to receive a further two hides at Rayne, which a certain Eadric rented annually for half a pound and one *gara* — a term that has defied interpretation.[34]

iii) Bishop Ælfstan of London also received woods and open lands (*feldas*) at Copford, which are described as lying 'to the east of the street' (Fig. 3.1), that is presumably the London-Colchester Roman road, and an enclosure or 'hay' at Glazen in Bradwell.

iv) next Æthelric divided his estate at an unidentified *Norðho* [that is the northern 'headland' or 'hill-spur'],[35] half to St Gregory's church at Sudbury and half to St Edmund's at *Bedericeswyrth* [that is Bury St Edmunds].

Finally Æthelric ends his will with the request that if Bishop Ælfstan were to outlive them, he protect his widow and support all these bequests.

This is a very unusual will indeed. After providing for his widow, Leofwynn, Æthelric arranged that thereafter everything was to pass to the Church. He made no provision at all for any kinsman (or kinswoman) —

[28] This was equivalent to 1,800 silver pence at the standard conversion of 1 gold mancus : 30 silver pennies (i.e. 360 West Saxon shillings or 450 Mercian shillings) . For the conversion rate, see H. Munro Chadwick, *Anglo-Saxon Institutions* (Cambridge, 1905), pp. 23–4 and 66.

[29] We are uncertain what variety of spear, perhaps characteristic of the Franks, the term *francan* may indicate; it occurs twice in Scragg, *The Battle of Maldon, AD 991*, lines 77 and 140 (pp. 20, 24). The rich variety of spear-types known from pagan burials is illustrated in M. J. Swanton, *The Spearheads of the Anglo-Saxon Settlements* (London, 1973), and his *A Corpus of Pagan Anglo-Saxon Spear-types*, BAR, Brit. ser., 7 (Oxford, 1974).

[30] II Cnut 71 (ed. Liebermann, *Gesetze*, I, pp. 356–8 and Robertson, *Laws*, pp. 208–10): '… and the heriots of the king's thegns, who are nearest to him: 4 horses – 2 saddled and 2 unsaddled – and 2 swords, and 4 spears and as many shields, and a helmet and byrnie, and 50 mancuses of gold; and of lesser thegns: a horse and its trappings, and his weapons or his *healsfang* in Wessex, and in Mercia £2, and in East Anglia £2; and the heriot of a king's thegn among the Danes who has his soke: £4; and if he is more closely beholden to the king: 2 horses, 1 saddled and 1 unsaddled, and 1 sword, and 2 spears and two shields and 50 mancuses of gold; and for him who is less close: £2.'

[31] Keynes, *Diplomas of Æthelred*, pp. 212, 237; Simon Keynes, *An Atlas of Attestations in Anglo-Saxon Charters, c. 670–1066* (Cambridge, 1998), list LXIII, where an Æthelric is found among the 'third group' of thegns. It is conceivable that Æthelric of Bocking was the thegn who had earlier attested charters of King Eadwig in 958 and 959: *Charters of Abingdon Abbey*, ed. S. E. Kelly, AS Charters 7–8 (London, 2000–1), nos. 78 (S 650), 79 (S651), 83 (S 658) and *Charters of New Minster Winchester*, ed. S. Miller, AS Charters 9 (London, 2001) no. 22 (S 660), but who thereafter was seldom if ever at court, perhaps just attesting BCS 1199 (S 748) of 967 and KCD 611 (S 831) of 977, but these charters all concern estates and churches in the West Saxon heartland (Berkshire, Wiltshire and Hampshire); none concern Essex or Suffolk.

[32] For other late Anglo-Saxon endowments of parish churches with 1 hide, see John Blair, *The Church in Anglo-Saxon Society* (Oxford, 2005), pp. 371-3.

[33] The version of the will preserved in the Bury St Edmunds cartulary adds the word *strete* here, making Æthelric's bequest that of Rayne 'to the west of the street'. For the Roman road that would be involved, see Fig.3.1.

[34] *Gara* is a masculine noun, meaning 'a gore' or triangular piece of arable land left unploughed in 'open-field' agriculture for plough-teams to turn, but that could not be a component of an annual rent. Here the word is feminine (*mid anre garan*). Could it mean a 'lappet' or triangular piece of ornate decoration or be a feminine variant of the masculine noun *gar*, 'spear'? Conceivably Eadric was a skilled smith, whom Æthelric wished to remain on his lease.

[35] For the interpretation of OE *hoh* in place-names and the peculiarities of its use in East Anglia, see Margaret Gelling and Anne Cole, *The Landscape of Place-Names* (Stamford, 2000), pp. 186-90. It might prove worth searching for this name in Suffolk near the Roman road running north from Bocking, and between Sudbury and Bury St Edmunds, which are near or on that road.

whether from his own or from his wife's family. Æthelric and Leofwynn may, of course, have had no offspring and have therefore preferred to make pious benefactions. But such total exclusion of all their kinsfolk is unique among extant wills and therefore needs explanation. Forfeiture of property and of the right to transmit possessions to heirs was a familiar penalty in Anglo-Saxon law for the most serious criminal offences, that is those that were *botleas* or uncompensatable. In Æthelred's laws, that penalty was particularly associated with desertion on the battlefield or with disloyalty to the king.[36] The underlying principles were to be summed up in clause 77 of Cnut's secular ordinance:

> And the man who, through cowardice, flees from his lord or his comrades, be it on a ship-*fyrd* or a land-*fyrd*, is to forfeit all that he owns and his own life; and the lord is to resume the property and the land which he had formerly given him; and if he has bookland, it is to pass into the king's hands.[37]

This enactment may be linked firstly with the fundamental 'hold-oath' or oath of fealty, widely found throughout early medieval Europe, by which a man on entering a lord's service vowed to 'love what his lord loved and to shun what he shunned';[38] and secondly with the treason law, which had been reinforced by King Alfred so that not only plotting against the king's life and against his men's lives, but also the harbouring of outlaws had been deemed punishable by forfeiture of life and of all property.[39] Though Æthelric is not known to have actually deserted from the battlefield at Maldon (or from any other battle), we learn from King Æthelred's confirmation of the bequest of Bocking to Christ Church (*Appendix*, no 2) that he had been suspected of colluding or plotting with the king's enemies. Indeed the king had told Archbishop Sigeric (990-994) that he understood Æthelric to have been in the plot to receive Swein into Essex when he first came thither with a fleet.

King Æthelred's Old English confirmation of Æthelric's bequest of Bocking to Christ Church is still preserved in the cathedral archives at Canterbury as the middle section of a tripartite chirograph. The document states that one copy was at Christ Church; one at the king's *haligdom*, that is the collection of relics that travelled

with the royal household, and one with the widow, i.e. Leofwynn. Like Æthelric's will, the confirmation bears no date, but the witness and participation of Archbishop Ælfric of Canterbury allows us to date it after his accession to the see in 995, and the presence of Abbot Lyfing (of Chertsey) among the witnesses places it before his consecration as bishop of Wells in 998 or 999.[40] This vernacular confirmation relates a fascinating series of events for which likely dates can now be proposed:

King Æthelred had been informed of Æthelric's involvement in a plot (*unræd*) to receive Swein in Essex, when he first came there with a fleet (991).

The king informed Archbishop Sigeric (990-994) — here said to have been Æthelric's advocate (*forespeca*) for the gift of Bocking to Christ Church — of the accusation.[41] The appointment of the archbishop as *forespeca* should be understood as an attempt to protect Æthelric and his wife from forfeiture and to allow them to retain the estate during their lifetimes.[42]

During Æthelric's lifetime, he remained unacquitted of this charge and unatoned (*ungeladod ge ungebett*). On his death, his widow brought his heriot to the king at the meeting of the *witan* at Cookham (? 995), presumably as the first step in the attempt to secure the royal lord's support for the terms of the will in her favour.

There, however, the king had sought to initiate proceedings against Æthelric before the witan because the events were known to Ealdorman Leofsige (of Essex, 991x4-1002) 'and many others'.[43] Proof of Æthelric's involvement in a plot to bring Swein into Essex, would have led to the forfeiture of all his properties, with his booklands passing to the crown. The king therefore had a strong financial interest that such charges of treason should be successfully proved.

The widow (Leofwynn) countered this development by informing her advocate, Archbishop Ælfric (who seems to have succeeded Sigeric in that role) and Æthelmær[44] that

---

[36] V Æthelred 28; VI Æthelred 35 (Liebermann, *Gesetze*, I, pp. 244, 256; Robertson, *Laws*, pp. 86, 102).

[37] II Cnut 77 and 77 §1 (Liebermann, *Gesetze*, I, p. 364; Robertson, *Laws*, p. 214): 'And ðe man ðe fleo fram his hlaforde oððe fram his geferan for his yrhðe, sy hit on scipfyrde, sy hit on landfyrde, ðolie he ealles ðæs ðe he age 7 his agenes feores, 7 fo se hlaford to ðam æhton 7 to his lande ðe him ær sealde. 7 gyf he bocland hæbbe, ga þæt þam cincge to handa'.

[38] For the Old English oath of fealty, see II Edward, c.1 (Liebermann, *Gesetze*, 1, p.140; Attenborough, *Laws*, p. 118) and *Swerian*, c.1 (Liebermann, *Gesetze*, 1, p.396).

[39] Alfred 4 (Liebermann, *Gesetze*, I, p. 50; *Laws of the Earliest English Kings*, ed. F. L. Attenborough (Cambridge, 1922), p.64-6): 'Gif hwa ymb cyninges feorh sierwe, ðurh hine oððe ðurh wreccena feormunge oððe his manna, sie he his feores scyldig 7 ealles þæs ðe he age.'

[40] The fact that neither Bishop Ælfstan, named in the will as Æthelric's advocate, nor his successor at London, Wulfstan (995x6–1002) is mentioned in the confirmation might indicate that it was written during the vacancy between them, 995–6.

[41] Sigeric is not named as Æthelric's advocate in the extant copy of the will (Canterbury, D and C, Chart Ant. B 1), which may have only been written after Archbishop Sigeric's death.

[42] For the role of advocate, see Andrew Rabin, 'Old English *forespeca* and the role of advocate in Anglo-Saxon law', *Medieval Studies* 69 (2007), 223-54.

[43] It is instructive that in 1002 Leofsige was himself to be Æthelred's envoy to negotiate the payment of Danegeld to the Viking army, but soon thereafter fell out of royal favour, being banished for killing Æfic, the king's high reeve (ASC 1002 CDE). His sister Æthelflæd later had her estates in Huntingdonshire confiscated for helping him after his banishment; see *Charters of Rochester*, Anglo-Saxon Charters 1, ed. A. Campbell (London, 1973), no.33 (S 926).

[44] He is not identified further in the text of the charter, but since he witnesses the confirmation first among the laymen in the king's following; he is likely to have been the king's thegn, Æthelmaer, son of Ealdorman Æthelweard and the future founder of Eynsham abbey and notable patron of reformed Benedictine monks. For his career, see Simon Keynes, 'King Æthelred's charter for Eynsham Abbey (1005)', *Early Medieval Studies in Memory of Patrick Wormald*, ed. Stephen Baxter, Catherine Karkov,

in return for the abandonment of the accusation against her husband, she would give her morning gift to Christ Church 'on behalf of the king and the nation' (*for ðone cincg ealne ⁊his leodscype*). That gift would presumably have secured regular prayers for both king and nation by the monastic community at Christ Church. Æthelred's confirmation does not locate Leofwynn's morning-gift, but the community at Christ Church later remembered Æthelric and Leofwynn as the donors not only of Bocking, but also of Mersea. There can be little doubt that her property had been the two hides on the west of the island of Mersea in the estuary of the Blackwater, which are recorded in the Domesday survey as being attached to the monks' 4½-hide manor of Bocking; they were later to be known as the estate of Bocking Hall (Fig. 3.1).[45]

Leofwynn's offer proved sufficient to persuade the king to lay aside the 'dreadful accusation' and to permit the will's bequest of Bocking to Christ Church (and of other properties to the other churches) to stand. A declaration to that effect was read before the witan.

Thus Æthelric's will and the king's confirmation of it reveals some of the tensions inherent in the upper levels of society in Æthelred's reign, not only in the royal court but especially in the shire community in Essex. At the battle of Maldon, Ealdorman Byrhtnoth and a substantial proportion of the shire nobility in the East Saxon *fyrd* had refused to pay tribute to the Viking army, choosing to fight and to die in battle against a better-armed force. That disastrous decision may well have caused further bitter divisions within the shire community. The widows and kinsmen of the slain will have wished to commemorate the fallen as heroes — as the extant poem clearly does. They will have had no interest in forgiving those Essex noblemen who were absent from the battle, since such men (along with those who actually fled from the battlefield) could be held responsible for the catastrophic defeat. Æthelric of Bocking may therefore have been seen as an arch-villain, particularly if he was believed to have been conducting negotiations with Swein at about the time of the battle. Moreover the fact that Æthelric engaged Archbishop Sigeric as his *forespeca*, or advocate, will not have helped endear him locally, since the archbishop was particularly associated with the national policy of offering tribute or Danegeld to buy off Viking armies — the policy that the poet declares Byrhtnoth and his men to have rejected. Moreover, if men like Æthelric were to be proved guilty of a *botleas* offence — that is of absenting themselves from

the land-fyrd or of plotting with the king's enemies — then their presumed fate would be to be hanged as criminals; moreover, their confiscated estates might provide rich pickings in a subsequent distribution to loyal men.

Such issues would have surfaced initially in the shire court of Essex, at its twice-yearly meetings under the joint presidency of the Ealdorman and the Bishop — that is of Byrhtnoth's successor, Ealdorman Leofsige, and Bishop Ælfstan of London. Æthelred's confirmation asserts that the king was aware that the charge was known to Ealdorman Leofsige 'and many men' and that phrase may to refer to the shire court, where Leofsige is likely have had especial responsibility for secular law and the judgment of secular men.[46] By making Ælfstan and the church of St Paul's the ultimate beneficiary of the Essex properties at Rayne, Glazen and Copford and by entrusting the Bishop with the protection of his widow and of the properties initially left to her, Æthelric may have found an effective way to continue in possession of his estates and to neutralize the anger of those in the court whose kinsmen had been slain at Maldon. If his properties were to pass safely to the Bishop, then Ælfstan would have needed to prevent any formal charge of plotting with the king's enemies from being heard in the shire court. Likewise at formal meetings of the *witan* before the king, the archbishop of Canterbury would need to exercise a similar influence. Æthelric had therefore made Sigeric his advocate both for his grant of Bocking to Christ Church and for his bequests to other churches. In the event the archbishop does seem to have been able to prevent the king from instituting formal proceedings before the witan. In consequence Æthelric of Bocking remained in legal limbo until his death. Widely suspected of treachery, but not charged with any crime, he had therefore never been acquitted of the accusation, nor had he atoned for the offence by making an appropriate penance; yet Æthelric had retained his properties and had also sought to ensure that his widow too would be supported from them until her death.

Æthelric's death (perhaps in early 995) and Leofwynn's consequent journey to the royal vill at Cookham to take his heriot to King Æthelred, her husband's lord, had put these arrangements to the test. For by then Leofwynn's two ecclesiastical protectors (Archbishop Sigeric and Bishop Ælfstan) had both died, and the danger was that a posthumous charge of treason would reopen the possibility that all Æthelric's properties would be forfeited. Leofwynn sought to defend her interests by securing Sigeric's successor, Archbishop Ælfric, as her advocate and by utilizing the one property of which her ownership was secure, namely her morning-gift — that is the property that she received from her husband in connection with their wedding. It is instructive

Janet Nelson and David Pelteret (Farnham, 2009), pp. 451-73, at 451-4.
[45] Little Domesday Book, 8r; *Domesday Book: Essex*, ed. A. Rumble (Chichester, 1983), 2: 2. For the main Christ Church cartulary's record of Æthelric and Leofwynn's gift of Bocking and Mersea, a conflation of the information in S 1501 and 939 with the community's memory of its benefactors, see Robin Fleming, 'Christ Church Canterbury's Anglo-Norman cartulary', in *Anglo-Norman Political Culture and the Twelfth-Century Renaissance*, ed. C. Warren Hollister (Woodbridge, 1997), pp. 83–155, at 142–3 and *Charters of Christ Church Canterbury*, no. 137A, ed. Nicholas Brooks and Susan Kelly, Anglo-Saxon Charters 18 (British Academy, 2013), pp. 1008-10. For Bocking Hall, see R. Morant, *History of Essex*, 2 vols (1768), I, 428.

[46] III Edgar 5. 1–2 (Liebermann, *Gesetze*, I, p. 204; Robertson, *Laws*, p. 26: '⁊ hæbbæ man þriwa on geare buruhgemot ⁊tuwa scirgemot . ⁊ðar beo on þare scire biscop ⁊se ealdorman, ⁊ðar ægðer tæcan Godes riht ge worldriht'; 'And the borough court shall be held three times a year; and the shire court twice . And the bishop and the ealdorman shall be in the shire [court] and shall there direct both God's law and secular law'. This was to be repeated in II Cnut 18.

that she did not offer this to the king, but rather promised to give it to Christ Church 'for the sake of the king and of all the nation' — so long as the king would remove the charge against her husband and allow the bequests that he had made in his will to stand . As the king's confirmation then states: 'Then — may God reward the king — he permitted it, for the love of Christ, of St Mary and of St Dunstan and of all the saints who rest at Christ Church'.

The fact that King Æthelred gave way to ecclesiastical pressure from Bishop Ælfstan and from Archbishops Sigeric and Ælfric and allowed Æthelric and Leofwynn to retain their lands before passing them on, posthumously, to St Paul's, to St Gregory's at Sudbury, to Bury St Edmunds and to Christ Church — instead of taking them back into the royal demesne — demonstrates the weakness of the king in the 990s. Against a background of the steadily growing ferocity of the Viking assaults during the period 984–1016, it is noteworthy that the king is not known to have ever led an English army in person against any of the Viking forces that were active in his kingdom. The task of responding to the Viking threat was left to his Ealdormen and to local forces. It is not surprising that, in the absence of royal leadership, noblemen often chose to negotiate for peace rather than to offer battle; such doubts were evident in the response in south-eastern England to the 'host' (*here*) and fleet of ninety or more ships that Swein and Olaf commanded in 991 and 994. We do not know the explanation for the king's apparent cowardice, nor how contemporaries sought to explain it, since we do not have a contemporary version of the *Old English Royal Annals* composed during Æthelred's reign. But a cowardly king was certainly scarcely in a position to take action against a cowardly noble.

Some hint of contemporary attitudes may indeed be gleaned from the royal diplomas of the reign. We do not have any charters from the year of the battle of Maldon or from the following year (992); but in 993 Æthelred's general charter of privileges to Abingdon Abbey makes explicit that the Viking raids were already being portrayed at that time as divine punishment for English sins in general, for the youthful sins of the king in particular, and for the greed of those who counselled him.[47] Archbishops

Sigeric and Ælfric and Bishop Ælfstan of London seem to have been among those counsellors of King Æthelred, who reacted to the battle of Maldon by advising that generosity towards the Church (and in particular towards the monastic communities of the kingdom, devoted to God's service)[48] was the best means to appease God's wrath. That is likely to have been a widely-held view. Ealdorman Byrhtnoth and his family themselves certainly made notable bequests to monastic houses.[49] The second component of Sigeric's advice, however, was that the Viking forces which threatened the safety of those churches should be bought off by negotiations and payments of tribute.

That had not been the choice made by Ealdorman Byrhtnoth in 991 and was seemingly not the view of the poet of *The Battle of Maldon*. But it may well have been a widely-held understanding of the military realities, shared by many Anglo-Saxon nobles, not just by ecclesiastics, and including in particular Æthelric of Bocking. We need therefore to ask whether it is possible to understand his viewpoint and to interpret his actions in 991 as anything other than that of a coward who treacherously preferred to negotiate with King Swein in 991 rather than to join Byrhtnoth's heroic band of warriors at Maldon. Here we need to take account of the topography (Fig. 3.1). We know from the account in the C, D and E manuscripts of the *Royal Annals* that in 991 the Viking force first ravaged around Ipswich, before moving to Maldon. We must therefore envisage Olaf and Swein's fleet of more than ninety ships operating in the estuaries of the Orwell as well as of the Blackwater. The island of Mersea, with the property that Æthelric gave to Leofwynn as her morning-gift, lies between those estuaries and specifically at the junction of the Blackwater with the Colne. Life on the island, and its access to the mainland by means of its causeway or 'bridge',[50] will certainly have been disrupted by the Viking incursion, when as the *Old English Royal Annals* state 'great terror was caused along the coast'. It is indeed entirely possible that Leofwynn had been residing there at the very time when the area came under Viking control. Faced with a king who was not prepared to fight, it would not be surprising if Æthelric had felt that his first priority was the safety of his wife and of their houses and households. Had he been seeking to ensure their

[47] Kelly, *Charters of Abingdon*, no.124, pp. cxi-v, 477–83 (=S 876). This charter survives as an original single-sheet charter (London, British Library, Cotton Augustus ii.38), in which Abbot Wulfgar of Abingdon's attestation states *hoc sintagma triumphans dictaui*; 'Rejoicing, I have dictated this document'. Moreover, the first witnesses listed after the king are Archbishop Sigeric, Bishop Ælfstan of London and Bishop Ælfric of Ramsbury (i.e. Sigeric's successor at Canterbury), exactly the men who protected Æthelric and Leofwynn from facing forfeiture of their properties and whose churches were the eventual beneficiaries. The Abingdon privilege of 993 makes the king assert that the present *infortunia* 'misfortune' arose '*partim ... pro meae juventutis ignorantiae ... partim etiam pro quorundam illorum detestanda philargiria qui meae utilitati consulere debebant accidisse*'; 'partly ... on account of the ignorance of my youth ... partly too on account of the covetousness of certain of those who happened to be obliged to advise about my service'. For the theme of the king's sins in charter-formulation after 991, see Keynes, *Diplomas of Æthelred*, pp. 95–114; for the Viking raids as divine punishment, see P. Stafford, 'Political ideas in late tenth-century England: charters as evidence', *Law, Laity and Solidarities*, ed. Pauline

Stafford, *et al.* (Manchester, 2001), pp. 68-82; Keynes, 'Re-reading King Æthelred', pp. 90–6; Simon Keynes, 'An abbot, an archbishop and the Viking raids of 1006–7 and 1009–12', *ASE* 36 (2007), 151–220, at 152-5.
[48] For the series of monastic foundation charters, pancartae and immunity privileges that punctuate the most difficult periods of Æthelred's reign, see Simon Keynes, 'King Æthelred's charter for Eynsham Abbey (1005)', in *Early Medieval Studies in Memory of Patrick Wormald*, ed. S. Baxter, *et al.* (Farnham, 2009), pp. 451–73, at 456-62.
[49] The Suffolk estate of Eleigh passed from Ealdorman Ælfgar to his daughter, Ælfflæd, wife of Byrhtnoth; and after she was widowed at Maldon and after her subsequent death to Christ Church; Byrhtnoth and his wife were also remembered at Canterbury as having bequeathed to the monks Lawling (Essex) and Hadleigh (Suffolk); see Fig. 3.1, above and Nicholas Brooks, *The Early History of the Church of Canterbury* (Leicester, 1984), pp. 285-6.
[50] For the 'bridge' of oak piles of late 7th-century date leading to the island, see P. Crummy, J. Hillam, and C. Crossan, 'Mersea island: the Anglo-Saxon causeway', *Essex Archaeology and History* 14 (1982), 77-86.

safekeeping from Swein at much the time that Ealdorman Byrhtnoth determined to fight the contingent encamped near Maldon on Northey island, then that might well have been perceived by some as involvement in a plot (*unræd*) to receive Swein in England. Equally it is understandable that leading churchmen might have inclined to a more charitable interpretation of Æthelric's motives, particularly if Æthelric was prepared to make it worth their while so to think.

In conclusion, it is here suggested that Æthelric's will needs to be understood as the key component of his post-991 defensive strategy to avoid the immediate loss of all his property. It provides another illustration how this period of extreme military and political stress proved to be a time of huge potential for the Church. Though churches and churchmen, like all landowners, suffered from Viking attacks — as the martyrdom of St Ælfheah, archbishop of Canterbury, in 1011 would soon show so graphically — the insecurity also made lay rulers and nobles more inclined to make bequests to churches in the hope of securing

continuing prayers for their souls. Moreover the loss of lives in the prolonged warfare meant that inheritances were without their expected heirs and charges of treachery or cowardice rendered others subject to forfeiture. The insecurity also created a situation in which those who controlled the law-courts had the greatest opportunities to manipulate the system to their own advantage. Such was the context in which the archbishops of Canterbury and the monks of Christ Church acquired the substantial estate at Bocking, which remained one of the major manors of the cathedral community for the rest of the Middle Ages and which in due course became a centre of peasant unrest. More fundamentally, however, Bocking may be said to have passed into the hands of the Church because in a time of military crisis the King failed in his fundamental obligation to lead the Christian English army in person against the pagan enemy. Æthelred was therefore vulnerable to secular disaffection and to ecclesiastical pressure. A pious and courageous king would not, they believed, have been so evidently punished by God by such fearsome assaults of pagans.

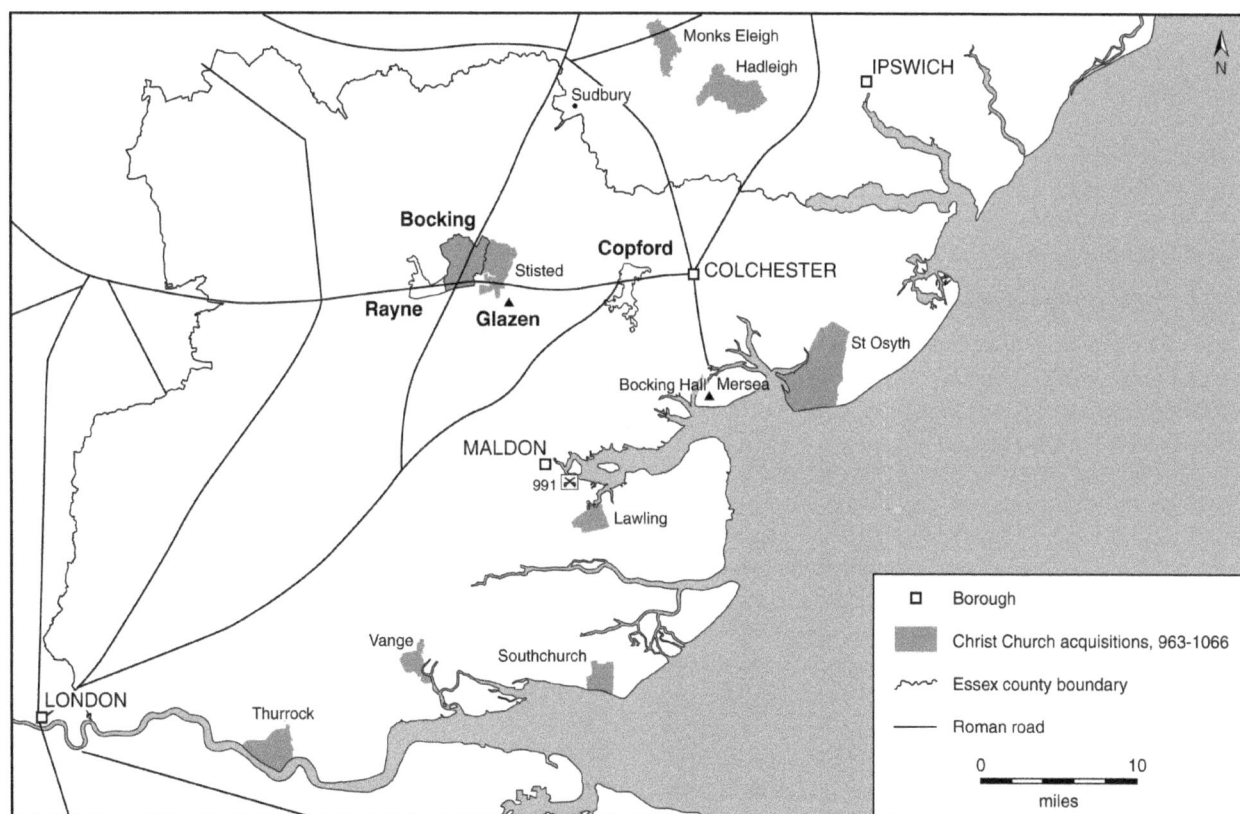

FIG 3.1 THE BEQUESTS OF ÆTHELRIC OF BOCKING AND THE ESTATES OF CANTERBURY CATHEDRAL IN ESSEX AND SUFFOLK.

APPENDIX[51]

I *Will of Æthelric* [AD *c.* 960 x (995 x 996)]

B. Canterbury, D. & C., Chart. Ant. B 2 (Red Book, no. 20): non-contemporary single-sheet copy, s. xi[med] or s. xi[2], parchment, 55 x 240 mm

Endorsements: (1) *in a hand of s. xi:* to Boccinge; (2) *in a hand of s. xii:* Eaþeric dedit Bockinge ecclesie Christi . Anno dcccc.xcvii.; (3) *in another hand of s. xii:* scrip' xiii [*numeral deleted*]; (4) *in a hand of s. xiii/xiv:* ·XIII·

W. Cambridge, University Library, Ff. 2. 33, 50r: copy of ME version, s. xiii[2] (from Bury St Edmunds)

Editions:

a. KCD 699, from B

b. *OSFacs.,* i. 16 (facsimile, transcript and translation of B)

c. Whitelock, *Wills*, no. 16/1 (p. 42, with translation p. 43), from B, W

Listed: S 1501; C. R. Hart, *The Early Charters of Eastern England* (Leicester, 1966) no. 27

Edited from B, with major variants from W

+ Her cyð `Æþeric´[a] on þissum gewrite hwam he geann . ofor his dæig þæra æhta þe him God alæned hæfð . þ is ærest sona minum hlaforde . syxti mancusa[b] goldes . ⁊ mines swyrdes mid fetele . ⁊ þarto twa hors . ⁊ twa targan . ⁊ twegen francan[c] . ⁊ ic geann Leofwynne minan wife ealles þæs þe ic læfe hire dæig . ⁊ ofor hire dæg gange þ land on Boccinge into Cristes circean þam hirede for uncera saule ⁊ for mines fæder þe hit ær begeat eall buton anre hide ic gean into þære cyrcean þam preoste þe þar Gode þeowaþ . ⁊ ic geann þæs landes æt Rægene be westan[d] . into sancte Paule þam bisceope to[e] geleohtenne . ⁊ þar on Godes folce cristendom to dælenne . ⁊ ic geann þarto twegra hida þe Eadric gafelaþ ælce geare mid healfum punde [f]⁊ mid anre garan[f] . ⁊ ic geann be eastan stræte æigþer ge wudas ge feldas Ælfstane bisceope into Coppanforde . ⁊ þæs heges on Glæsne[g] . ⁊ ic geann þæs landes æt Norðho . healf into sancte Gregorie . on Suðbyrig . ⁊ healf into sancte Eadmunde on Bedericeswyrþe . Nu bidde ic þone

bisceop Ælfstan . þ he amundige mine lafe ⁊ þa þincg þe ic hyre læfe . ⁊ gif him God[h] lifes geunne lencg þonne unc þ he gefultumige þ ælc þara þinga stande þe ic gecweden hæbbe;

[a] *Added above the line in B, by the same hand and marked for insertion with three commas;* ⁊ Æþeric W

[b] markes W

[c] speres *substituted for* francan *in ME copies in Christ Church cartularies*

[d] strete *included* W

[e] repetition by scribal error?

[f...f] mid are garen W

[g] Glesene W

[h] *Followed by erasure of 1-2 letters* B

+ Here in this document Æthelric declares to whom after his day he grants the possessions that God has lent to him. That is first, straightway, to my lord: sixty mancuses of gold and my sword with belt and besides two horses and two shields [targes] and two spears. And I grant to Leofwynn my wife for her day everything that I leave. After her day, the estate at Bocking is to go to the community of Christ Church, for our souls and for that of my father, who first acquired it — all but one hide [which] I grant to the church for the priest who serves God there. And I grant the land on the west of Rayne [*or* the land at Rayne to the west of the street] to St Paul's to the bishop for the lighting and for spreading Christendom to God's people there. And in addition I grant the two hides which Eadric rents annually for half a pound and one gore (*gara*). And I grant, on the east of the street, both the woods and the open land at Copford to Bishop Ælfstan, and the enclosure at Glazen[wood]. And I grant the estate at *Northho*, half to St Gregory's at Sudbury, half to St Edmund's at *Bedericeswyrthe* [Bury]. Now I beseech the bishop, Ælfstan, that he protect my relict and the possessions that I leave to her; and— if God grant him long[er] in life than us— that he give support, so that all the things that I have bequeathed may stand.

[51] The editions of Æthelric's will and King Æthelred's confirmation provided here are simplified versions of those that will appear as nos 136 and 137 in *Charters of Christ Church Canterbury*, ed. Brooks and Kelly, (A-S Charters, 18), pp. 999-1008. Particular thanks are due to Dr Kelly, who undertook most of the fundamental editorial work on these and other documents in that edition, but who is not responsible for any errors that I have introduced.

II *King Æthelred confirms the will of Æthelric.* [A.D. 995 x 999]

A. Canterbury, D. & C., Chart. Ant. B 1 (Red Book, no. 18): original, s. x^ex, central portion of tripartite chirograph, parchment, 160/180 x 345 mm

Endorsements: (1) *in a hand of s. xii¹:* Eðelred cing uðe Æðerices quide ⁊ his lafe into Cristes circe . ðet his Boccing . Tempore Æluric archiepiscopi . (2) *in a hand of s. xii^med:* anglice; (3) *in a hand of s. xiii:* Eðelredus Rex confirmauit testamentum Edrici qui nobis legauit Bockinge anno .dcccc°.xcvii° . (4) *in a hand of s.xiii:* scriptum *and* Elurici archipeiscopi xiiii; (3) *in a hand of s. xiii/xiv:* ·XIII·

Ed.:

a. KCD 704

b. *OSFacs.,* i. 17 (facsimile, transcript and translation of A)

c. Whitelock, *Wills,* no. 16/2 (pp. 44-6, with translation pp. 45-7)

Translated: Whitelock, *EHD,* no. 121 (pp. 579-80)

Listed: S 939; Hart, *Early Charters of Eastern England,* no. 29

Edited from A

+ C Y R O G R A P H U M

+ Her swutelað on þison gewrite hu Æðelred kyning geuðe þ Æþerices cwyde æt Boccinge standan moste . Hit wæs manegon earon^a ær Æðeric forðferde þ ðam kincge wæs gesæd þ he wære on þam unræde þ man sceolde on Eastsexon Swegen underfon ða he ærest þyder mid flotan com . ⁊ se cincg hit on mycele gewitnysse Sigerice arcebisceope cyðde þe his forespeca þa wæs for ðæs landes þingon æt Boccinge ðe he into Cristes cyrcean becweden hæfde . Þa wæs he þisse spæce ægþer ge on life . ge æfter ungeladod ge ungebett oð his laf his hergeatu þam cincge to Cocham brohte þær he his witan widan gesomnod hæfde . Þa wolde se cing ða spæce beforan eallon his witan uphebban ⁊ cwæð þ Leofsige ealdorman . ⁊ mænige men þære spæce gecnæwe wæron . Þa bæd seo wuduwe Ælfric arcebisceop ðe hire forespeca wæs . ⁊ Æðelmær þ hig þone cincg bædon þ heo moste gesyllan hire morgengyfe into Cristes cyrcean for ðone cincg . ⁊ ealne his leodscype wið ðam ðe se cing ða egeslican onspæce alete . ⁊ his cwyde standan moste þ is swa hit herbeforan cwyð . þ land æt Boccinge into Cristes cyrcean . ⁊ his oðre landare into oðran halgan stowan swa his cwyde swutelað . Þa God forgylde þam cincge getiðode he ðæs for Cristes lufan . ⁊ sca Marian . ⁊ sce Dunstanes . ⁊ ealra þæra haligra ðe æt Cristes cyrcean restað . þæs costes ðe heo þis gelæste . ⁊ his cwyde fæste stode . þeos swutelung wæs þærrihte gewriten . ⁊ beforan þam cincge ⁊ þam witon gerædd ; Þis syndon ðæra manna naman ðe ðises to gewittnesse wæron . Ælfric arcebisceop . ⁊ Ælfheh bisceop on Wintaceastre . ⁊ Wulfsige bisceop on Dorsæton .

⁊ Godwine bisceop on Hrofeceastre . ⁊ Leofsige ealdorman . ⁊ Leofwine ealdorman . ⁊ Ælfsige abbod . ⁊ Wulfgar abbod . ⁊ Byrhtelm abbod . ⁊ Lyfincg abbod . ⁊ Alfwold abbod . ⁊ Æðelmær . ⁊ Ordulf . ⁊ Wulfget . ⁊ Fræna. ⁊ Wulfric Wulfrune sunu : ⁊ ealle ða ðegnas ðe þær widan gegæderode wæron ægðer . ge of Westsexan . ge of Myrcean . ge of Denon . ge of Englon ᵇ. Þissa gewrita syndon ðreo . an is æt Cristes cyrcean . oðer æt þæs cinges haligdome . ðridde hæfð seo wuduwe.ᵇ

+ C Y R O G R A P H U M

ᵃ *Error for* gearon

ᵇ⁻ᵇ *Written by same scribe in smaller script*

+ Here in this document is declared how King Æthelred granted that Æthelric's will might stand in relation to Bocking.

It was many years before Æthelric had passed away that the King was told that he was in the plot that Swein should be received in Essex when he first came thither with a fleet. And the King before many witnesses made it known to Archbishop Sigeric — who was his advocate for the estate at Bocking which he had bequeathed to Christ Church. Then, both in his lifetime and afterwards, he both remained unacquitted of this charge and [the crime remained] unatoned, until his widow brought his *heriot* to the King at Cookham, where he had assembled his *witan* from afar. Then the king wished to raise the charge before all his *witan* and declared that Ealdorman Leofsige and many men were aware of the charge. Then the widow bade Archbishop Ælfric, who was her advocate, and Æthelmær that they request the King that she might give her morning-gift to Christ Church, for the King and for all his people, provided that the King would lay aside the dreadful accusation and that his [Æthelric's] testament might stand, namely as it says herebefore: the estate at Bocking to Christ Church and his other landed possessions to the other holy places as his will declares. Then, may God reward the King!, he permitted this — for the love of Christ, of St Mary, and of St Dunstan and all the saints who rest at Christ Church — with the understanding that she should carry this out and that his will should [then] stand.

This declaration was immediately written and read before the King and the *witan*. These are the names of the men who served as witnesses of it: Archbishop Ælfric, and Bishop Ælfheah of Winchester, and Bishop Wulfsige of Dorset, and Bishop Godwine of Rochester, and Ealdorman Leofsige, and Ealdorman Leofwine, and Abbot Ælfsige, and Abbot Wulfgar, and Abbot Byrhthelm, and Abbot Lyfincg, and Abbot Ælfwold, and Æthelmær, and Ordulf, and Wulfgeat, and Fræna, and Wulfric Wulfrun's son, and all the thegns who were gathered there from far: both West Saxons and Mercians, and Danes and English.

There are three of these documents: one is at Christ Church; another with the king's *haligdom* [relic collection]; the widow has the third.

Chapter 4 Promoting Royal Authority in Anglo-Saxon England: The Making of Edmund 'Ironside'

Ian Howard

There is evidence that in Anglo-Saxon times public opinion was being manipulated in a sophisticated manner. This can be shown by considering the propaganda role of some early Old English and Latin documentary sources in reinforcing royal authority in England particularly during the tenth and eleventh centuries.

Clearly, influential marketing cannot succeed in a vacuum. There are necessary concomitants. For instance, the Old English vernacular was transformed into a written language in a sophisticated process supported directly by kings and royal officials as well as by the Church.[1] In most of Europe there was a restriction on communications from central authority since, in the first and often the final instance, royal communications were restricted to those who could readily understand Latin. This restriction did not apply to the Anglo-Saxon peoples because the Old English vernacular was developed as a written language. The prime purpose of this written vernacular was not so much that it should be a record – Latin served that purpose very well – but rather that it could be read aloud to audiences all over the territories governed by the Anglo-Saxon kings. In the vernacular Old English there are homilies written and frequently amended for the edification and moral and social discipline of the people;[2] there are the 'Laws', an exposition of the legal precepts which were of particular importance and which, consequently, could be amended to reflect changes in emphasis;[3] and there are annals, which are known collectively as the *Anglo-Saxon Chronicle*,[4] incorporating political messages of great significance, and so also subject to amendment, examples of which are provided below. In addition, the Latin charters incorporate passages in the vernacular containing the boundaries of property; passages which could be read to the people for the avoidance of dispute.[5]

Anglo-Saxon homilies and laws were important in creating moral and social discipline. Their underlying principles were Christian and hierarchical and this was important in bringing cohesion to provinces inhabited by different peoples some of whom were still influenced by a pagan tradition.[6] That the reading of homilies and extracts from the laws should be influential in underpinning the authority of the establishment will be readily understood. However, consideration is rarely given to the propaganda function of the annals which are so eagerly read to form an idea of historical incident and social development. It is this aspect of communication, and how it supported royal authority, which is considered here.

The earliest and perhaps the most obvious example of the propaganda value of the annals in the *Anglo-Saxon Chronicle* is to be found in what is commonly regarded as the 'Alfredian original'. These are the annals which form the basis of the extant versions of the *Chronicle*. They consist of a translation of parts of the chronological summary to Bede's *Historia ecclesiastica* and other early historical information, to which were added a series of annals glorifying the exploits of King Alfred. Annals covering the last decade of Alfred's reign and the reign of his son, Edward (the Elder) were added to the *Anglo-Saxon Chronicle* in what is known as 'the First Continuation'. A revised version of these annals is available in the tenth-century *Chronicle of Æthelweard* and provides an example of how a political message can easily be revised for propaganda purposes. Alistair Campbell, in the preface to his edition of the *Chronicle of Æthelweard*, says:

> Æthelweard's ... account of the events of 893 appears to be based on a revision of the [Anglo-Saxon Chronicle] annal ..., made to meet political conditions in the reign of Eadweard the Elder, and to glorify that king and his supporter Æthelred of Mercia, while completely suppressing the part played by Ælfred in the fighting of that year.[7]

---

[1] King Alfred is an obvious ninth-century example of enthusiastic royal support for the development of a written Old English vernacular. Ealdorman Æthelweard and his son Æthelmær are tenth-century examples of secular interest in the development of Old English, as well as in scholarship generally, particularly in their encouragement of the work of churchmen such as Abbot Ælfric.

[2] For examples see *English Historical Documents*, Vol. I, *c. 500-1042*, ed. Dorothy Whitelock (London, 1955), pp. 849-59 which provides extracts from the work of the homilists Ælfric and Archbishop Wulfstan under the general heading of 'Vernacular Prose Literature'.

[3] From at least Alfred's time, legal precepts or 'Laws' were written in Old English and Alfred quotes Ine's Laws in the same vernacular. The earliest such Law, ascribed to King Æthelberht of Kent by Bede, was also written in Old English; Bede specifically records the important point that 'these were written in English speech'. See Patrick Wormald, *The Making of English Law: King Alfred to the twelfth century*, Vol. I, *Legislation and its Limits* (Oxford, 1999) p. 29.

[4] Earlier writers refer to 'The Old English Chronicle' or 'The Saxon Chronicle'.

[5] This was an instance where a message in the vernacular was not supposed to be amended. However, scribes did make good what they would no doubt have regarded as 'omissions' in the charter records.

[6] Because of Scandinavian connections, eastern and northern regions of England were influenced by pagan traditions well into the tenth century; Ian Howard, *The Reign of Æthelred II, King of the English, Emperor of all the Peoples of Britain 978 – 1016*, BAR, British Series 522 (Oxford, 2010), p. viii. Norway was forcibly converted to Christianity at the end of the tenth century by King Olaf Tryggvason. The king of Denmark, Harold Gormsson (Bluetooth), accepted Christianity about three decades earlier. For Olaf Tryggvason, see *Hér hefr sogu Óláfs konungs Tryggvasonar* in *Snorri Sturluson: Heimskringla, Nóregs Konunga Sogur*, ed. Finnur Jónsson (Copenhagen, 1911) pp. 105-81. The earliest record of Harold's conversion is the famous 'Jelling Stone'; see *Cultural Atlas of the Viking World*, ed. J. Graham-Campbell *et al.* (Abingdon, 1994), pp. 118-19 and the illustration on p. 120.

[7] *The Chronicle of Æthelweard*, ed. Alistair Campbell (London, 1962), p. xviii.

Another example of manipulation is to be found in Asser's *Life of King Alfred*, where the annals in the Alfredian original were taken up and expanded to emphasis the king's love of learning and his many saintly characteristics, together with some territorial aspects of Alfred's authority which had not featured in the original version, for instance the submissive relationship of the Welsh provinces towards King Alfred.[8]

These examples of the manipulation of chronicle history are well known and are relatively straightforward and benign in objective. Other examples are more complex, for instance the manipulations of historical records occurring in the eleventh century that transformed perceptions of an Anglo-Saxon king so that he became known as 'King Edmund Ironside'. The early records of his career are not especially propitious. The first extant record of Edmund's activities is a charter by which he made a payment securing title to land which he was forcing a monastery to give to him.[9] He was not a candidate for kingship until his elder brother, Athelstan, died in 1014,[10] less than two years before the death of their father, King Æthelred. When Athelstan died an important faction at Court, which had the ear of the king, argued that his younger half-brother, Edward, should be recognised as heir to the throne. When his enemies gained the upper hand, Edmund fled from court, seized a widow from a monastery, married her, and took possession of all her dead husband's estates.[11] He conspired with northern leaders against his father,[12] until eventually his father feared for his life when in his company.[13]

This was a far from propitious start to a royal career. Yet King Edmund Ironside is now commonly regarded as one of the great hero kings of the Anglo-Saxon period. We can trace the manipulation of his reputation in three eleventh-century sources, two of which are extant, the other being known because it was used as a source for a twelfth-century chronicle.

The Anglo-Saxon Chronicle

The first of these sources is the *Anglo-Saxon Chronicle*; specifically annals for the years 1015 and 1016 which are to be found in manuscripts C D and E.[14] The annals for 1015 and 1016 in MSS C D E are part of a series of annals covering the reign of King Æthelred II (the Unready) which are so similar that they must be derived from a common exemplar.[15] From internal evidence it can be deduced that the annals were written in or before 1023: the annal for 1012 refers to St Ælfheah's body being in St Paul's Minster, London, but it was translated to Canterbury in 1023. The detail in later annals, particularly in the annal for 1016, is such as to suggest that they are a contemporary record of events.

Edmund's character is developed in two distinct phases in these annals. The first phase begins in the year 1015, when he is mentioned for the first time in the *Chronicle*, and ends in the annal for 1016 on 23 April, the date when his father, King Æthelred, died. The annals make reference to incidents which must have been well known at the time they were written, since they are a near-contemporary account of events. They describe how Sigeferth and Morcar, the chief thegns of the Danelaw, were killed whilst attending a royal assembly at Oxford and their property confiscated by the king; how the Ætheling Edmund opposed this royal policy, married Sigeferth's widow and went with her into the Danelaw where the people accepted him as their ruler and he took possession of all Sigeferth's estates and Morcar's estates. Whilst this was happening, England was invaded by King Cnut. King Æthelred was too ill to lead the opposition to the invasion personally so his leading adviser, Ealdorman Eadric, collected an army, as did the Ætheling Edmund, and they joined forces for a short time. The armies soon parted, however, without opposing the invaders because Edmund discovered that

[8] Whitelock's extracts from this 'Life' provide valuable illustrations of the point; see *EHD* pp. 264-76, in particular chapters 76, 79 and 80. There has long been discussion about the provenance of Asser's annals. Whitelock assessed the evidence and decided that the annals are, in essence, early and that Asser was their author (*EHD*, p.120) Others have given greater emphasis to evidence that, in all or in part, the annals were written at the turn of the tenth century at a time when King Æthelred's court was encouraging the cult of royal saints. Whatever the provenance, *Asser's Life of King Alfred* shows how annals can be enhanced to introduce specific points; in this case to emphasise the saintly aspects of Alfred's character and to make political claims.

[9] The charter is S. 1422, dated 1012 by the witness list. It is a lease, for life, of land at Holcombe Rogus, Devon from the community at Sherborne to Edmund the Ætheling. The key sentences are: '*Eadmund æþeling bæd þone hyred æt Scireburnan þ(æt) he moste ofgan þ(æt) land æt Holancumbe; ða ne dorste se hyred hym þæs wyrnan . ac cwæþon þ(æt) hy þæs wel uðon . gyf se cing 7 se bisceop þe heora ealdor wæs þæs geuðon*'; 'Ætheling Edmund required of the community at Sherborne that he must be allowed to acquire the estate at Holcombe. Then the community did not resist to refuse him that [i.e. did not dare to refuse him], but agreed that they would fully grant it, if the king and the bishop, who was their superior, granted it'. *Anglo-Saxon Charters*, ed. A. J. Robertson (Cambridge, 1939), p. 146; my translation.

[10] Professor Keynes has argued very persuasively that Athelstan died on 25 June 1014; Simon Keynes, *The Diplomas of King Æthelred 'The Unready' 978-1016* (Cambridge, 1980), p. 267.

[11] Whitelock, *EHD, ASC* CDE *s.a.* 1015: 'Then after a short interval, the atheling Edmund went and took the woman against the king's will and married her'.

[12] Whitelock, *EHD, ASC* CDE *s.a.* 1015: 'Then before the Nativity of St. Mary (8 September) the atheling went from the west, north to the Five Boroughs, and at once took possession of all Sigeferth's estates and Morcar's, and the people all submitted to him'. In a hierarchical society, the 'people' acted in accordance with their lords' wishes – hence northern leaders were supporting Edmund.

[13] Whitelock, *EHD, ASC* CDE *s.a.* 1016: 'When they all came together, it availed nothing, no more than it had often done before. The king was

then informed that those who should support him wished to betray him; he then left the army and returned to London'.

[14] More exactly, manuscripts C, D and E are: British Library, MS Cotton Tiberius B. i; British Library, MS Cotton Tiberius B. iv; and Oxford, Bodleian Library MS Laud 636. A comparative edited version of the annals for 1015 and 1016 may be found in *The Anglo-Saxon Chronicle according to the Several Original Authorities*, Vol. I, *Original Texts*, ed. Benjamin Thorpe, Rolls Series (London, 1861) pp. 274-85. More recently, edited versions have been published in a series entitled The Anglo-Saxon Chronicle: A Collaborative Edition, ed. David Dumville and Simon Keynes (Cambridge). The respective volumes in this series are: Volume 5, *MS C*, ed. Katherine O'Brien O'Keeffe (pp. 99-103); Volume 6, *MS D*, ed. G. P. Cubbin (pp. 59-62); Volume 7, *MS E*, ed. Susan Irvine (pp. 71-4). In quoting from the *Chronicle*, I have followed the *MS D* version. For discussion of the provenance of these manuscripts, see Howard, *The Reign of Æthelred II*, Appendix 2, pp. 91-109.

[15] Each version differs to a limited extent from the other versions but differences are not material for the purposes of this paper.

Eadric was planning to have him killed. In the annal for 1015 the king's chief adviser, Ealdorman Eadric, is revealed as a villain. The policy by which Sigeferth and Morcar were killed is ascribed to him and described as a 'betrayal'.[16] He personally brought about their deaths in a thoroughly treacherous manner;[17] he sought to betray the Ætheling Edmund likewise and when he failed he betrayed his master, King Æthelred, and went over to King Cnut to help the invaders. The *Chronicle* emphasises the extent of this betrayal by stating that Eadric 'seduced' 40 ships away from the king at this time;[18] effectively the whole of King Æthelred's mercenary army of Scandinavians. There is no criticism of King Æthelred himself, who is exonerated to a large extent from any blame because he was incapacitated by illness[19] and there is no criticism of the Ætheling Edmund whose opposition to royal policy, tantamount to rebellion, is exonerated to a large extent by the implied misdirection of royal policy by the king's chief adviser, the treacherous Ealdorman Eadric.

The annal for 1016 describes how King Cnut, aided by Ealdorman Eadric, ravaged large parts of England. The Ætheling Edmund joined his father who was preparing to defend London against King Cnut. However, before the enemy arrived, King Æthelred died, on 23 April, and Edmund was chosen as king.[20] After that, London was besieged.

The second phase of the *Chronicle* account of Edmund's activities commences immediately after King Æthelred's death on 23 April 1016 and ends with Edmund's own death on 30 November of that year. By the *Chronicle* standards it is a long account and so appears to be very significant, although in truth it covers only a seven-month period. Edmund had gone out of London before it was surrounded. He raised an army in Wessex and fought the Danish army near Gillingham and then again, after midsummer, at Sherston. Ealdorman Eadric supported the Danish army. The battles were hard-fought and inconclusive. Then Edmund gathered another army, raised the siege of London and defeated the Danes near Brentford. Unfortunately, Edmund suffered a setback because many of his men broke away to seek booty after the battle and a large number were drowned crossing the Thames through their own carelessness. So Edmund had to retire to Wessex to collect another army and the Danes were able to lay siege to London again and harried throughout Mercia for provisions.

Edmund collected an army for the fourth time, crossed the Thames at Brentford, and drove the Danish army away, killing many stragglers and forcing the Danes to seek refuge on the Isle of Sheppey. Then Ealdorman Eadric deserted the Danish army and went over to King Edmund. Describing Eadric's acceptance by King Edmund the Chronicler observes that '*Næs nan mare unræd geræd þænne se wæs*'; 'no greater folly was ever agreed to than that was'.

Next the Danes raided in Mercia. Edmund gathered his army, pursued the Danish army and overtook it in Essex, where he joined battle with it at a hill called *Ashingdon*. Ealdorman Eadric and his contingent were the first to flee the battlefield, thereby ensuring Edmund's defeat. Many of the English leaders were slain. In the words of the Chronicle, 'all the nobility of the English people was destroyed there.'[21] However, Edmund escaped and fled to Gloucester. King Cnut and his Danish army pursued King Edmund there. Then Ealdorman Eadric intervened and persuaded the kings to agree a truce, following which Edmund and Cnut divided England between them.

The *Chronicle* annal for 1016 ends with the death of King Edmund on 30 November. The following annal, for the year 1017, commences with King Cnut succeeding to all the kingdom of England, without any observations about events between Edmund's death and Cnut's accession. Cnut rewarded Ealdorman Eadric with high office, but soon afterwards had him killed as part of a purge of the English nobility.

The account of these events in the *Anglo-Saxon Chronicle* is largely factual and also credible. However, there are interesting features. Throughout the earlier annals of King Æthelred's reign action is taken with the advice of his councillors and the king is not described as proactive. Nor is King Cnut described in proactive terms during the seven months following the death of King Æthelred. By contrast, King Edmund is referred to frequently in the annal for 1016 in a manner which shows him to be a decisive leader with enormous energy. It is first implied and then declared openly that King Edmund's failure to dislodge the Danes from England was due to the treachery of Ealdorman Eadric, continuing to blacken the ealdorman's character as the *Chronicle* had done previously, in earlier annals. It will be seen how this manner of describing events and the leading characters influenced later sources. What should not be overlooked at this stage is the fact that, as originally crafted, the *Anglo-Saxon Chronicle* annals for 1015 and 1016 were politically motivated to support the cause of a king, who in reality was a faction leader, as is explained later in this paper.

---

[16] '*7 þær Eadric ealdorman beswac Siferð 7 Morcer*'; 'And there Ealdorman Eadric betrayed Sigeferth and Morcar'.

[17] Eadric '*beþæhte hi into his bure, 7 hi mon þærinne ofsloh ungerysenlice*'; Eadric 'enticed them into his chamber, and they were basely killed inside it'. I have followed Whitelock's interpretation of *ungerysenlice* (otherwise 'unbecoming', 'improper'). Swanton has 'dishonourably'.

[18] '*Eadric ealdorman aspeon ða feowertig scipa fram þam cyninge, 7 beah þa to Cnute*'; 'Then Ealdorman Eadric seduced forty ships from the king, and then submitted to Cnut'.

[19] '*Þa læg se cyng seoc æt Cosham*'; 'The king then lay sick at Cosham'.

[20] '*7 þa æfter his ende ealle þa witan þe on Lundene wæron 7 seo buruwaru gecuron Eadmunde to cyninge*'; 'And then after his [Æthelred's] death, all the councillors that were in London and the burghers [i.e. citizens] approved Edmund as king'.

[21] *Þa wearð þær ofslægen ... 7 eall seo duguð of Angelcynnes þeode*'. A list of some of the important people who were slain has been omitted from the middle of this sentence.

The Encomium Emmae Reginae

The second source is the *Encomium Emmae Reginae*,[22] which was written by a continental author to please Queen Emma of England. She had been the wife of King Æthelred and then of King Cnut and, after suffering exile during Harold Harefoot's reign, she returned to England to exert considerable authority during the reign of her son, Harthacnut. She hoped to retain her influence after Harthacnut's death through her eldest son, Edward (the Confessor). The extant version of the *Encomium* denigrates King Harold Harefoot and underpins the legitimacy of the reigns of Kings Cnut and Harthacnut. Finally, it justifies Edward's rights of succession, describing how Harthacnut invited Edward back to England where Harthacnut, Edward and Queen Emma shared power in perfect agreement, comparing their shared earthly rule with the heavenly rule of the Holy Trinity.

The *Encomium* begins by explaining how King Swein of Denmark became rightful king of England, through conquest. After Swein's early death, his son Cnut, rightful successor to the English throne, was forced to retire to Denmark for a period. He later returned to England with an army where he was opposed by the English. Cnut's generals, Thorkell the Tall and Eric of Lade, won victories over the English and then Cnut besieged the leaders of the English opposition in London. God took mercy upon the English and created an opportunity for peace by taking away the life of their leader. The Londoners sued for peace but this was thwarted because the son of the dead English leader escaped from London and gathered an army to oppose Cnut. This new leader of English resistance is named for the first time; it is Edmund. Cnut suspected that the citizens of London might prove treacherous and retired to the Isle of Sheppey for the winter, leaving Edmund to spend the winter in London.[23]

The *Encomium* introduces Ealdorman Eadric stating that on Edmund's side 'Eadric was the chief supporter, a man skilful in counsel but treacherous in guile, and Eadmund afforded him hearing in all affairs.'[24]

The next year, after Easter, Edmund raised an army to attempt to drive the Danes out of England. They met at the Battle of Ashingdon. Ealdorman Eadric and his force fled early in the battle. The Encomiast indicates that this flight was an act of treachery and suggests that Eadric had been bribed by the enemy. Nevertheless, Edmund's English army still outnumbered the army of King Cnut. After a hard fought battle, Cnut's army was victorious. Many of the English leaders were killed but Edmund escaped. At this stage, Cnut was in difficulties because many of his men had been killed or wounded in the battle and he could not obtain reinforcements quickly. The defeated Edmund by contrast could gather another English army. So Cnut accepted Ealdorman Eadric's advice whereby Cnut and Edmund divided the kingdom between them. God then intervened again, taking pity upon a divided country to take away the life of King Edmund so that there should be only one king, leaving Cnut as the only king in England.[25]

In the Encomiast's account, Edmund features as a leader of English opposition. He is only accorded the title of 'king' by the Encomiast after Cnut agrees to divide the country with him. Edmund's courage and resilience in battle is underlined, the Encomiast's motive clearly being to explain Cnut's difficulties and the division of the country. At no time does Ealdorman Eadric feature as an ally of Cnut. He is Edmund's chief adviser, but he is described as being full of guile and, when he deserts King Edmund at the battle of Ashingdon, his action is ascribed to bribery. The Encomiast explains that, after the death of King Edmund, Ealdorman Eadric went to Cnut and claimed that it was his actions that had enabled Cnut to gain the victory at Ashingdon. Cnut had the treacherous Eadric killed immediately. Thus the Encomiast avoids any suggestion that Cnut retained Eadric in high office and justifies Cnut's actions in having him killed.[26]

Being some twenty years further removed from the events, the Encomiast can and does manipulate the facts to suit his political objectives more readily than the writer of the *Anglo-Saxon Chronicle* annals for 1015 and 1016. Although the Encomiast was very well informed about events, presumably by Queen Emma, he apparently wrote without having had access to a version of the *Anglo-Saxon Chronicle*. So his chronological ordering of events and the seasons when events occurred is inaccurate, but no more than might be expected in such circumstances.

Life of King Edmund Ironside

The final development of the story of King Edmund took place over a decade later in the mid-eleventh century. Edward the Confessor was king and it was increasingly apparent that he would have no son to succeed him. There were several potential candidates for the English throne, one of whom was Edward, a son of King Edmund who had been removed from England as a child after the death of his father. He was brought back from exile in Eastern Europe,

[22] The manuscripts of the *Encomium Emmae Reginae* are: (1) London, BL Additional 33241, a vellum manuscript dating from the mid-eleventh century which was copied from an original version of the *Encomium*, possibly for Queen Emma; (2) Aberystwyth, National Library of Wales, Hengwrt 158 (= Peniarth 281), a late, paper copy derived from BL Add. 33241; (3) BL Additional 6920, a later, paper copy, ultimately derived from BL Add. 33241; (4) Paris, Bibliothèque Nationale Fonds Lat. 6235, a vellum manuscript probably dating from the sixteenth century. Although it has not been copied well and appears to omit certain passages it is probably derived from an independent transmission of the original version of the *Encomium*; see Ian Howard, *Harthacnut, The Last Danish King of England* (Stroud, 2008), pp. 74-100. For an edited version of the *Encomium*, see *Encomium Emmae Reginae*, ed. Alistair Campbell, Camden 3rd series, LXXII, Royal Historical Society (London, 1949), reissued with a supplementary introduction by Simon Keynes (Cambridge, 1998).
[23] Campbell, *Encomium*, I.2-5, pp. 10-15; II.1-8, pp. 14-25.
[24] Campbell, *Encomium*, II.8, pp. 24-5.
[25] Campbell, *Encomium*, II.9-15, pp. 24-33.
[26] Campbell, *Encomium*, II.8-15, pp. 24-33.

partly at the instigation of Ealdred, bishop of Worcester.[27] An account of the early life and career of Bishop Ealdred is provided in the *Anglo-Saxon Chronicle*,[28] perhaps written by members of his circle, and in these annals there is a reference to the Ætheling Edward's father as 'King Edmund Ironside'.[29]

The twelfth-century Latin *Chronicle of John of Worcester* used a source in which King Edmund is given the by-name 'Ironside' and Ealdorman Eadric is given the by-name 'Streona' meaning 'acquisitive'.[30] The *Chronicle of John of Worcester* does not acknowledge its sources and the passages used in the annals for 1015 and 1016 have not been fully identified although they clearly draw upon a version of the *Anglo-Saxon Chronicle* for structure and some of their content. For present purposes, this source is described as 'a lost *Life of King Edmund Ironside*', since Edmund is the hero of the passages. Edmund's by-name 'Ironside' is mentioned some eight times in the annal *s.a.* 1016 and it is possible that John of Worcester's source is the origin of this usage. If so, the relevant passages may be dated to the mid-eleventh century because of a contemporary reference to 'King Edmund, [who] was called 'Ironside' for his bravery' in MS D *s.a.* 1057, indicating that the by-name was already known.[31]

The extracts from the *Life of Edmund Ironside* source in the *Chronicle of John of Worcester* have all the hallmarks of melodrama. In them, King Edmund shows extraordinary courage and leadership but he is thwarted throughout by the equally extraordinary treachery of Ealdorman Eadric Streona, who finally brings about Edmund's downfall at the battle of Ashingdon. King Edmund Ironside's heroic qualities are enhanced to legendary levels, as is the treachery of his nemesis, Ealdorman Eadric Streona. The following passages illustrate how the original author develops his theme:

> King Edmund Ironside made his presence felt in fierce hand-to-hand fighting in the front line. He took thought for everything; he himself fought hard, often smote the enemy; he performed at once the duties of a hardy soldier and of an able general.

Furthermore he continues:

> The king [Edmund] would have crushed all the Danes if it had not been for the wiles of Eadric Streona, the treacherous ealdorman; for, when the battle was at its height and he observed that the English were stronger, he cut off the head of a certain man called Osmear, very like King Edmund in face and hair, and raising it aloft he shouted, saying that the English fought in vain: 'You men of Dorset, Devon, Wiltshire, flee in haste, for you have lost your leader. Look, I hold here in my hands the head of your lord, King Edmund. Flee as fast as you can.' When the English perceived this they were appalled, more by horror at the action than by any trust in the announcer, whence it happened that the waverers were on the verge of flight.[32]

It is this highly imaginative account that has been fixed into historical perspective to create in King Edmund Ironside one of the greatest hero monarchs in the history of England. Equally, it has ensured that Ealdorman Eadric should be remembered for all time as the personification of treachery. Once again, however, we should recognise that this account was politically motivated. By celebrating the extraordinary kingly qualities of King Edmund Ironside, it was creating a political platform from which his son, Edward, could be brought forward as the best candidate to succeed Edward the Confessor to the English throne. This objective was thwarted by Edward's sudden death shortly after he was brought back to England:

> Here the ætheling Edward came to England; he was son of King Edward's brother, King Edmund, [who] was called 'Ironside' for his bravery. King Cnut had sent this ætheling away into Hungary to betray, but he there grew to be a great man, as God granted him and became him well, so that he won the emperor's relative for wife, and by her bred a fine family; she was called Agatha. We do not know for what cause it was arranged that he might not see his relative King Edward's [face]. Alas! that was a cruel fate, and harmful to all this nation, that he so quickly ended his life after he came to England, to the misfortune of this wretched nation.[33]

King Edmund as a faction leader

When King Æthelred II died on 23 April 1016, King Cnut was already in England and his claim to the throne was recognised by the provinces which had accepted him or had been overrun by his Danish forces and his English allies. The three sources discussed above concentrate upon the conflict between King Cnut and King Edmund. However,

---

[27] F. M. Stenton, *Anglo-Saxon England* (Oxford, 1971) p. 571; Ian Howard, 'Harold II: a Throneworthy King', in *Harold II and the Bayeux Tapestry*, ed. Gale R. Owen-Crocker (Woodbridge, 2005), pp. 35-52.
[28] An account of Bishop Ealdred's career is provided in *ASC* D, *s.aa.* 1047, 1050, 1052-4, 1056, 1058, 1060-1, 1066-8. Some of the annal numbers do not align with the calendar year of the events recorded therein.
[29] *ASC* D, *s.a.* 1057, which is amongst the annals that provide an account of Bishop Ealdred's career.
[30] There are many manuscripts of the *Chronicle of John of Worcester*. The passages for the years 1015 and 1016 used in this paper are to be found in *The Chronicle of John of Worcester*, Vol. II, *The Annals from 450 to 1066*, ed. R. R. Darlington and P. McGurk (Oxford, 1995) pp. 478-97.
[31] The quotation is taken from *The Anglo-Saxon Chronicle*, ed. Michael Swanton (London, 1996) pp. 187-8; see note 29, above, and note 33, below, for the context of this quotation. It is among the *MS D* annals for 1046 to 1068 which contain much information about the activities of Bishop Ealdred, who, according to John of Worcester, was responsible for arranging the return of King Edmund's son, Edward, to England.

[32] Darlington and McGurk, *Chronicle of John of Worcester*, pp. 486-9.
[33] *ASC* D, *s.a.* 1057 in Swanton, *Anglo-Saxon Chronicle*, pp. 187-8. *ASC* E *s.a.* says Edward returned and soon died and was buried in St Paul's Minster in London.

Scandinavian and German sources point to the existence of a third claimant to the throne. It is the existence of a third candidate which makes sense of Ealdorman Eadric's opposition to Edmund, and which explains London's independence in relation to the activities of the two kings, Cnut and Edmund.

King Æthelred had been married twice. In 1014, when he returned from exile, he was joined by three sons of his first marriage, the Æthelings Athelstan, Edmund and Eadwig. It seems that Athelstan had long been regarded as the heir to the throne. By his second wife, Queen Emma, Æthelred had two sons, Edward and Alfred. Although still a boy, Edward was deemed old enough to represent King Æthelred in the negotiations which preceded the king's return to England.[34] Nothing special should be read into this other than to deduce that Edward was in Normandy with his father at the appropriate time and that his elder (half) brothers were elsewhere. It was the death of the Ætheling Athelstan, coupled with the king's illness, which appears to explain the crisis described in the *Anglo-Saxon Chronicle* for the year 1015, although there is no mention of the Ætheling's death in the *Chronicle*.[35] Ealdorman Eadric's actions in that year were supported by the king and led to the Ætheling Edmund retiring from the royal court and defying his father. Clearly, Eadric had no claim to the throne himself, so these events suggest that he was supporting another candidate. If the boy Edward was deemed old enough to 'lead' an important delegation in 1014 it is likely that he was also deemed old enough to be a candidate to succeed his father. All the indications point to a contest for recognition between the eldest surviving son, Edmund, and Æthelred's son by Queen Emma, Edward, in which Ealdorman Eadric and Queen Emma supported Edward's candidature. The actions of Æthelred and Edmund suggest that the king favoured Edward's candidature also, especially as he was greatly influenced by Ealdorman Eadric. Thus, Cnut was able to invade a country which was politically divided in 1015. The king's death in April 1016 would only have enhanced the rivalry between Edmund and the supporters of Edward. It is against this background that German and Scandinavian sources should be considered.

The *Chronicle* written by Bishop Thietmar of Merseburg is a contemporary source for the events in England during the years 1015 and 1016.[36] Merseburg, in Germany, is some distance from the coast and a significant distance from England and the bishop relied for his knowledge of important English events upon information he received from travellers.[37] Thus, he knew about the murder of the archbishop of Canterbury in 1012 and that Thorkell the Tall ('*Thurkil*' or '*dux Thurcil*') was with the Scandinavian army in England at the time; but he did not know the *name* of any archbishop of Canterbury subsequent to St Dunstan ('*Dunsten*'), who was well known on the Continent having spent a period of exile in Flanders.[38] He knew that Æthelred's eldest surviving sons were Athelstan and Edmund ('*cum Ethelsteno ac Ethmundo*') but he did not know that Athelstan had died in England in 1014.[39] He knew about the battle of Sherston and that many important men had died in this hard-fought battle but he wrongly supposed that the English leader, Edmund ('*Æthmun*'), and the Scandinavian leader, Thurgut ('*Thurgut*'), were killed in the battle; nor does he seem to have realised that the leader he called 'Thurgut' was one and the same person as Thorkell the Tall.[40] It is Thietmar's *Chronicle* that reveals how Queen Emma was in the burh of London when King Æthelred ('*Æthelred rex Anglorum*') died and that it was she who led the opposition to Cnut when London came under siege.[41] Thietmar also explains that the queen entered into negotiations with King Cnut and contemplated handing over the æthelings, her stepsons, to him together with other inducements to raise the siege and make peace.[42] This explains why Edmund (and Eadwig) had to escape from London before it was surrounded.[43] As it happened the negotiations came to nothing at that time and the queen continued to defy King Cnut.

Thietmar's sources of information were spasmodic and sometimes unreliable. However, his description of Queen Emma's activities is supported by Scandinavian sources. In those sources there are skaldic verses which apparently once formed a poem about the Danish siege of London in 1016.[44] They are evidently a song about the shipmen[45] – the Danes who besieged London in 1016 after Æthelred's death – and refer to the resistance of London and the woman, or widow, who resided within the burh. Verse 3 boasts that the woman ('*mær*') will learn about the heaps of slain and the bravery of their prince. Ashdown recognises that 'a love motif and a battle motif are here combined' but is

[34] *ASC* CDE *s.a.* 1014.

[35] The death, in 1014, is not recorded in any extant version of the *Anglo-Saxon Chronicle*. By contrast, the death of King Edgar's eldest son in 971 was recorded in all versions of the *Chronicle*, although it was subsequently erased in *ASC* A.

[36] *Thietmari Merseburgensis Episcopi: Chronicon*, trans. W. Trillmich, in *Ausgewählte Quellen zur Deutschen Geschichte des Mittelalters, in Verbindung mit vielen Fachgenossen*, ed. R. Buchner, IX (Darmstadt, 1974). See also, *Thietmari Merseburgensis Episcopi: Chronicon*, ed. J. M. Lappenberg, in *Monumenta Germaniae Historica* III (Hanover, 1889), pp. 723-871. There is an English translation: David A Warner, *Ottonian Germany; The Chronicon of Thietmar of Merseburg* (Manchester, 2001).

[37] In Book 7.42, Thietmar names one of his informants, *Sewald*.

[38] Thietmar, *Chronicon*, 7.42-3.

[39] Thietmar, *Chronicon*, 7.40.

[40] Thietmar, *Chronicon*, 7.41.

[41] Thietmar, *Chronicon*, 7.40. Thietmar does not refer to Emma by name; she is *Regina*.

[42] Thietmar, *Chronicon*, 7.40.

[43] It also calls into question the *ASC* CDE statement that Edmund was chosen as king in London after Æthelred's death. For a more detailed explanation of these events, see Howard, *The Reign of Æthelred II*, pp. 70-1.

[44] The extant verses have been brought together and are published in *English and Norse Documents Relating to the Reign of Ethelred the Unready*, ed. Margaret Ashdown (Cambridge, 1930). It should be recognised, however, that there remain some uncertainties about the verses, including the order in which they were delivered, see Ashdown's notes. The verses are identified in more than one saga.

[45] Ashdown names the verses '*LIÐSMANNAFLOKKR*' because the verses taken from *Knytlinga saga*, c. 14, are described as having been taken from the poem composed by Cnut's troops ('*af liðmonnum*'). See also, *Knytlinga Saga; The History of the Kings of Denmark*, trans. Hermann Pálsson and Paul Edwards (Odense, 1986), pp 36-7.

unable to identify 'the mysterious lady'. An identification of the prince as Cnut and the lady as Emma makes sense since the resistance at London was eventually concluded by their marriage. Verse 5 again refers to 'the fair woman' using the word '*ekkja*' which has connotations of widow, which is appropriate to the newly widowed Queen Emma. This 'fair woman' dwells '*i steini*' a phrase which caused Ashdown considerable difficulty, since she could not decide whether it should be translated as 'a cave in a rock' or as a place-name. In the context of the siege, however, '*i steini*' is probably a kenning for the burh of London with its stone fortifications. This emphasises the strength of the burh and is particularly appropriate since *Knytlinga saga* concludes its quotation of verses from this poem by noting that despite many attempts, Cnut 'failed to win the town'.[46]

Neither the *Anglo-Saxon Chronicle*, which did not want to distract attention from Edmund as the representative of Anglo-Saxon resistance, nor the *Encomium*, which did not want to dwell on Queen Emma's earlier marriage, nor her defiance of Cnut, mention these events. The *Encomium* speaks vaguely of Cnut sending for Queen Emma to be his wife, but later hints at the real political background by saying that there would not have been peace in England without the marriage and that Danish and English armies were thankful that the marriage brought about peace and union[47] – references to the queen's political power, a power which would indeed have been very great with control of London.[48] This explains why

the political accord between Emma and Cnut was necessary after Edmund's death, and why London made a separate peace after the battle of Ashingdon.[49]

In effect, therefore, when King Æthelred died on 23 April 1016, there were three claimants for the throne: King Cnut, the Ætheling Edmund, and the Ætheling Edward, who was represented by his mother and her supporters.

Conclusion

Edmund Ironside came to prominence in 1015 in rebellious circumstances; he was one of three candidates for the throne of England after King Æthelred's death in 1016; and he died within seven months of King Æthelred. His story provides an excellent case study, illustrating how historical perceptions have been created in three separate sources that were written on different occasions to serve three quite different political objectives. As a result our history books celebrate the life of a great hero king. Each of these three sources was intended to promote the royal authority, respectively of Edmund himself, then King Cnut and, finally, the pretensions to the throne of the Ætheling Edward. This study also underlines the importance of careful chronological analysis in researching our sources and demands that we should consider who sponsored the creation of each source and what were his or her political affiliations.

---

[46] *Knytlinga Saga*, c. 14.
[47] *Encomium*, 2.16: 'This is what the army had long eagerly desired on both sides, that is to say that so great a lady, bound by a matrimonial link to so great a man ... should lay the disturbances of war to rest.' and 2.17: 'Both armies also rejoiced indescribably, looking forward to increasing their possessions by joining forces ...'. Campbell's translations.
[48] Emma continued to hold out in London on behalf of her son. Although Edmund had raised the siege of London (*ASC* CDE *s.a.* 1016) and he and his brother Eadwig may have been admitted to the burh with their bodyguard and other attendants (as indicated by the *Encomium*, 2.8), the bulk of his army must have remained outside. Inside, the burh was occupied by a garrison loyal to the queen (Thietmar, *Chronicon*, 7. 40).

[49] *ASC* CDE *s.a.* 1016, 1018.

Chapter 5 Coins and Kingship in Anglo-Saxon England

Gareth Williams

Many historians have commented on the association between coins and kingship in early medieval Europe, and Anglo-Saxon England. While an individual coin may convey less information than a charter or a law-code, the issuing of coins, like charters or law-codes, was closely associated with royal power. Coinage was also an important vehicle for royal authority and control over standards, prices, fines and taxation. Furthermore coinage was arguably the most widely visible expression of royal authority among the population as a whole, as well as a medium for rulers to promulgate particular political messages and imagery. In a period in which coinage was the only real form of mass media, the die-cutters, or at least the people who selected the designs of the coinage, were the spin-doctors of their day. However, it is important to keep in perspective the limitations which literacy, and learning more generally, placed on the ability of the population as a whole to interpret both images and inscriptions on coins. Even in periods in which coin use was widespread, the conscious messages in coin design which will be discussed throughout this article must be seen as aimed primarily at an elite.

Both coins and kings existed throughout the whole of the period between the Anglo-Saxon settlement and the Norman Conquest, and the late Anglo-Saxon coinage was sufficiently successful to survive with only minimal reform throughout the Norman period as well. However, the nature of both coinage and kingship changed more than once between the fifth century and the eleventh, and this paper will argue that a number of distinct phases in the development in the coinage reflect broader developments in Anglo-Saxon kingship. These phases are, of course, artificial constructs to a great extent, and it is important to note that the shift from one phase to another did not always take place in all areas at the same time, reflecting the political fragmentation of Anglo-Saxon England, and particularly the different dates at which the separate kingdoms bought into an ideological concept of Romanised Christian kingship of which the issuing of coinage was one aspect. Nevertheless, I believe that the visible shifts in the coinage provide a useful perspective for considering developments in other aspects of royal authority. The scope of this paper does not permit me to go into those other aspects in detail, but I hope that it may stimulate others to explore such relationships more closely.

Phase 1: The pre-Christian period, c. 410-600

On current evidence, it seems safe to state that no coinage was officially minted or issued in England between the departure of the Roman administration in the early fifth century and the conversion of Æthelberht of Kent in the late sixth century.[1] Production of coinage in Roman Britain had stopped long before 410, but the end of the Roman administration and the withdrawal of the armies brought an end to the large-scale importation of Roman coinage to underpin that administration. There is thus no doubt that the Anglo-Saxon settlements which coincided with the end of Roman Britain also coincided with a major change in the nature of monetary circulation and function. In an influential article in 1961, John Kent argued that there was, effectively, a complete break in the coinage, and that there was no monetary economy in early Anglo-Saxon England. Those coins which were found in graves re-used as weights or jewellery were deemed to represent chance finds which were being re-used, rather than the re-use of circulating currency.[2] This view of the coinage reflected a broader interpretation of the end of Roman Britain, but while a number of approaches to the nature of Anglo-Saxon settlement (and continuity, or the lack of it) have been considered, Kent's interpretation of the coinage has remained the orthodox position until very recently. This approach has coloured interpretations not only of the fifth and sixth centuries, but even the seventh, entering the period of the earliest Anglo-Saxon coinage, considered in phase 2 below. Even where coin finds showed no sign of re-use, the assumption that there was no monetary circulation meant that alternative explanations had to be provided for the presence of the coins.

More recently, this view has been questioned. Ken Dark has noted the presence of coins in a number of fifth-century archaeological sites. Peter Guest has argued that the Roman hoards of the fifth century, while supporting a massive reduction in the supply of coinage on the Roman withdrawal, are consistent with continued circulation

---

[1] Many late Roman hoards, now believed to date from the 5th century (see below) contain both clipped siliquae and imitative siliquae. (A siliqua is a small silver Roman coin of the 4th-5th centuries, worth 1/24 of a gold solidus.) Both clipping and imitation had already begun in the 4th century, but it now seems likely that clipping intensified in the 5th century, and it is possible that both the clipping and the issue of the imitative siliquae may represent attempts by legitimate authorities to stretch out a limited coin stock, rather than unofficial abuse of the coinage. However, this currently remains only a hypothesis, and requires a detailed study of the imitative types and their chronology either to support or disprove the argument. No such study has as yet been undertaken, nor does it appear likely in the near future. Gareth Williams, 'Anglo-Saxon gold coinage. Part 1: the transition from Roman to Anglo-Saxon coinage', *BNJ* 80 (2010), 51-75.
[2] 2 John P. C. Kent, 'From Roman Britain to Anglo-Saxon England', in *Anglo-Saxon Coins: studies presented to F. M. Stenton on the occasion of his 80th birthday 17 May 1960*, ed. Michael R. H. Dolley (London, 1961), pp. 1-22. For a recent re-statement of this position on Roman coins from Anglo-Saxon graves, including extensive reference to earlier literature on the subject, see Thomas S. N. Moorhead, 'Roman bronze coinage in sub-Roman and early Anglo-Saxon England', in *Coinage and History in the North Sea World, c.500-1200. Essays in Honour of Marion Archibald*, ed. Barrie J. Cook and Gareth Williams (Leiden and Boston, 2006), pp. 99-109.

of existing coinage beyond 410, while as early as 1987, Michael Metcalf suggested that the growing number of coin finds from the late sixth and seventh centuries, most of which showed no signs of re-use, indicated a greater volume of monetary circulation than had previously been recognised.[3] Metcalf correctly predicted that the number of finds would continue to increase, and a survey by Richard Abdy and myself published in 2006 included 379 single finds (including 288 probable imported coins (253 gold and silver, and 35 copper)) and 18 hoards deposited in Britain between *c*. 410 and *c*. 675.[4] The number of imported gold and silver coins had risen to 309 by the beginning of 2010, and the number continues to increase each year.[5] The overwhelming pattern of the survey was that finds from graves predominantly showed signs of re-use, but that finds which were not from graves did not. Earlier interpretations were predominantly derived from grave finds, and both the increased volume of the corpus and the greatly increased proportion of coins showing no signs of re-use point much more clearly towards monetary circulation. This was certainly not as well regulated and controlled as the late Roman monetary system, but that does not mean, as Kent suggested, that monetary circulation effectively ceased completely. A number of late Roman numismatists have recently argued that elements of the Roman monetary system survived well into the fifth century, and I have argued for an economy based on the use of imported coinage throughout the settlement and conversion period.[6] The majority of these imported coins were gold *solidi* and *tremisses,* but some silver and bronze also continued to enter England, and there was probably also some re-use of earlier Roman low-value coins.[7] Alongside imported coin

there is clear evidence of the monetary use of bullion, as demonstrated by the Patching hoard (*terminus post quem c*. 475), but it is unclear whether or not this was officially sanctioned. Single finds of gold coin-shaped blanks and cut fragments of imported gold coins indicate that bullion continued to be used north of the Thames in the early seventh century.[8]

The nature of this economy is still not well understood, and would repay further and more detailed study. More detailed analysis of the fifth and sixth centuries would almost certainly allow this period to be divided into a number of shorter sub-phases, but that lies beyond the scope of this paper, and I will merely summarise the key characteristics of the period as a whole, at least from the mid-fifth century, if not before. These characteristics are:

- Continued use of the residual late-Roman coin-stock, possibly with some minting of imitative coinage, and with some use of bullion

- Use of a variety of residual and imported coinage, with little or no official regulation

- Some re-use of coinage in jewellery, although this represents a small minority in stray finds.

- Widespread circulation, especially in eastern England, but in relatively low volumes

- The majority of the imported coinage was specifically regal/imperial until the late sixth century, after which Frankish mint-and-moneyer types became increasingly dominant

- Virtually all of the imported coinage was explicitly Christian[9]

The evidence that coinage provides for kingship in this phase is thus largely negative. Early Anglo-Saxon kings did not issue coinage, nor did they apparently regulate the circulation of such imported coinage as there was. However, the presence of that coinage, along with other archaeological evidence, clearly points to contacts with coin-issuing kingdoms in western Europe as well as with the Byzantine empire These contacts were apparently based in part on monetary trade, while the imported coins provided models once the Anglo-Saxons chose to begin

[3] Ken Dark, *Britain and the End of the Roman Empire* (Stroud, 2000); Peter Guest, 'Hoards from the end of Roman Britain', in *Coin Hoards from Roman Britain, Volume X,* ed. Roger Bland and John Orna-Ornstein (London, 1997), 411-23; David Metcalf, 'The availability and uses of gold coinage in England, c. 670: Kentish primacy reconsidered', *Festskrift Lagerqvist, Numismatiska Meddelanden* 37 (1989), 267-274.

[4] Richard A. Abdy and Gareth Williams, 'A catalogue of hoards and single finds from the British Isles, *c*. AD 410-680', in Cook and Williams, *Coinage and History in the North Sea World*, pp. 11-74.

[5] For the 2010 listing, see Williams, 'Anglo-Saxon gold coinage. Part 1'. For ongoing finds, an online database, the *Corpus of Early Medieval Coin Finds*, is maintained by the Fitzwilliam Museum at www.fitzmuseum. cam.ac.uk/coins/emc. This is regularly updated, and provides an invaluable resource in making recent finds available for study alongside the established corpus.

[6] Guest, 'Hoards'; R. Abdy, 'After Patching: imported and recycled coinage in fifth- and sixth-century Britain', in Cook and Williams, *Coinage and History in the North Sea World*, pp. 75-98; Gareth Williams, 'Monetary circulation in England in the Age of Conversion, c. AD 580-680', in Cook and Williams, *Coinage and History in the North Sea World*, pp. 145-92; *Idem*, 'Anglo-Saxon gold coinage. Part 1'; Thomas S. N. Moorhead, Roger Bland, and Penelope Walton, 'Finds of late Roman silver coins from England and Wales', in *Silver in the Post-Roman World*, ed. Fraser Hunter and Kenneth Painter, Society of Antiquaries of Scotland Monograph (Edinburgh, forthcoming). Abdy ('After Patching') also suggests that although authorities in fifth-century Britain did not have enough silver to issue coinage, they may have made payments using clippings from existing coins as a sort of official issue.

[7] Abdy and Williams, 'Catalogue'; Williams, 'Monetary circulation', pp. 159-61; *Idem*, 'Anglo-Saxon gold coinage. Part 1'; Thomas S. N. Moorhead, 'Early Byzantine copper coins found in Britain: a review in the light of new finds recorded by the Portable Antiquities Scheme', in *Ancient History, Numismatics and Epigraphy in the Mediterranean World: studies in memory of Clemens E. Bosch and Sabahat Atlan and in honour of Nezahat Baydur,* ed. Oğuz Tekin (Istanbul, 2009), pp. 263-74.

[8] Abdy, 'After Patching'; *Idem*, 'Patching and Oxborough: the latest coin hoards from Roman Britain or the first early medieval hoards from England?', in *Coin Hoards from Roman Britain, Volume XII, Collection Moneta* 97, ed. Richard A. Abdy, Eleanor Ghey, Celine Hughes and Ian Leins (Wetteren, 2009), 394-5; *Idem*, 'The Patching Hoard', in *Silver in the Post-Roman World*, ed. Fraser Hunter and Kenneth Painter, Society of Antiquaries of Scotland Monograph (Edinburgh, forthcoming); Gareth Williams, 'The circulation, minting and use of coins in East Anglia, *c*. AD 580–675', in *North Anglia and the North Sea World*, ed. D. Brown, Robert Liddiard and Lucy Marten (Woodbridge, forthcoming); *Idem*, 'Hack-silver and precious metal economies: a view from the Viking age', in Hunter and Painter, *Silver in the Post-Roman World*.

[9] The exceptions are two Sasanian drachms with Zoroastrian imagery (Abdy and Williams, 'Catalogue', nos. 252-3).

to issue coinage of their own. Interestingly, the areas showing the strongest evidence of coin use in the fifth to seventh centuries are the main areas of Anglo-Saxon settlement, rather than the areas in which Dark and others have suggested the existence of Romano-British kingdoms providing an element of post-Roman continuity. If anything, this suggests that the Anglo-Saxons (or possibly their employers) in the east and south-east, showed greater continuity. Distribution of the coins also suggests that there were direct contacts between several emergent Anglo-Saxon kingdoms and the Continent, and while the kingdom of Kent shows the strongest evidence for contact, this is less dominant, and also less unusual, than formerly appeared to be the case.[10]

Phase 2: Early Anglo-Saxon gold coinage, c. 600-675

Production of native Anglo-Saxon coinage appears to have begun during the reign of Æthelberht of Kent, although the introduction of coinage cannot be precisely dated, nor are there any coins recorded in the name of Æthelberht himself. The introduction of coinage seems to have been closely linked with conversion to Christianity, and the spread of coin production in different kingdoms probably mirrored the gradual spread of Christianity. This phase therefore overlapped considerably with the previous phase, with individual kingdoms making the transition at different times. The general characteristics of the phase are as follows:

- All coinage in gold, following continental pattern of solidi and tremisses

- Coins issued locally, but coinage continued to be imported

- Limited re-use of coins in jewellery continues

- Variety of designs, predominantly imitative

- Rarely explicitly regal

- Many types have illegible legends, or no legend at all.

- No control of circulation

- Most coins explicitly Christian

Following a wider pattern throughout monetary history, the coinage was heavily influenced by the imported coins with which the Anglo-Saxons were already familiar. The combination of larger solidi and smaller tremisses was common to the Frankish, Byzantine and Visigothic coinage, but the designs were predominantly influenced by Frankish coins, with a smaller direct influence from Byzantine designs.[11] There was also a strong influence

from earlier Roman coins of the late third to mid-fourth centuries. This Roman influence is particularly apparent towards the end of this phase, as the coinage became debased into pale gold, but the Licinius type was issued at the height of the gold coinage, while a solidus imitating coinage of Constantine's mother Helena is probably also not particularly late.[12] The designs were predominantly sub-Roman profile busts combined with variations on the form of the cross, although one type carries a facing bust without numismatic parallels, although it may be derived from ecclesiastical art.[13]

The strong Frankish influence on design reflects the dominance of Frankish coinage within the archaeological record, but it may also reflect Frankish political influence. Ian Wood has argued for a period of Frankish hegemony over Kent in the late sixth century, and this would certainly be consistent with the Frankish influence on the coinage.[14] Although, as mentioned, the coinage shows a clear link with Christianity, its introduction in Kent may predate the arrival of Augustine. A pendant bearing the inscription LEVDARDVS EPS can be identified with reasonable certainty with Bishop Liudhard, who accompanied Æthelberht's Frankish wife Bertha when she came to Kent. Although this piece has often been described as a medalet, other pendants from the same site (and possibly from the same grave) incorporate coins mounted with suspension loops, and it is unclear whether the Liudhard piece represents a coin re-used as jewellery or a piece of pseudo-coin jewellery reflecting a wider taste for coin jewellery.[15]

Other early types follow the Frankish pattern of naming mints and moneyers rather than rulers, and the only certain explicitly regal type is interpreted as an issue of Æthelberht's son Eadbald (AD 616-40).[16] Although known from a few examples, the use of at least five different reverse dies suggests that this was a coinage of some size. Interestingly, the reverses all seem to carry blundered versions of a London mint signature. The

[10] Williams, 'Monetary circulation', pp. 170-73; *Idem*, 'Anglo-Saxon gold coinage. Part 1'; *Idem*, 'East Anglia'.
[11] For the prototypes, see Philip Grierson and Mark A. S. Blackburn, *Medieval European Coinage: Volume 1, The Early Middle Ages* (Cambridge, 1986).
[12] Duncan Hook and Gareth Williams, 'Analysis of gold content and its implications for the chronology of the early Anglo-Saxon coinage', in Anna Gannon (with contributions by Marion M. Archibald, Duncan Hook and Gareth Williams), *Sylloge of Coins of the British Isles, 63. British Museum. Anglo-Saxon Coins.* Part I. *Early Anglo-Saxon Coins and Continental Silver Coins of the North Sea, c.600-760* (London, forthcoming). Gareth Williams, 'Anglo-Saxon gold coinage. Part 2: corpus, chronology and attribution of Anglo-Saxon gold coinage', *BNJ* 83 (forthcoming).
[13] Anna Gannon, The *Iconography of Early Anglo-Saxon Coinage. Sixth to Eighth Centuries* (Oxford, 2003), p. 25.
[14] Ian Wood, *The Merovingian North Sea* (Alingsås, 1983)..
[15] Carol Sutherland, *Anglo-Saxon Gold Coinage in the Light of the Crondall Hoard* (Oxford, 1948), p. 74; Williams, 'Anglo-Saxon gold coinage. Part 2'.
[16] Sutherland, *Anglo-Saxon Gold Coinage*; David M. Metcalf, *Thrymsas and Sceattas in the Ashmolean Museum, Oxford*, Royal Numismatic Society Special Publication no. 276, 3 vols (London, 1993-4); Mark A. S. Blackburn, 'A new coin of King Eadbald of Kent (616-40)', *Chris Rudd List* 34 (1998) 2-4; Gareth Williams, 'The gold coinage of Eadbald, king of Kent (AD 616-40)', *BNJ* 68 (1998) 137-40. Another type with an inscription beginning EAN- is more ambiguous, as this could be the beginning of the name of a ruler (although it is difficult to identify a plausible candidate) or a moneyer. Williams, 'Anglo-Saxon gold coinage. Part 2'.

status of London in this period is difficult to interpret, and it seems at various times in the early seventh century to have fallen under the influence of the East Saxons, Mercia and Kent. While Bede seems to suggest that London was under East Saxon or Mercian rule throughout Eadbald's reign, the East Saxon king was Eadbald's cousin, and the London coins may thus point to some sort of political accommodation not specifically recorded by Bede.[17] A recent find of a related coin type with a clear Canterbury mint signature may also carry Eadbald's name, or may be a mint and moneyer type.[18] Apart from other Kentish mint and moneyer types, the only issue to carry a legible mint signature is the facing bust issue mentioned above, which has a clear London signature. This may perhaps be an episcopal issue, with the facing bust representing a bishop rather than a king, and has been tentatively associated with Bishop Mellitus (604-16/18).[19]

Other early gold types either carry only blundered legends, or no legends at all, so that the attribution to a particular kingdom can only be deduced from the distribution of coin finds. One group can be assigned with reasonable certainty to the kingdom of Northumbria, and probably more specifically within the smaller kingdom of Deira, which together with the more northerly kingdom of Bernicia and elements of the British kingdoms of Rheged and Elmet came to form the kingdom of Northumbria in the course of the seventh century. The majority of the provenanced finds come from Yorkshire, with another from north Lincolnshire, reflecting Northumbria's intermittent dominance of the sub-kingdom of Lindsey in the seventh century.[20] Metallurgical analysis suggests that this coinage was established in the late 620s or 630s, after the extension of the Augustinian mission to Northumbria under Paulinus.[21] The attribution of other types is complicated by the presence of several of them in the Crondall hoard, deposited c. 640, along with one Byzantine and several Frankish tremisses.[22] The presence of such a mixture demonstrates very clearly the lack of any regulation of the currency in Hampshire at that period, and the presence of individual types in the Crondall hoard says little about

their attribution, although the variety of Anglo-Saxon types suggests that they represent the coinage of more than one kingdom. By the time of the introduction of the late 'pale gold' phase of the gold coinage in the mid-seventh century, a number of issues can be identified as coming from north of the Thames, probably East Anglia.[23] These are derived from Roman rather than Frankish issues, and it is possible that earlier Roman-derived types copying coins of Licinius and Helena may also have come from north of the Thames, reflecting the conscious Romanisation which has been suggested in one interpretation of the Sutton Hoo burial.[24] A final group, containing both runic coins and related issues with Roman lettering, seems to have been struck somewhere along the Thames valley, or slightly to the north, dating from c. 620-40. The attribution of this type is problematic, owing to the uncertain political geography of the period, and attribution to a specific kingdom depends on the interpretation of the Tribal Hidage, a subject too large to be addressed here.[25]

With growing numbers of single finds, it may prove possible to attribute other early types more firmly, and work is currently under way on the distribution, chronology and scale of the early gold coinage.[26] On the current evidence, however, coinage seems to have begun in Kent by the beginning of the seventh century, to have been established in Northumbria in the second quarter of the century, and to have been issued in East Anglia and/or Essex certainly by the 650s, and quite possibly before c. 640. The introduction of the Kentish coinage shows most clearly the link with the introduction of Christianity, and with a style of Romanised Christian kingship in which the king and the Church supported each other, and issuing coinage was one of a number of recognised regal activities. The spread of coinage to other early kingdoms is also consistent with the growing success of the Augustinian mission. It should be noted that this is a specifically continental connection, rather than simply a link with Christianity. The Christian kingdoms in Ireland, Scotland and Wales did not issue coins throughout the Anglo-Saxon period, with a single exception in the tenth century which will be discussed below.[27]

[17] Bede, HE II.iii; The Ecclesiastical History of the English People, ed. and trans. Judith Maclure and Roger Collins (Oxford, 1994), pp. 74-5. I am grateful to Alex Burghart for discussion of this point.
[18] Mark A. S. Blackburn, 'Two new types of Anglo-Saxon gold shillings', in Cook and Williams, Coinage and History in the North Sea World, pp.127-40.
[19] Sutherland, Anglo-Saxon Gold Coinage, pp. 41-5, 856; Gannon, Iconography, pp. 25-6.
[20] Bruce Eagles, 'Lindsey', in The Origins of Anglo-Saxon Kingdoms, ed. Steven Bassett (London and New York, 1989), pp. 202-12; David P. Kirby, The Earliest English Kings (London, 1991), passim; Williams, 'The gold coinage of seventh-century Northumbria revisited', Numismatic Circular 115.1 (February 2007), 6-8.
[21] Williams, 'Gold coinage of seventh-century Northumbria'; Hook and Williams, 'Analysis of gold content'.
[22] John Y. Akerman, 'Description of some Merovingian, and other gold coins, discovered in the parish of Crondale, in Hampshire, in the year 1828', Numismatic Chronicle 6 (1843-4) 171-182; Ponton d'Amécourt, le vicomte de, 'Farther notes on the gold coins discovered in 1828 at Crondal, Hants', Numismatic Chronicle new series 12 (1872) 72-82; Carol H. V. Sutherland, Anglo-Saxon Gold Coinage; Philip Grierson, 'The purpose of the Sutton Hoo coins', Antiquity 44 (1970) 14-18; Williams, 'Monetary circulation', pp. 174-5.

[23] Metcalf, Thrymsas and Sceattas, I, 47-9; Williams, 'East Anglia'; Idem, 'Anglo-Saxon gold coinage. Part 2'.
[24] William Filmer-Sankey, 'The "Roman emperor" in the Sutton Hoo ship burial', Journal of the British Archaeological Association 149 (1996) 1-9; Leslie Webster, 'From Hoxne to Dover: recent gold finds in Britain and their political geography c. 400-600 AD', in Treasure in the Medieval West, ed. Elizabeth Tyler (York, 2000), pp. 251-262.
[25] For overviews of the debate concerning the interpretation of the Tribal Hidage, see Alexander R. Rumble, 'Appendix III The Tribal Hidage: an annotated bibliography', in The Defence of Wessex, The Burghal Hidage and Anglo-Saxon Fortifications, ed. David Hill and Alexander R. Rumble (Manchester, 1996), pp.182-8; Peter Featherstone, 'The Tribal Hidage and the Ealdormen of Mercia', in Mercia: an Anglo-Saxon kingdom in Europe, ed. Michelle P. Brown and Carol A. Farr (London and New York, 2001), pp. 23-34; for dating and attribution of the 'Benutigoii' type, see Hook and Williams, 'Analysis of gold content'; Williams, 'Anglo-Saxon gold coinage. Part 2'.
[26] Williams, 'Anglo-Saxon gold coinage. Part 2'.
[27] Williams, 'Currency and circulation', 167-8, 186-8; Idem, 'Kingship, Christianity and coinage: monetary and political perspectives on silver economy in the Viking Age', in Silver Economy in the Viking Age, ed. James Graham-Campbell and Gareth Williams (Walnut Springs, CA,

The use of coinage in Kent is corroborated by references to 'shillings' in early Kentish law-codes. Philip Grierson has argued convincingly that the term refers to the smaller size of gold coin in circulation, equivalent to the Frankish tremissis, and sometimes referred to misleadingly by modern scholars as 'thrymsas'.[28] The absence of early surviving law-codes from other kingdoms may again give a misleading impression that Kent was something of a special case. Nevertheless, the fact that in Kent at least the introduction of written law coincided closely with the introduction of locally-issued coinage reinforces the link between coinage and the style of Romanised Christian kingship promoted by both the Frankish and the Augustinian missions. While the laws tell us little about general monetary use of coinage in the period, they use shillings to measure the levels both of fines owed to the king and of compensation payments to victims of crime (or their relatives). This shows a link between coinage, law and royal authority, but the use of coins as a measure of value indicates their increasing importance and suggests that their use was becoming fairly widespread. This does not necessarily indicate that such payments were necessarily made in coin, but at the very least there must have been established prices and values, in order for payments defined in shillings to be paid in kind. The fact that these values appear in relation to fines and compensation payments also indicates that kings felt that they had had a right to regulate such values, as well as the right (and responsibility) to regulate the use of violence within society.[29]

Phase 3: Anonymous silver, c. 675-760

The next phase of the coinage is in many ways one of the richest in the Anglo-Saxon period, but also one of the hardest to interpret, and the phase in which the association with kingship is hardest to trace. Following the gradual debasement during the previous gold phase, gold coinage ceased altogether, and was replaced c. 675 by the small silver pennies sometimes referred to as sceattas.[30] These were minted in large numbers until the mid-eighth century, in a variety of designs. Most of the varieties lack literate inscriptions, so the attribution of particular types within this varied coinage to specific areas, or even specific mint towns, is largely based on the distribution of coin finds. Interestingly, some areas seem to have had very tightly controlled circulation, with only certain types permitted. Other types circulated more widely, and circulated alongside each other, within a broad monetary zone that

spanned the North Sea, with links to Frisia and western Jutland as well as the Anglo-Saxon and Frankish kingdoms, and it now seems clear that some types commonly found in England are Frisian, rather than Anglo-Saxon, although some of these may then have spawned Anglo-Saxon imitations.[31] The characteristics of this phase can be summarised as follows:

• Coins issued locally, sometimes with more than one mint per kingdom

• Wide variety of design, featuring both imitative and original coin types

• Coinage anonymous, and predominantly without literate legends

• Variable control of circulation

• Not explicitly regal

No coin from this phase is explicitly regal, to the extent of carrying a ruler's name. Types carrying the names PADA and ÆTHILIRED, which were formerly thought to represent the Mercian rulers Peada and Æthelred are now generally accepted as the names of moneyers,[32] and the few other types that carry inscriptions (whether in runes or the Latin alphabet) are probably also predominantly more or less blundered versions of Anglo-Saxon or Frankish moneyers' names. The exceptions are a literate London mint signature, and an intriguing inscription MONITA SCORVM, which will be discussed further below.

The absence of explicitly regal inscriptions does not mean that none of the coins were regal in character. In the absence of inscriptions, the imagery of the coins often carried a symbolic message and Anna Gannon, in her detailed studies of the iconography of the coinage of this period, has argued that the symbolism of these images would have been more clearly understood than inscriptions in a largely illiterate society.[33] The finds record makes it clear that this was a much more substantial coinage than the gold phase which preceded it, and one which must have penetrated to a much lower level in the social hierarchy. This period

2007), pp. 177-214, at 184, 206.
[28] Philip Grierson, 'La Function sociale de la monnaie en angleterre aux VIIe-VIIIe siècles', in *Moneta e scambi nell'alto medioevo: 21-27 aprile 1960*, Settimane di studio del Centro italiano di studi sull'alto Medioevo 8 (Spoleto, 1961), pp. 341-85; see also John Hines. 'Units of account in gold and silver in seventh-century England: scillingas, sceattas and pæningas', *Antiquaries Journal* 90 (2010), 153-73.
[29] Guy Halsall, *Warfare and Society in the Barbarian West, 450-900* (London, 2003), pp. 14-20.
[30] This term is probably a misnomer, based on a misunderstanding of the term used for a small weight of gold in early law codes (Grierson, 'La Function sociale'). However, for a proposed rehabilitation of the link between the term *sceattas* and coinage, see Hines, 'Units of account'.
[31] Metcalf, *Thrymsas and Sceattas*; *Idem*, 'Variations in the composition of the currency at different places in England', in *Markets in Early Medieval Europe: trading and 'productive' Sites, 650-850*, ed. Tom Pestell and Katharina Ulmschneider (Bollington, 2003), pp. 37-47; W. Op den Velde and David M. Metcalf, 'The monetary economy of the Netherlands, c. 690–c. 715 and the trade with England: a study of the sceattas of Series D', *Jaarbook voor Munt-en Penningkunde* 90 (2007 for 2003); C. Feveile, 'Series X and coin circulation in Ribe', in *Studies in Early Medieval Coinage 1: Two Decades of Discovery*, ed. Tony Abramson (Woodbridge, 2008), pp. 53–67; David M. Metcalf and W. Op den Velde, 'The monetary economy of the Netherlands, c. 690–c. 760 and the trade with England: a study of the "Porcupine" sceattas of Series E', *Jaarboek voor Munt- en Penningkunde* 96–7 (2011 for 2009–10); Gannon *et al.*, *Sylloge*.
[32] Mark A. S. Blackburn, 'A survey of Anglo-Saxon and Frisian coins with runic inscriptions', in *Old English Runes and their Continental Background*, ed. A. Bammesberger (Heidelberg, 1991) pp. 137-89; Metcalf, *Thrymsas and Sceattas*, I, 73; Gannon, *Iconography*, p. 180.
[33] Gannon, *Iconography, passim*.

coincides with the expansion of the coastal and riverine trading centres known as *wics*, and in some cases individual coin series can be associated with specific *wics*, such as Series H with *Hamwih* (Southampton).[34] In addition to clearly defined *wics* in the historical and/or archaeological record, this period also saw a marked increase in the so-called productive sites identified through metal detecting, many of which provide evidence of both production and exchange, including in some cases concentrations of coins.[35] The spread of coinage in this phase must be seen at least in part as reflecting the everyday use of money within a coin-based economy, focused on pre-urban trading centres. At the same time, a growing corpus of coin finds of this period from rural areas indicates that coin-use was not limited to trading centres.[36]

Against that background, it is important to recognise that many of the designs on the coinage of this period continue to symbolise royal power. Royal/imperial busts remain common, although sometimes crudely copied, with Anglo-Saxon kings continuing to portray themselves as the heirs of Roman emperors.[37] Other images, such as the lion, were also associated with kingship in Christian iconography.[38] These images therefore suggest a continued link between coinage and royal authority, rather than minting by a merchant class without legitimate authority and purely in response to economic need. Other images, however, are harder to link directly to kingship. Many have religious motifs, and Gannon has argued that some types may have been ecclesiastical rather than royal issues.[39] This would be consistent with Marion Archibald's suggestion that MONITA SCORVM is a contraction of *moneta sanctorum*, or 'money of the saints', which also suggests an ecclesiastical issue.[40] Gannon links these ecclesiastical coinages with John Blair's work on minster sites. Blair has argued that many productive sites were monastic sites rather than purely secular centres of trade and production, and thus that the Church was closely linked with trade and commerce.[41] This would certainly be consistent with ecclesiastical issues, and would also help to explain the

apparently simultaneous production of different types within individual kingdoms. There are also parallels for ecclesiastical issues in the Frankish coinage.[42]

It is also notable that explicitly episcopal coins appear in the following phase of regal coinage (see below), and it may well be that some of the issues of the anonymous phase are also episcopal issues. In the absence of documentary evidence for minting rights, it is equally possible that these were a new development in the late eighth century or that episcopal coins were an established tradition within the anonymous coinage, and that episcopal coinage only becomes explicitly visible at the same time as regal coinage because the use of inscriptions became standard in this phase. How far ecclesiastical issues represent a departure from the normal pattern of a firm link between coins and kingship depends on whether one believes that churchmen simply assumed for themselves the right to issue coins, or whether this remained an essentially royal prerogative which might be granted to others in the same way as land or other privileges. The latter certainly appears to be the case at least from the tenth century (see below), but since this represents a later phase of both coinage and kingship, one must be wary of assuming that this had necessarily always been the case.[43]

The difficulty that we have in interpreting this phase of the coinage is that the history of the period is comparatively poorly documented, except in Northumbria, and Northumbria falls slightly apart from the general pattern of the development of Anglo-Saxon coinage, as discussed under the following phase. What does seem clear is that this phase coincides with the spread and consolidation of Christian kingship, including the promulgation of written law-codes, and the spread of bookland tenure and, arguably, the beginnings of formalised military organisation. What is less clear is how effective royal authority and the manipulation of royal prerogatives really were in this period. Bede's often-cited letter to Egberht points to the dangers of granting bookland to purely nominal monasteries without sufficient safeguards to ensure that the needs of either kingdom or Church were properly met.[44] If, as suggested above, legitimate minsters were issuing coins of their own, it is possible that the same is true of the sort of pseudo-monasteries described by Bede.

Equally, the written sources present a somewhat confusing account of over-kings, kings and sub-kings, as well as of internal conflict between rival contenders for the kingship of individual kingdoms. Within this period, the exact relationships between different levels of kingship is not

[34] For a recent survey and reassessment of *wics*, see Tom Pestell, 'Markets, *emporia*, *wics*, and "productive" sites: pre-Viking trade centres in Anglo-Saxon England', in *The Oxford Handbook of Anglo-Saxon Archaeology*, ed. Helena Hamerow, David A. Hinton and Sally Crawford (Oxford, 2011), pp. 556–79. For the attribution of Series H to Hamwih, see David M. Metcalfe, 'The coins', in *Southampton Finds, Vol. 1: the coins and pottery from Hamwic*, ed. Philip Andrews (Southampton, 1988), pp. 17–59. For an overview, with references of current thinking of attributions of other series, see Gannon *et al.*, *Sylloge*.
[35] Mark A. S. Blackburn, '"Productive" sites and the pattern of coin-loss in England, 600-1180', in Pestell and Ulmschneider, *Markets in Early Medieval Europe*, pp. 20-36; Pestell, 'Markets, *emporia*, *wics*, and "productive" sites'.
[36] For overall distribution of coins of this phase, see the *Corpus of Early Medieval Coin Finds*, as n. 5.
[37] Gannon, *Iconography*, pp. 23-62.
[38] Gannon, *Iconography*; Anna Gannon, 'King of all beasts – beast of all kings. Lions in Anglo-Saxon coinage and art', in *Medieval Animals*, ed. Aleksander Pluskowski, Archaeological Review from Cambridge 18 (Cambridge, 2002), pp. 22–36.
[39] Gannon, *Iconography*, pp. 190-1.
[40] Marion M. Archibald, 'Coins', in *The Making of England. Anglo-Saxon Art and Culture AD 600-900*, ed. Leslie Webster and Janet Backhouse (London, 1991), pp. 62-7, at 66, no. 56.
[41] John Blair, *The Church in Anglo-Saxon Society* (Oxford, 2005).
[42] Grierson and Blackburn, *Medieval European Coinage*, p. 139.
[43] A detailed discussion of the issue of ecclesiastical coinage in Anglo-Saxon England is provided by Rory Naismith, 'Money of the saints: Church and coinage in early Anglo-Saxon England', in *Studies in Early Medieval Coinage 3*, ed. Tony Abramson and Gareth Williams (forthcoming).
[44] Blair, *Church in Anglo-Saxon Society*, pp.100-108; Naismith, 'Money of the saints'.

always clear, not least because they mostly seem to have depended on the temporary and personal relative positions of individual rulers, rather than permanent institutional relationships between different kingdoms. Traditional interpretations of the *bretwalda* as an institutionalised 'high king' have been rejected by most modern commentators, but there seems no doubt that at varying points in this phase (and the preceding one), individual rulers exercised varying degrees of authority and overlordship over others, and that the balance of power shifted between different kingdoms in the course of this period. Over-kingship almost certainly involved the imposition of tribute and perhaps military service, but it is less clear that in this phase it also involved curtailing symbols of authority such as the issue of coins, laws and charters within individual sub-kingdoms.[45] A large number of different types can be identified in a series of sub-phases within this coinage, and not all of these can yet be attributed to a particular area.[46] There are probably not enough different types for each of the individual kingdoms or peoples listed in the Tribal Hidage to have issued their own, but too many simply to attribute one coinage to each of the major kingdoms. This might be explained if some of the types are ecclesiastical issues, as discussed above, but it may also be explained by the issue of coins by the rulers of minor kingdoms, or even some which only appear in the historical sources as sub-kingdoms.

A number of issues about the interpretation of coinage within this phase remain opaque. If coins were, as suggested, a powerful symbol of kingship, were they perhaps issued by pretenders as well as by 'legitimate' kings? How far down the hierarchy of rulers did the right to issue coins extend? Did grants of the right to issue coin proliferate in the same way as grants of bookland, with coin-issue temporarily extended to become an elite prerogative rather than simply a royal one? The short answer is that we do not know, but the body of evidence for coinage within this phase is growing steadily. This is a very active area of research, and as our understanding of the chronological and geographical distribution of the different coin types continues to improve, a systematic attempt to map the distribution of coin-types onto a political landscape derived from written sources might well prove to be instructive.

Phase 4: Explicitly regal coinage in separate kingdoms, c. 760-924

The relationship between coins and kings is more apparent in the next phase, which saw the introduction of literate inscriptions on all coins, the vast majority of which were explicitly regal, and many of which identify in some form the kingdoms in which they were issued. There were a number of episcopal issues, but many of these were joint issues with kings, and therefore probably represent the granting of minting rights by kings, as seen in later law codes (see below). Like claims to landholding through bookland tenure, this was therefore effectively a restatement of royal power rather than a weakening of it. This is probably also the case with the majority, if not all, of sole issues in the names of archbishops of Canterbury and York, although it has been suggested that some of the solely archiepiscopal issues of Canterbury under Offa and Coenwulf may represent attempts to challenge the authority of the Mercian kings over Canterbury.[47] This phase extends from the eighth century to the early tenth, and the main factor that differentiates this from later phases is that coins were issued by a number of different kings in different kingdoms, a pattern which disappeared with the gradual unification of England in the tenth century, which represents the subsequent phase. Within the broad phase of regal coinage of separate kingdoms, a number of developments are apparent, and this phase has therefore been divided into sub-phases. Nevertheless, there are a small number of key characteristics which cover the whole phase:

- Coins explicitly regal, and literate
- Some control of circulation
- Coins issued by individual kingdoms, often reflected in designs/inscriptions
- Various sub-phases

Phase 4a: Regal coinage: Images of authority

The first sub-phase covers the eighth to the mid-ninth centuries, with overlap in some kingdoms with both the preceding phase and the next sub-phase. This phase began much earlier in Northumbria than in the other kingdoms, in the reign of Aldfrith (685-704), at a time when other kingdoms were still firmly in the anonymous coinage of phase 3.[48] Aldfrith's coinage was of similar fabric, but now carried a regal inscription. Pursuing the link between coinage and Romanised Christianity discussed above, it is perhaps not surprising that Northumbria

[45] James Campbell, *Bede's Reges and Principes*, Jarrow Lecture 1979; Barbara A. E. Yorke, 'The vocabulary of Anglo-Saxon overlordship', *Anglo-Saxon Studies in Archaeology and History* 2 (1981), 171-200; Thomas Charles-Edwards, 'Early medieval kingships in the British Isles', in Bassett, *The Origins of Anglo-Saxon Kingdoms*, pp. 28-39; David N. Dumville, 'The terminology of overkingship in early Anglo-Saxon kingship', in *The Anglo-Saxons from the Migration Period to the eighth century: an ethnographic perspective*, ed. John Hines (Woodbridge, 1997), pp. 345-73.
[46] The most comprehensive discussion of this coinage, including a number of attributions, remains Metcalf, *Thrymsas and Sceattas*. However, for discussion of chronology and attributions informed by more recent finds, see Gannon *et al.*, *Sylloge*, while Tony Abramson, *Sceatta List* (Leeds, 2012) offers a new classification of the different types within the series, including new types and mules discovered since the last major classification of this series, in Stuart E. Rigold, 'The principal series of English sceattas', *BNJ* 47 (1977), 21-30.
[47] Christopher E. Blunt, Colin S. S. Lyon and Bernard H. I. H. Stewart, 'The coinage of southern England, 796-840', *BNJ* 32 (1963), 1-74; Naismith, 'Money of the saints'.
[48] David M. Metcalf, 'The coinage of King Aldfrith of Northumbria (685-704) and some contemporary imitations', *BNJ* 76 (2006), 147-58; Elizabeth J. E. Pirie, 'Contrast and continuity within the coinage of Northumbria, c. 670–867', in Cook and Williams, *Coinage and History in the North Sea World*, pp. 211-39.

should adopt regal coinage so early, given the evidence for a strong Romanising influence on the Northumbrian Church in the late seventh century, under figures such as Wilfred, Ceolfrith and Benedict Biscop. It is unclear how far our picture of the relative importance of Northumbria in this period is distorted by the comparative wealth of Northumbrian narrative sources compared with the rest of England, but Aldfrith's coinage does seem to provide some corroboration for this. What is particularly striking is that this innovation appears to have been unrelated to any change in the Frankish coinage, and is thus unlikely to be the result of direct political influence. However, this appears to have been something of a false start, with a break in explicitly regal issues between (on current evidence) the coinage of Aldfrith and the resumption of a continuous Northumbrian regal coinage in the reign of Eadberht (737-57/8).[49]

This coincides more closely with the introduction of regal coinage in other Anglo-Saxon kingdoms. This seems to have been inspired in part by developments in the Frankish coinage, which continued to influence Anglo-Saxon coinage at various points throughout this phase. Pepin the Short (751-68), following his seizure of the throne, issued a regal coinage, struck on very slightly larger and thinner flans. It has been suggested that the increased size of the flan was intended to accommodate explicitly regal legends, and royal authority over the coinage is also demonstrated by Pepin's regulation of the weight of the coinage in a clause in a capitulary of 754/5. Regal coinage continued under his son Charlemagne (768-814). Charlemagne's initial issues followed the pattern of Pepin's, but he introduced a type with a standardised obverse in 771, demonstrating his authority by abolishing all coins in the names of other issuers. A fully standardised national type, struck to a higher weight standard, and including the name of the mint, was issued from 793/4, and another standard type showing an imperial bust, probably from 812.[50]

The coins of this period from England share many of the characteristics of the Carolingian coinage, and its progressive reforms, with the significant difference that Anglo-Saxon issues of this period typically identify moneyers rather than mints, suggesting a slightly different structure in the organisation of minting, although a similar level of royal control. The general characteristics of this phase are as follows:

• Explicitly regal inscriptions

• Often regal/imperial imagery

• Projecting authority internally and externally

• Symbol of overlordship/independence

• Moneyers identified, signifying devolved authority

With the possible exception of Eadberht of Northumbria, it seems likely that all of the Anglo-Saxon regal coinage of the mid-eighth century followed that of Pepin, although the exact chronology is uncertain, and the sequence may therefore be debated.[51] An initial transitional phase, characterised by coins struck on flans slightly broader and flatter than the earlier pennies, is discernable in the names of three kings, Æthelberht, Beonna and Offa. Æthelberht, who is known from a single coin, is probably to be identified with the 'Alberht', who according to the *Historia regum* divided the East Anglian kingdom with 'Hunbeanna' in 749, whereas Beonna, whose coinage was rather more extensive, has been identified both with 'Hunbeanna' and the 'Beorna' described as king of the East Angles in 758 by John of Worcester. The coins of the two kings are closely related, and the provenances of the known examples strongly support an East Anglian origin.[52] Offa of Mercia (757-96) has only a few coins of comparable size, and it is likely that he progressed very quickly from this transitional phase to the Light Coinage that represents the bulk of the coinage of his reign. This returned to an earlier weight standard of *c.* 1.3g, but was now on a significantly broader, flatter flan than the coins of the previous phase, with a further increase in both size and weight in the final years of his reign, probably intended to bring Offa's coins up to the same standard as those of Charlemagne. In addition to his Mercian kingdom, Offa also conquered the kingdoms of East Anglia and Kent, and apparently issued coins in all three kingdoms. Almost all of Offa's coins carry the name of the moneyer responsible for issuing them, as well as Offa's own name and title, thus serving as symbols of authority, but with an element of delegated local authority, as the moneyers were responsible to the king for the quality of the coins. The moneyers are identifiable with different kingdoms either because they are known to have issued coins for Kentish or East Anglian rulers, or through stylistic similarities with those who do. The Kentish coins were minted in Canterbury, and those of Mercia are conventionally attributed to London, while it has also become customary to attribute the East Anglian issues to Ipswich.[53] However, caution is required

---

[49] Pirie, 'Contrast and continuity'; Rory Naismith, 'Kings, crisis and coinage reforms in the mid-eighth century', *Early Medieval Europe* 20.3 (2012), 291-332.
[50] Grierson and Blackburn, *Medieval European Coinage*, pp. 204-10.
[51] An alternative chronology and relative sequencing has recently been proposed by Naismith, 'Kings, crisis and coinage'.
[52] Marion M. Archibald, 'The coinage of Beonna in the light of the Middle Harling hoard', *BNJ* 55 (1985), 10-54; Marion M. Archibald and V. Fenwick, with Michael R. Cowell, 'A *sceat* of Æthelberht I of East Anglia and recent finds of coins of Beonna', *BNJ* 65 (1995), 1-31; Marion M. Archibald, 'Beonna and Alberht: coinage and historical context', in *Æthelbald and Offa: two eighth-century kings of Mercia*, ed. David Hill and Margaret Worthington, BAR, British Series 383 (Oxford, 2005), pp. 123-32; Naismith, 'Kings, crisis and coinage'.
[53] Christopher E. Blunt, 'The coinage of Offa', in Dolley, *Anglo-Saxon Coins*, pp. 39-62; Grierson and Blackburn, *Medieval European Coinage*, pp. 278-82; Bernard H. I. H. Stewart, 'The London Mint and the coinage of Offa', in *Anglo-Saxon Monetary History*, ed. Mark A. S. Blackburn (Leicester, 1986), pp. 27-43; Derek Chick, 'Towards a chronology for Offa's coinage: an interim study', *The Yorkshire Numismatist* 3 (1997), 47-64, reprinted with minor revisions in Derek Chick (ed. by Mark A. S. Blackburn and Rory Naismith), *The Coinage of Offa and his Contemporaries*, British Numismatic Society Special Publication 6 (London, 2010), pp. 1-16; *Idem*, 'The coinage of Offa in the light of recent discoveries', in Hill and Worthington, *Æthelbald and Offa*, pp. 111-22, reprinted with minor revisions in Chick, *The Coinage of Offa*, pp. 17-29; Gareth Williams, 'Mercian coinage and authority', in Brown

in the absence of mint signatures. Although stylistic similarities may indicate that groups of moneyers obtained their dies from common sources, this only enables us to identify patterns of die-cutting, and linking moneyers to specific towns purely on stylistic grounds is rather more conjectural than the tone of much numismatic literature would suggest. The distribution of Offa's Mercian types is largely concentrated in the south-eastern part of the kingdom, which would support an attribution to London, and it is notable that as yet neither stylistic analysis nor distribution suggests minting in the Mercian heartland of the West Midlands. The numismatic evidence for Offa's reign thus does nothing to support the idea of a network of Mercian *burhs* foreshadowing those of Alfred and his successors (see below).[54] However, distribution within East Anglia is widespread. While the suggestion that Ipswich was a mint in this period is likely, given its significance as a *wic,* it is difficult to argue on stylistic grounds that all East Anglian coins in this phase were minted in one place, or on the grounds of distribution that Ipswich is the only possible location for a mint.

Offa's coinage in many ways sets the pattern for the rest of the phase, although his long reign and the breadth of his dominions mean that his coinage is both larger and more varied than that of most kings. Like the Carolingian coinage, Offa's coinage shows increasing royal authority, and in some areas his reforms appear to be earlier than those of Charlemagne. Offa's coins lack the standardisation of design of Charlemagne's coinage post-771, but show reasonable standardisation in both size and weight, while the variety of design shows experimentation with different approaches to the expression of regal identity. Some of his coins, like those of Pepin, use initials and abbreviations rather than his full royal title. Others include, in full, or in abbreviated form, his title of king of the Mercians. The lack of standardisation also has parallels in the earlier phases of Charlemagne's coinage, which became increasingly standardised as his reign progressed.[55] Complete standardisation of design did not become the norm within any Anglo-Saxon kingdom before the late ninth century, but the extreme variety in Offa's reign raises interesting questions about the roles of king, die-cutter and moneyer respectively in deciding on the designs for individual dies.[56] Although many of the coins are based

around inscriptions and geometric designs, a number of them show royal busts. These are stylised busts, rather than an attempt at realistic portraiture, and the majority of these designs are derived from Roman imperial busts, and this use of the imperial image predates the use of imperial busts on Charlemagne's coinage.

The Roman theme is also apparent in the coinage issued in the name of Offa's wife Cynethryth. These coins in the name of a king's wife are unparalleled in Europe in this period, and although it has been suggested that there may have been a model in the coins of the Byantine empress, Irene,[57] it appears that the Cynethryth coins predate those of Irene. More plausible models are the coins issued by a number of Roman emperors in the names of their empresses, something which must have been known in Offa's time, since female as well as male Roman busts were imitated. Since all of the coins in the name of Cynethryth were issued by a single moneyer, Eoba, it is possible that Offa may have granted Cynethryth the right to the royal profits derived from that particular moneyer.[58] Another bust type of Offa has been identified by Anna Gannon as a possible representation of the biblical King David, based on parallels elsewhere in Anglo-Saxon art. This would be consistent both with the general importance of David as a model of kingship promoted by the early medieval Church, and more specifically with the fact that Charlemagne in particular sought to identify himself with David.[59] Once again, Offa appears to be using coins to make a statement about his own royal identity against the background of broader shared European concepts of kingship.

Like Charlemagne, Offa seems to have had firm authority over the coinage wherever and whenever he had control of the constituent kingdoms of his domains. As mentioned above, he issued coins in East Anglia and Kent as well as in Mercia, and he does not seem to have permitted any of his *subreguli* to issue coins of their own. Coins of this period are known in the names of the Kentish kings Ecgberht and Heaberht, but these only survive in small numbers, suggesting a very limited period of circulation. Both kings are known to have ruled in Kent c. 765, but Ecgberht appears again in the 770s. Sir Frank Stenton argued that Offa's authority in Kent may have been severely diminished after the battle of Otford in 776,[60] and the most obvious interpretation of the coinage of Ecgberht,

and Farr, *Mercia*, pp. 210-28; Naismith, 'Kings, crisis and coinage'; *Idem, Money and Power in Anglo-Saxon England: the southern English kingdoms, 757-865* (London, 2012).
[54] Jeremy Haslam, 'Market and fortress in England in the time of Offa', *World Archaeology* 19.3 (1987), 76-93; Steven Bassett, 'Divide and rule? The military infrastructure of eighth- and ninth-century Mercia', *Early Medieval Europe* 15 (2007), 53-85; *Idem,* 'The middle and late Anglo-Saxon defences of western Mercian towns', in *Anglo-Saxon Studies in Archaeology and History* 15 (Oxford, 2008),180-239.
[55] Grierson and Blackburn, *Medieval European Coinage*, pp. 205-10; Georges Depeyrot, *Le Numéraire carolingien, corpus des monnaies: troisième édition augmentée,* Collection Moneta 77 (Wetteren, 2008).
[56] This issue is discussed in some detail in Naismith, *Money and Power.* This publication, and its companion publication by the same author, *The Coinage of Southern England, 796-865,* British Numismatic Society Special Publication 7, 2 vols (London , 2011), present a fascinating and thorough re-examination of the coinage of the period 757-865, but were unfortunately published after this article was essentially complete, and

it has not been possible to incorporate here any detailed discussion of the arguments presented there. Suffice it to say that while I have minor disagreements with some of Dr Naismith's conclusions, these books are now essential reading for anyone wishing to understand Anglo-Saxon coinage of the eighth and ninth centuries in the context of the history of both England and the Continent in this period.
[57] Stewart, 'London Mint', p. 41.
[58] Blunt, 'Coinage of Offa', pp. 46-7; Sybille Zipperer, 'Coins and currency – Offa of Mercia and his Frankish neighbours', in *Völker an Nord- und Ostsee und die Franken,* ed. Uta Von Freeden, Ursula Koch and Alfried Wieczorek (Bonn, 1999), pp. 121-7; Williams,'Mercian coinage and authority', p. 216.
[59] Gannon, *Iconography,* pp. 31-3.
[60] Frank M. Stenton, *Anglo-Saxon England,* 3rd ed. (Oxford, 1971), pp. 206-7.

Heaberht and Offa is that Offa established authority in Kent, lost it and then regained it, although the precise sequence of both authority and coinage is problematic. The most recent sequence, proposed by Derek Chick, sees a brief coinage by Heaberht, *c.* 765, immediately followed by coinage in the name of Offa. Following the battle of Otford, Kentish control was reasserted by Ecgberht, with the reappearance of coins in the name of Offa after he re-established Mercian overlordship in Kent around the end of the decade.[61] Although this interpretation is not certain, it is very plausible, and has been generally accepted in numismatic circles.

Similarly, a very small coinage survives in the name of Æthelberht of East Anglia, who was executed on the orders of Offa in 794, having previously been accepted as a sub-king, and a suitable husband for one of Offa's daughters.[62] Æthelberht's coinage is distinctive, showing a Roman imperial bust on one side, and Romulus and Remus suckling Roma in the form of a wolf on the other, an image derived from Roman coins. This suggests that Æthelberht also wished to be seen as a 'Roman' king, although it has been suggested that the wolf image was also a pun on the name of the Wuffingas, the native East Anglian royal dynasty. In either case, the coinage appears to assert Æthelberht's independence of Offa, and it may have been such attempts to assert East Anglian independence that led to his death.[63] Interestingly, a recent find of Offa also shows a wolf and twins, although the relative chronology of the two is uncertain, and it seems likely that this was a specific statement of Offa's sovereignty over East Anglia.[64]

The importance of coinage as a vehicle for statements of political autonomy is also apparent on Offa's death in 796. His son Ecgfrith succeeded him for only a few months before he too died, and no coins are recorded in his name. It is possible that this represents the security of his power within Mercia, and that there was no urgency for him to issue coins, but it is also possible that he had lost control of all the mints, including London. Certainly the absence of his coinage contrasts with the brief re-emergence of independent coinage in Kent, in the name of the historically documented Eadberht Praen, and in East Anglia in the name of an otherwise unknown Eadwald. In the case of Kent, Coenwulf of Mercia (796-821) quickly re-established Mercian supremacy, crushing Kentish independence but initially allowing a degree of autonomy under his brother Cuthred, who issued coins as sub-king of Kent, although following Cuthred's death in 807 Coenwulf apparently resumed full authority without difficulty. In the absence of independent historical evidence, the situation in East Anglia is less clear, as Eadwald is known only from his coins. Their size places them after the introduction of Offa's heavy coinage shortly before the end of the reign,

and the moneyer Lul struck coins for Æthelberht of East Anglia, Offa, Eadwald and Coenwulf, so there is little doubt that Eadwald's coins are East Anglian issues between Offa and Coenwulf, but it is less certain whether he represents a failed attempt at independence, like Eadberht Praen, or an authorised sub-king, like Cuthred.[65] It is also notable that the coinage of Beorhtric of Wessex (786-802) is extremely rare. Married to another of Offa's daughters, it is possible that his coinage was also only issued after the death of Offa, and that the degree of his independence implied by later West Saxon sources is exaggerated.

This link between coinage and sovereignty and/or independence reflects a broader shift in Anglo-Saxon kingship. As discussed above, over-kingship was nothing new in the mid-eighth century, and was very much a feature of the preceding phase. However, the over-kingship of the late eighth century and beyond was very different from what had gone before. The many small kingdoms of Bede and the Tribal Hidage either disappeared entirely, or lost much of their separate identity and autonomy.[66] Arguably, the same process began in both in East Anglia and Kent, and had Mercian power not fragmented on the death of Coenwulf in 821, this change might have been lasting in East Anglia, while the reassertion of Kentish independence after Coenwulf's death was quickly and permanently crushed by the West Saxon expansion under Ecgberht. This expansion of royal authority is visible in, for example, the assumption of direct control over military service in Kent by Offa, rather than simply demanding service and tribute from a semi-autonomous sub-king as appears to have been case in the earlier period.[67] The closer definition in this period of royal rights such as military service and building obligations also points to a more highly structured royal administration,[68] which is also consistent with the pattern of devolved authority shown through the combination of king and moneyer on the coinage. This combination continued on most issues of this phase and those which followed, with the king's name indicating the authority by which coins were issued while at the same time providing the ultimate guarantee of the quality of the coinage, but the naming of individual moneyers added an intermediate level of both authority and accountability between coin-users and the king. The emphasis on regal inscriptions on the coins, rather than simply relying on the iconography of the previous phase, may also reflect a growing emphasis on literacy as a key to legitimacy, as seen in both written law and bookland tenure.

[61] Chick, 'Chronology for Offa's coinage'.
[62] Sheila Sharp, 'Æthelberht, king and martyr: the development of a legend', in Hill and Worthington, *Æthelbald and Offa*, pp. 59-64.
[63] Gannon, *Iconography*, p. 147.
[64] Chick, *The Coinage of Offa*, Type 171; Naismith, *Money and Power*, pp. 118-20.

[65] Gareth Williams, *Early Anglo-Saxon Coins* (Oxford, 2008), p. 38.
[66] Simon D. Keynes, 'The kingdom of the Mercians in the eighth century', in Hill and Worthington, *Æthelbald and Offa*, pp. 1-21, at 10.
[67] Damien Tyler, 'Orchestrated violence and the "Supremacy of the Mercian Kings"', in Hill and Worthington, *Æthelbald and Offa*, pp. 27-34.
[68] Nicholas Brooks, 'The development of military obligations in eighth-and ninth-century England', in *England before the Conquest: studies in primary sources presented to Dorothy Whitelock*, ed. Peter Clemoes and Kathleen Hughes (Cambridge, 1971), pp. 69-84; Richard Abels, *Lordship and Military Obligation in Anglo-Saxon England* (London, 1988); Gareth Williams, 'Military institutions and royal power', in Brown and Farr, *Mercia*, pp. 295-309; *Idem*, 'Military obligations and Mercian supremacy in the eighth century', in Hill and Worthington, *Æthelbald and Offa*, pp.101-110.

The same link between sovereignty and coinage apparently continued after Wessex replaced Mercia as the dominant kingdom. Kentish independence was reflected in a short-lived coinage under Baldred (823-25), but Canterbury simply became a West-Saxon mint after Ecgberht's conquest of Kent in 825.[69] Ecgberht pointedly issued coins as king of the Mercians following his conquest of Mercia in 828, and although Wiglaf 'obtained' his kingdom again the following year, he appears not to have resumed issuing coinage, perhaps suggesting that he held Mercia as a sub-king under Ecgberht, with carefully circumscribed authority, rather than as an independent king.[70] East Anglia, however, remained independent of the West Saxon sphere of influence, although there was a confused period in the aftermath of the collapse of the Mercian hegemony, in which some Mercian rulers apparently struck coins in Mercia, others only in East Anglia, while an independent East Anglian coinage also re-emerged, surviving until the collapse of the East Anglian kingdom, c. 870. A striking feature of this coinage is the use of imagery copied from Frankish coins, such as the Temple type of Louis the Pious, and the ship type found on coins of the important ports of Quentovic and Dorestad.[71] Frankish links across the North Sea were mentioned in earlier phases. The lack of surviving documentation from East Anglia means that one can only speculate whether the use of Frankish images on East Anglian coins was simply the result of familiarity with imported Frankish coins through trade, or whether it reflects a political affiliation, perhaps with a more remote Frankish overlordship or alliance as a balance to the growing power of the West Saxons.

Northumbria, which had initiated this phase of regal coinage, maintained both its political independence and its independent coinage until the fall of the kingdom in 867. The coinage remained regal throughout and, like the coinage south of the Humber, adopted the standard pattern of the king's name and title on one side, and the moneyer's name on the other. However, for reasons which are not well understood, the Northumbrian coinage underwent a different series of physical developments in this period. Unlike the broader, flatter southern coins, they retained the small, thick flans of the anonymous silver phase, as well as the large scale of minting, but the silver content of the coinage became increasingly base until by the end of the coinage in the 860s it contained virtually no silver at all.[72] This difference in scale of production and in silver content demonstrates a clear economic difference between coinage

north and south of the Humber, but there is less obvious difference in those aspects of the coinage which relate to kingship.

It is true that a number of coins were issued in the ninth century with blundered inscriptions, and it is therefore difficult to be certain whether royal control over the coinage was always firmly maintained. However, it is also true that political power changed hands, often abruptly, and sometimes reversibly, with both Æthelred I and Æthelred II having split reigns. Issuing coins with blundered legends may perhaps have been a way for moneyers to hedge their bets, since at least with blundered coins they could not be accused, in the case of a sudden political reversal, of issuing coins in the name of the 'wrong' king. The blundered inscriptions are interpreted as being struck in two phases, one in the 840s (certainly a time of civil war) and the other in the 850s or 860s. This latter phase also coincided with civil war between the rivals Osberht and Ælle in the final years of the kingdom, and it is notable that while coins of Osberht were minted in some numbers, none are recorded in the name of Ælle. It is also possible that some of these anonymous blundered coins may have been issued after the fall of Northumbria in 867, as the presence of large numbers of stycas in Viking camps of the 870s suggests that they were still being used at this point.[73] In the matter of the adoption of Roman imperial busts, the small flans did not permit both inscriptions and busts, and this reinforces the importance of literate demonstrations of royal authority, as discussed briefly above. Furthermore, Northumbrian rulers were not averse to the idea of using comparable imagery to their southern neighbours. A silver penny does survive in the name of Eanred, in a similar style to those of Æthelwulf of Wessex (c. 839-58) and Berhtwulf of Mercia (840-52), and was perhaps intended for use in trade south of the Humber,[74] while a unique gold solidus of Archbishop Wigmund couples a bust type similar to that found on coins of the archbishops of Canterbury with a reverse found on coins of Louis the Pious (814-40).[75]

This raises two other points which are features of the coinage of this period, episcopal coinage and issues in gold. Coinage was struck in the name of the archbishops of Canterbury from Jaenberht (766-92) to Plegmund (890-23) and more intermittently in the name of various archbishops of York from Ecgberht (732/4-766) to Wulfhere (854-900). Rarer issues are also recorded in the name of Bishop Eadberht of London (787-9). These episcopal issues should

[69] Christopher E. Blunt, Colin S. S. Lyon and Bernard H. I. H. Stewart, 'The coinage of southern England, 796–840', *BNJ* 32 (1963), 1–74; Naismith, *Money and Power*, pp. 106-12.

[70] Williams, 'Mercian coinage', p. 224.

[71] Marion M. Archibald, 'A Ship Type of Athelstan I of East Anglia', *BNJ* 52 (1982), 34–40; Gareth Williams, 'The influence of Dorestad coinage on coin design in England and Scandinavia', in *Dorestad in an International Framework: new research on centres of trade and coinage in Carolingian times*, ed. Annemarieke Willemsen and Hanneke Kik (Turnhout, 2010), pp. 75-81.

[72] Elizabeth J. E. Pirie, *Coins of Northumbria* (Llanfyllin, 2002); *Idem*, 'Contrasts and continuity within the coinage of Northumbria, c.670–867', in Cook and Williams, *Coinage and History in the North Sea World*, pp. 211-40.

[73] Gareth Williams, 'Viking camps and the means of exchange in Britain and Ireland in the ninth century', in *Viking Ireland and Beyond*, ed. Ruth Johnson and Howard B. Clarke (Dublin, forthcoming).

[74] David M. Metcalf, Hugh Pagan and Veronica Smart, 'The Eanred penny', in *Coinage in Ninth-Century Northumbria*, ed. David. M. Metcalf, BAR, British Series 180 (Oxford, 1987), pp. 36-40; Elizabeth J. E. Pirie, 'Eanred's penny: a Northumbrian enigma', *The Yorkshire Numismatist* 3 (1997), 65-8.

[75] Bernard H. I. H. Stewart, 'Anglo-Saxon gold coins' (with appendix by W. Andrew Oddy), in *Scripta Nummaria Romana: essays presented to Humphrey Sutherland*, ed. Robert A. Carson and Colin M. Kraay (London, 1978), pp. 143-72; Mark A. S. Blackburn, 'Gold in England during the 'Age of Silver' (eighth–eleventh centuries)', in Graham-Campbell and Williams, *Silver Economy in the Viking Age*, pp. 55–98.

probably not be seen as a challenge to royal authority, but as a reinforcement of it, since it would appear that the right to issue coin might be granted to the Church, in just the same way as a piece of land. By accepting the grant, the Church effectively recognised the authority of the king in this matter. It is also notable that with the exception of a single issue in the name of Jaenberht, all of the early issues were joint issues in the names of both king and (arch)bishop, while the short-lived coinage of the bishop of London may well have been a ploy in Offa's attempts to increase his authority over the English church, in parallel to his documented attempts to have the archbishopric transferred from Canterbury to Lichfield.[76] Once the right of archiepiscopal minting was established, the king's name was dropped from the coins, and the ninth-century issues from both Canterbury and York were struck in the names of the archbishops alone. It does not seem likely, however, that this was done without the consent of the respective kings.

A few examples of Anglo-Saxon gold coins are also recorded from this period. Apart from the Wigmund solidus already mentioned, four are known from the late eighth to mid-ninth centuries, together with a number of anonymous imitations of imported Islamic and Frankish gold which may well also be of Anglo-Saxon manufacture.[77] Two of the four carry only the names of moneyers, Pændræd and Ciolheard, while two carry the names of the Mercian rulers Offa and Coenwulf. Unlike later Anglo-Saxon gold issues from the tenth and eleventh centuries, these were not struck from the same dies as the silver pennies, and whereas the later coins have generally been accepted as representing part of the circulating currency, the function of these early coins has been debated, with some preferring to see them as presentation pieces rather than genuine monetary issues. This is certainly plausible in the case of the Pændræd mancus, which carries a bust of Augustus in much higher relief than normal Anglo-Saxon coins, and was apparently designed more for show than for practicality. If the Pændræd coin is a presentation piece, the same may also be true of the Ciolheard coin, although its appearance is less remarkable, while the Wigmund solidus may well have been specially struck in celebration of his investiture as archbishop, just as its prototype is likely to have celebrated the imperial coronation of Louis the Pious.[78]

In contrast, the Offa dinar and the Coenwulf mancus have the appearance of being coins designed to fit in with established international trade coinages, but making firm statements of Mercian royal authority. The Offa dinar copies a dinar of the caliph al-Mansur, with the title OFFA REX inscribed upside-down in relation to the slightly blundered Arabic inscription. This combination of factors suggests that the original dinar was copied by an

Anglo-Saxon die-cutter with good copying skills but no knowledge of Arabic. Although the coin, first recorded (without provenance) in a coin sale in Rome, has been linked with documented accounts of payment in gold from Offa to the Papacy, it is likely that the design reflects the dominance of the Islamic dinars in the gold currency of eighth-century Europe.[79] Quite simply, Offa's coin appears to be designed to look like a coin of accepted currency value, but with his own name on it, a recurrent pattern in the adoption of new coinage throughout history. Offa seems to have used the coin to make a statement of his own international importance, both economically and politically. This is even more the case with the Coenwulf coin, which couples Coenwulf's name and title with an imperial bust on one side, and a stylised ornamented cross (paralleled in his silver coinage) with the inscription DE VICO LVNDONIAE. This has clear parallels with a unique gold coin of Charlemagne, issued as king of the Franks and Lombards, also with an imperial Roman bust, with the reverse inscription VICO DURISTAT. The design of the Coenwulf coin is consistent with his silver coinage, suggesting that it is suitable for domestic use, while the parallels with Charlemagne's coin suggest an international role, and an element of the sort of one-upmanship associated with the relationship between Offa and Charlemagne, but not previously documented for Coenwulf.[80] The precise significance of the description of London as a 'vicus' rather than a 'civitas' is unclear, but seems to emphasise London's importance as a trading centre, by analogy with Dorestadt, and also the king's role in controlling trade, a role which can be seen more clearly in the law-code of Alfred later in the century.[81] Like other aspects of the coinage of this phase, the Coenwulf mancus is thus an expression of both personal royal power and national sovereignty.

Phase 4b: Monetary alliances

While the previous sub-phase continued in East Anglia and Northumbria, a distinct sub-phase is visible in the coinage of Mercia and Wessex from the 840s to the collapse of the Mercian kingdom c. 879-80. In many respects, this is similar to the previous sub-phase. The coins are still explicitly regal, and continue to use Roman imperial busts, and the coins continue to carry the king's name on one side and the moneyer's name on the other, indicating that the

[76] Williams, 'Mercian coinage', p. 217; Naismith, 'Money of the saints'.
[77] Blackburn, 'Gold in England', *passim*; Williams, 'Anglo-Saxon gold coinage. Part 2.'
[78] Williams, *Early Anglo-Saxon Coins*, pp. 41-2.

[79] Blunt, 'Coinage of Offa', p. 51; Marion M. Archibald, 'Pecking and bending: the evidence of British finds', in *Sigtuna Papers. Proceedings of the Sigtuna Symposium on Viking-Age Coinage 1-4 June 1989* (*Commentationes de nummis saeculorum IX-XI in Suecia repertis n.s. 6*), ed. Kenneth Jonsson and Brita Malmer (Stockholm, 1990) pp. 11-24, at p. 12; Williams, 'Mercian coinage', p. 219; Blackburn, 'Gold in England', pp. 61-2.
[80] Blackburn, 'Gold in England', pp. 62-4; Gareth Williams and Michael R. Cowell, 'Analysis of a gold mancus of Coenwulf of Mercia (AD 796-821) and other comparable material in the BM collection', *The British Museum Technical Research Bulletin* 3 (2009), pp. 31-36; Williams, 'Influence of Dorestad', pp. 108-9.
[81] Williams, 'Influence of Dorestad', pp.108-9. Naismith (*Money and Power*, pp. 114-16) prefers to see the *vicus* on this coin as a reference to a royal estate near London rather than to the trading centre of *Lundenwic*, but makes no attempt to explain the similarity to the Dorestad coin.

coins were being issued through devolved royal authority. What sets this apart from the previous sub-phase is that the two kingdoms moved away from using coins to emphasise the sovereignty of the separate kingdoms, and entered into a series of monetary alliances, in which coinage was issued in both kingdoms to common standards, and sometimes with common designs, although each coin carries the names of either a Mercian or a West Saxon king, rather than the two together. Although in most cases individual moneyers can be associated with one kingdom or the other, a number of moneyers seem to have issued coins for both kingdoms, and it seems clear that coins from one kingdom would have been permitted to circulate in the other.

This sub-phase began during the reigns of Æthelwulf of Wessex (839-58) and Berhtwulf of Mercia (840-52), following a period in which Mercia had issued no coinage, probably, as I argued above, because the kingdom was under some kind of West Saxon domination rather than being fully independent. It would, therefore be possible to interpret Berhtwulf's coinage not in terms of a monetary alliance, but as a statement of independence, like the East Anglian and Kentish issues discussed in the previous sub-phase. However, there are too many indications of co-operation and West Saxon support for the new Mercian coinage, and it has even been suggested that Berhtwulf's coins might have been struck for him by West Saxon moneyers in Kent. It seems likely at the very least that a West Saxon die-cutter provided dies for Berhtwulf's earlier issues, and some moneyers struck coins for both kings, whether or not there was a full monetary alliance of the sort that was to follow under Burgred.[82] A more likely explanation is that the monetary economies of the two kingdoms had become so close during the 830s when no Mercian coinage was issued, that it was beneficial to maintain the monetary links once Mercia regained fuller political independence. The monetary alliance may also indicate a political alliance. This period saw an escalation in Viking attacks on England, and one which placed pressure on the military and monetary resources of all the Anglo-Saxon kingdoms. If my interpretation of Mercia as a semi-autonomous sub-kingdom during the 830s is correct, Æthelwulf may have felt that it was better to have Mercia as a willing ally than to attempt to continue to exercise domination in the face of an additional external threat. This is, of course, speculation, but it is notable that only a little later Æthelwulf was unable to maintain control of the whole of the West Saxon kingdom south of the Thames, and had to cede power in Wessex itself to his son Æthelbald. Simon Keynes has noted documentary evidence for 'close, and apparently friendly' relations between the two kingdoms at this time, although nothing that necessarily amounts to military alliance.[83]

The pattern of the alliance shifts somewhat under Burgred (852-74), although in his reign the evidence for political alliance is clearer. Burgred married Æthelwulf's daughter Æthelswith, and West Saxon forces aided Burgred against the Welsh in 853 and the Vikings in 868. Æthelwulf's youngest son Alfred also married a Mercian noble's daughter in 868, while charter evidence also supports strong links between the two kingdoms throughout Burgred's reign. Burgred initially issued his own coinage, apparently breaking the monetary alliance. However, the monetary alliance was re-established under Æthelwulf's son Æthelred I (865-71) and continued under Æthelred's brother Alfred (871-99) until Burgred's abdication in 874. However, in contrast to the earlier monetary alliance between Æthelwulf and Berhtwulf, in which Wessex seems to have been the dominant partner, Æthelred adopted the designs of Burgred's coinage. Both this and the great size and variety of Burgred's coinage suggest very clearly that Burgred was the senior partner in this monetary alliance, although narrative accounts of the period, written after the event under West Saxon patronage, tend to give the impression that Mercia was the weaker partner in military alliance.[84]

West Saxon re-writing of history after the event is even more apparent with regard to Burgred's successor Ceolwulf II (874- c. 879), probably a descendant of the dynasty of Coenwulf and his brother Ceolwulf I. Dismissed in West Saxon sources as 'a foolish king's thegn' and effectively a puppet of the Vikings who had driven Burgred into exile, it is clear from his charters that Ceolwulf acted as a fully independent king. Furthermore, it is clear that his kingship was accepted by Alfred, as again the two issued a joint coinage, even carrying out a monetary reform improving the silver content of the coinage. There are two types issued in the names of both rulers, a substantive Cross-and-Lozenge type, and the rarer Two Emperors type, of which a single example survives in the name of each ruler. Both types copy Roman busts, while the Two Emperors type pairs this with a fourth-century Roman reverse design showing two emperors side by side, an ideal image for a monetary alliance.[85] The interpretation of this joint coinage is not necessarily as straightforward as has sometimes been suggested. Although the same basic designs appear on the coinage of both kings, and two moneyers struck coins in the names of both kings, Mark Blackburn has argued that the quality of the bust shows

[82] J. Booth, 'Monetary alliance or technical co-operation? The coinage of Berhtwulf of Mercia (840-852)', in Kings, Currency and Alliances: history and coinage of southern England in the ninth century, ed. Mark A. S. Blackburn and David N. Dumville (Woodbridge, 1998), pp. 63-103.
[83] Simon Keynes, 'King Alfred and the Mercians', in Blackburn and Dumville, Kings, Currency and Alliances: history and coinage of southern England in the ninth century, pp.1-46.
[84] Hugh Pagan, 'Coinage in the age of Burgred', BNJ 34 (1974), 45-65; Simon Keynes, 'King Alfred and the Mercians', pp. 4-11; A. W. Lyons and W. A. MacKay, 'The coinage of Æthelred I (865-871)', BNJ 77 (2007), 71-118; A. W. Lyons and W. A. MacKay, 'The Lunettes coinage of Ælfred the Great', BNJ 78 (2008), 38-110; Gareth Williams, 'Burgred "Lunette" type E reconsidered', BNJ 78 (2008), 222-7.
[85] Mark A. S. Blackburn, 'The London mint in the reign of Alfred', in Blackburn and Dumville, Kings, Currency and Alliances, pp. 105-23; Idem, 'Alfred's coinage reforms in context', in Alfred the Great. Papers from the Eleventh-Centenary Conferences, ed. Timothy Reuter (Aldershot, 2003), pp. 199–218; Keynes, 'King Alfred and the Mercians', pp. 12-19; Mark A. S. Blackburn and Simon Keynes, 'A corpus of the cross-and-lozenge and related coinages of Alfred, Ceolwulf II and Archbishop Æthelred', in Blackburn and Dumville, Kings, Currency and Alliances, pp. 125–50.

a marked deterioration throughout the type, with the best of Alfred's coins close to the Roman prototype, and the rest progressively deteriorating, with Ceolwulf's designs even further removed from the prototype. On this basis he suggests that Ceolwulf's coins followed those of Alfred rather than being issued concurrently. This he explains by Alfred exercising power in London and perhaps other parts of southern Mercia at the end of Burgred's reign, and subsequently ceding power in this area to Ceolwulf once he had established himself as king in western Mercia, with the coinage thereafter being produced in Ceolwulf's name in London and one other mint in southern Mercia which received its coins from West Saxon Winchester. This would also be consistent with the use of the title REX ANGLO[RUM] on Alfred's Two Emperors coin, and REX SM, interpreted as *Rex Saxonum et Merciorum* on what appears to be one of the earliest Cross-and-Lozenge issues, since these could then indicate an aspirational claim over southern Mercia.[86] However, as Blackburn noted in a later article, the discovery of new finds of apparently early style in the name of Ceolwulf casts some doubt on the previously suggested chronology.[87] This could support an interpretation of shared minting rights in London, or that minting in Alfred's name in London was replaced by minting in the name of Ceolwulf, but with the change taking place much more quickly. In any case, it seems likely that minting in this type continued at both Canterbury and Winchester, as there would otherwise be a gap in Alfred's coinage, which seems unlikely in a period which saw both substantial payments to the Vikings, and a decisive victory over the Vikings at Edington in 878. Furthermore, the apparent provision of dies from Winchester for one of Ceolwulf's moneyers also suggests official sanction. Provenances offer little evidence, since most of the known examples either derive from the Cuerdale hoard or are unprovenanced, but the few provenances we have are consistent with shared circulation both north and south of the Thames. Ceolwulf's full participation in the Cross-and-Lozenge coinage and the reforms involved is also indicated by the survival of a halfpenny of this type in Ceolwulf's name, although none are currently recorded in the name of Alfred. On the current balance of evidence, a joint issue from the beginning is as likely as the earlier interpretation of a coinage begun unilaterally by Alfred after Burgred's departure in 874, but which developed into a joint issue and monetary (and perhaps political) alliance later in the 870s.

Phase 4c: Alfred's sole rule (c. 880-99)

Interpretation becomes more straightforward in the next sub-phase. The official Northumbrian coinage had apparently already come to an end in 867 before Alfred's reign began, as had the East Anglian coinage in *c.* 869, with the Viking conquest of the two kingdoms although, as noted above, it is possible that anonymous issues continued to be struck in Northumbria for a few years.

Coinage of East Anglian style in the names of Æthelred and Oswald apparently preserves the identities of two otherwise unknown royal pretenders using coinage in the well-established manner as a statement of their regal aspirations, and possibly even power, but these issues are so rare that any power they may have exercised did not last long, while aspects of the production of these coins seem more consistent with Anglo-Scandinavian issues than official East Anglian coinage, raising the possibility that Æthelred and Oswald should be considered as puppets rather than fully independent East Anglian rulers.[88] The Mercian kingdom, already divided following Burgred's abdication in 874, also disappeared as an entirely separate entity on the disappearance from the records of Ceolwulf II, *c.* 879, leaving Alfred as the sole surviving Anglo-Saxon king. This created a slightly altered context for the expression of regal authority. While it was still important for Alfred to be seen as a king, and to do all the things associated with kingship, it became less important to stress a strictly West Saxon identity for his kingship in the absence of rival kings.

It is true that the exact status of Alfred's son-in-law Æthelred is not entirely clear, as he seems to have been regarded as a king in Mercia and Wales, but is referred to as an ealdorman in West Saxon sources.[89] In either case, he seems to have accepted Alfred's overlordship, and subsequently that of Alfred's son Edward the Elder (899-924), and one aspect of that is that he did not issue coins in his own name, a situation with parallels for the interpretation suggested above for Wiglaf's relationship with Ecgberht in the 830s. The period following Ceolwulf's disappearance or death coincided with the relative stability created by Alfred's victory at Edington and the Treaty of Wedmore. Alfred was thus well-placed to define his kingship on his own terms. The surviving evidence gives us a good view of Alfred's ideas on the rights and responsibilities of kingship, or at least how he wished these to be perceived. The combined documentary output of Alfred's court, too large a subject to tackle in any detail here, presents a picture of strong kingship, a concern with the organisation and structure of royal power, and emphasis on the importance of law, learning and literacy, and the Church. Alfred's coinage needs to be seen against this background.[90]

[86] Blackburn, 'London Mint', p. 120.
[87] Blackburn, 'Alfred's coinage reforms', pp. 212-4.
[88] Mark A. S. Blackburn, 'Expansion and control: aspects of Anglo-Scandinavian minting south of the Humber', in *Vikings and the Danelaw: select papers from the Proceedings of the Thirteenth Viking Congress*, ed. James Graham-Campbell, Richard Hall, Judith Jesch and David N. Parsons (Oxford, 2001), pp. 125–42; *Idem*, 'Presidential address 2004. Currency under the Vikings. Part 1: Guthrum and the earliest Danelaw coinages', *BNJ* 75 (2005), 18–43.
[89] Keynes, 'King Alfred and the Mercians', pp. 19-39; *Idem*, 'Edward, king of the Anglo-Saxons', in *Edward the Elder, 899-924*, ed. Nicholas J. Higham and David H. Hill (London, 2001), pp. 40-66.
[90] Blackburn, 'Alfred's coinage reforms', pp. 205-8; Gareth Williams, 'Civil defence or royal power base? Military and non-military functions of the late Anglo-Saxon burh', in *Landscapes of Defence in the Viking Age: Anglo-Saxon England and comparative perspectives*, ed. J. Baker, Stuart Brookes, David Parsons and Andrew Reynolds (Turnhout, forthcoming).

With such strong authority, it comes as no surprise that Alfred's coins remained explicitly and exclusively regal, with the exception of the established franchise of the archbishops of Canterbury. What is more surprising is that in most of Alfred's later coinage he abandoned the use of imperial busts, as seen on his joint issues with both Burgred and Ceolwulf, and on the London monogram type which followed. The Two-line type, issued *c.* 880-899, carried no imagery beyond a simple cross. Whether this was because, having acquired a quasi-imperial status, he felt that he no longer need to proclaim it, or whether the simpler design reflects the image of personal humility portrayed in much of Asser's *Life*, or whether it was for some other reason, we do not know.

What does seem clear is that the coinage reflects three aspects of his kingship known from other sources. The first of these is his assumption of power over Mercia on Ceolwulf's death. The London monogram coinage appears to celebrate the fact that London was now formally under Alfred's control. While older books link this coinage with the 'restoration' of London in 886, current thinking places this earlier, not long after Wedmore, and probably immediately after Ceolwulf's death, placing it somewhere in the period *c.* 878-80.[91] By referring to himself simply as ÆLFRED REX on this and the Two-line type, Alfred left the full extent of his kingdom ambiguous, leaving room for further expansion, but by avoiding the use either of the Mercian name or any Mercian symbol, the coinage made it easier to present any expansion in the context of a unified kingdom rather than as kingship over two distinct areas. Coinage with the mint signatures of Gloucester and Oxford may similarly celebrate the extension of Alfred's authority into the former kingdom of Mercia. Alfred also issued coins from the traditional Kentish mint of Canterbury, some of which carry the mint signature after the king's name and title, but the bulk of Alfred's later coins carry no mint name and can only be assigned to individual mints on stylistic grounds, or where individual moneyers can be identified on the basis of mint-signed coins. The dispersed minting of coins in Alfred's name at mints in all three of the former kingdoms of Wessex, Mercia and Kent reflects his desire for unity, and the creation of a new 'Anglo-Saxon' identity which transcended the traditional political boundaries. The same desire is apparent in the introduction to Alfred's law-code, in which he explicitly stated that he was drawing on the legal traditions of all three kingdoms.[92]

This new emphasis on urban centres reflects another aspect of Alfred's kingship, the creation of a network of fortified towns, or *burhs*. Some of these were established centres, while others were old Roman towns which were probably re-settled or at least redeveloped at this time, and others

again were new foundations. The burghal system seems to represent an unprecedented strategic approach to control of the kingdom, in military, economic and administrative terms. As Alfred and his descendants widened the area under their control, so this burghal system expanded, facilitating a level of integration and authority which went far beyond the imposed over-kingships of the eighth and early ninth centuries. While the coins of London, Gloucester and Oxford merely point to the importance of towns within Alfred's vision (and perhaps to the celebration of his acquisition of formerly Mercian towns), the importance of an integrated approach shows through in coins of identical style issued in Winchester and Exeter. Coins from these established West Saxon centres cannot represent conquest or expansion, and the standardisation fits well with the idea of an integrated network of *burhs*.[93] It seems likely that coins were issued to the same pattern at other *burhs* (or were at least planned), but that these have not survived. This may reflect the timing of the issue. The type reflects the heavier weight of Alfred's second coin reform *c.* 880, but the Winchester and Exeter coins carry the title REX SAXONVM. The rarity of this type, and the absence of other types, may indicate that it was only briefly issued, to be replaced by types with the more neutral description of REX without further qualification.[94] The full significance of *burhs* as centres of royal authority and administration, in addition to their military and economic functions, is more explicit in the phase which followed, and especially from the reign of Alfred's grandson Athelstan (924-39), but the roots of Athelstan's burghal policy are probably to be traced in the reign of Alfred, and in the intervening reign of Edward the Elder.[95] Alfred's *burhs* represent the beginning of a new phase of urbanisation under royal authority. In his influential discussion of the defining characteristics that distinguished early medieval towns from other pre-urban centres of production and trade, Martin Biddle included minting, and it is in Alfred's reign that this appears to become systematised for the first time across a network of emerging towns, even if minting had been focused in a limited number of pre-urban centres throughout the whole of the phase of regal coinage, and very probably through the two preceding phases discussed above.[96]

[91] Marion M. Archibald, 'Coins', in Webster and Backhouse, *The Making of England*, pp. 284-9; Keynes, 'King Alfred and the Mercians, pp. 21-4'; Blackburn, 'The London Mint', pp. 120-22; *Idem*, 'Alfred's coinage reforms', pp. 205-14.

[92] Simon Keynes and Michael Lapidge, ed. and trans., *Alfred the Great. Asser's Life of King Alfred and other contemporary sources* (Harmondsworth, 1983), p. 164.

[93] Blackburn, 'Alfred's coinage reforms', p. 208; Williams, 'Civil defence or royal powerbase?'.

[94] Williams, 'Civil defence or royal powerbase?'.

[95] Mark A. S. Blackburn, 'Mints, burhs and the Grately code, cap. 14.2', in *The Defence of Wessex, The Burghal Hidage and Anglo-Saxon Fortifications*, ed. David Hill and Alexander R. Rumble (Manchester,1996), pp. 160-75; Colin S. S. Lyon, 'The coinage of Edward the Elder', in Higham and Hill, *Edward the Elder*, pp. 67-78; Elina Screen, 'Anglo-Saxon law and numismatics: a reassessment in the light of Patrick Wormald's *The making of English law*', *BNJ* 77 (2007), 150-72; Williams, 'Civil defence or royal powerbase?'.

[96] Martin Biddle, 'Towns', in *The Archaeology of Anglo-Saxon England*, ed. David M. Wilson (Cambridge, 1976), pp. 99-150; David H. Hill, 'The origin of Alfred's urban policies', in Reuter, *Alfred the Great*, pp. 219-34; Richard A. Hall, 'Burhs and boroughs: defended places, trade and towns. Plans, defences, civic features', in Hamerow, Hinton and Crawford, *Oxford Handbook*, pp. 600–21; Williams, 'Civil defence or royal powerbase?'; *Idem*, 'Towns and minting in northern Europe in the early Middle Ages', in *The City and the Coin in the Ancient and Early Medieval Worlds*, ed. Fernando Lopez Sanchez, BAR, International Series 2402 (Oxford, 2012), pp. 149-60.

A third important aspect of Alfred's kingship, as revealed both in his own (attributed) writings and in the contemporary accounts, is a recognition of the importance of the Church within the state. The distinction between fighting men, praying men and working men, and the recognition that all had an important contribution to make is clear in Asser's *Vita*, and Alfred's generosity to the Church is also noted.[97] It is therefore unsurprising that a rare coinage survives, larger and heavier than the regular coinage, which pairs Alfred's name and title with the inscription ELI MO, short for *elimosina*, or alms. In addition, ecclesiastical issues in the names of the archbishops of Canterbury continued throughout his reign, with changes in purity and weight reflecting Alfred's own coinage reforms.[98] The link between Anglo-Saxon kingship, Christianity and coinage has been a recurrent theme throughout this paper, but is rarely easier to substantiate than in the reign of Alfred.

Phase 4d: Viking England (c. 880-927)

A similar element of Christianised kingship runs firmly through the coinage of the Viking settlements in England. Despite the popular image of Vikings as militantly anti-Christian heathen barbarians, the Anglo-Scandinavian coinage of the period largely conforms to the characteristics of this general phase of Anglo-Saxon regal coinage, and the Anglo-Scandinavian coinage can be summarised as follows:

- Largely explicitly regal

- Transition from bullion economy to regal coinage

- Explicitly Christian

- Initially imitative, then original designs

- Limited control of circulation

- Assimilation to Anglo-Saxon-kingship

This pattern is largely very similar to the rest of the phase. The main differences can be attributed to the fact that the majority of Vikings came from a background of more fragmented kingship, with no established Christian Church, and with no locally issued coins across most of Scandinavia, although imported coins were used, apparently for their bullion value. The Viking world thus has close parallels with the first phase of Anglo-Saxon coinage/kingship discussed above, yet the Viking settlers in England rapidly made the transition to catch up with the general pattern of Anglo-Saxon coinage which had become established by the late ninth century. It is true that many of the earliest Anglo-Scandinavian coinages were blundered derivatives of the coinage of Alfred, just as many of the earliest Anglo-Saxon coins were blundered

imitations of Frankish prototypes. As mentioned above, this is typical of a much wider pattern in the adoption of new coinage. However, even the production of these imitative coinages is significant. The Vikings already had an established silver economy, in which imported coin could function alongside ingots and hack-silver within a bullion economy, apparently regulated by mutual consent rather than by royal authority, and based on a combination of measured weight and tested purity.[99]

Coinage, like any other form of 'good' silver, could function as a medium for exchange and for storage of wealth, but it is not clear that coinage was preferred over other forms of silver, and the continued presence of mixed silver hoards in northern England for some decades after the introduction of locally issued Anglo-Scandinavian coinage, together with test marks on coins, indicates that coinage was not necessarily trusted, and that royal authority over monetary circulation (rather than minting) remained limited at least until the late 920s.[100] Thus, the adoption of coinage by the Vikings does not appear to be due to the perceived superiority of a coin-based economy. Two other explanations seem possible. One is that the Viking settlers in northern and eastern England wished to engage in trade with the inhabitants of the areas which remained under Anglo-Saxon rule, and since this involved the use of coinage it became convenient for them to produce their own. The second is that the Viking settlers assimilated to some extent with the Anglo-Saxon population, and adopted Anglo-Saxon customs, including some of the concepts of Anglo-Saxon kingship, of which the issuing of coinage was one aspect. These two explanations are not, of course, by any means mutually exclusive.

If all of the Anglo-Scandinavian coinage took the form of anonymous imitations, it would be possible to argue that the transition was primarily driven by the needs of

---

[97] Keynes and Lapidge, *Alfred the Great*, pp. 103-7; Richard Abels, *Alfred the Great: war, kingship and culture in Anglo-Saxon England* (London and New York, 1998), pp. 243-6.

[98] Naismith, 'Money of the saints'.

[99] James A. Graham-Campbell, 'The dual economy of the Danelaw. The Howard Linecar Memorial Lecture 2001', *BNJ* 71 (2001), 49-59; Mark A. S. Blackburn, 'The coin-finds', in *Means of Exchange: dealing with silver in the Viking Age*, ed. Dagfinn Skre, University of Oslo/Aarhus University Press/Kaupang Excavation Project Publication Series 2: Norske Oldfunn XXIII (Oslo, 2008), pp. 29–74; Gareth Williams, 'Kingship, Christianity and coinage: monetary and political perspectives on silver economy in the Viking Age', in Graham-Campbell and Williams, *Silver Economy*, pp. 177-214; *Idem*, 'Silver economies, monetisation and society: an overview', in *Silver Economies, Monetisation and Society in Scandinavia AD 800–1100*, ed. James Graham-Campbell, Søren M. Sindbæk and Gareth Williams (Aarhus, 2011), pp. 337–72.

[100] Archibald, 'Pecking and bending'; *Idem*, 'Testing', in *The Cuerdale Hoard and Related Viking-Age Silver and Gold, from Britain and Ireland, in The British Museum*, ed. James Graham-Campbell, *et al*, British Museum Research Publication no. 185, (London, 2012), pp. 51-64; Graham-Campbell, 'Dual Economy'; Blackburn, 'Aspects of Anglo-Scandinavian minting', pp. 134-5; Williams, 'Kingship, Christianity and coinage', pp. 178-85, 196-7; *Idem*, 'Hoards from the northern Danelaw from Cuerdale to the Vale of York', in *The Huxley Viking Hoard: Scandinavian settlement in the North West*, ed. James Graham-Campbell and Robert Philpott (Liverpool, 2009), pp. 73-83; *Idem*, 'Coinage and monetary circulation in the Northern Danelaw in the 920s in the light of the Vale of York Hoard', in *Studies in Early Medieval Coinage 2: New Perspectives*, ed. Tony Abramson (Woodbridge, 2011), pp. 146-55. Mixed hoards continued in all parts of Viking Britain and Ireland not directly under Anglo-Saxon authority, and similarly continued in Scandinavia into the eleventh century, despite the introduction of regal coinage in Denmark, Norway and Sweden in the 990s.

trade. However, the designs of many of the coins clearly represent the kind of links with Christian kingship that are apparent throughout the Anglo-Saxon period. This is apparent from an early stage, with the coinage of the Viking leader Guthrum. After his defeat at Edington, Guthrum was obliged, as part of the peace process, to accept baptism, with Alfred as his godfather, taking as his baptismal name Æthelstan, a royal name in both the East Anglian and West Saxon dynasties. He then retreated to East Anglia where his kingship was accepted by Alfred according to the Treaty of Wedmore.[101] Shortly after this, a substantial coinage was issued in East Anglia which imitated the Two-line type of Alfred. Although many of the coins in this series have blundered inscriptions, literate examples show clearly that these coins were issued in the name of EDELSTAN REX, or King Æthelstan. This can only be Guthrum, having followed up his submission to Alfred with the adoption of at least some aspects of Anglo-Saxon kingship. The close relationship with Alfred's coinage suggests that Æthelstan/Guthrum was consciously reflecting his relationship with the West Saxon kingdom, but other issues of Æthelstan/Guthrum follow a more East Anglian pattern, and even his Alfred-derived coins follow the traditional East Anglian weight standard rather than the heavier weight standard of Alfred's reformed coinage.[102] The next East Anglian coinage, introduced in the mid 890s, also shows a clear desire to identify with established Anglo-Saxon kingship in the area. Rather than carrying the name of the current Viking ruler, it directly imitates the coinage of Eadmund, the last effective Anglo-Saxon king of East Anglia, whose death in 869 has traditionally been portrayed as Christian martyrdom and subsequently led to his canonisation. The St Eadmund coinage also followed the established East Anglian weight standard rather than following the weight reforms of Alfred's Wessex. The striking thing about this coinage is that it modifies the inscription of Eadmund's own coinage to give him the title S[an]C[tus as well as REX, providing the earliest evidence for the veneration of Eadmund as a saint.[103] How much this says about the religious views of the bulk of the Viking settlers of East Anglia is unclear, but it does indicate very clearly that the ruler or rulers who issued the coins chose to identify themselves as the Christian heirs and successors to Eadmund, within living memory of Eadmund's martyrdom. The reference to Eadmund may also be expressing a sense of political identity, since it refers back to the period in which East Anglia was an independent Christian kingdom with its own royal dynasty. By identifying themselves with this dynasty, the rulers who adopted the St Eadmund coinage could be seen as distancing themselves from the West Saxon overlordship implied by Alfred's sponsorship of Guthrum and Guthrum's adoption of a West Saxon style of coinage.[104]

The latter part of Alfred's reign also saw the introduction of another regal coinage, in the name of Guthfrith, king of Northumbria, although it is uncertain whether this was issued in Northumbria itself, or somewhere in the Midlands, and the fact that this is currently known from a single example suggests that it was never a large coinage.[105] The same applies to coin types from the 880s or later which appear to carry the names VLFDENE and HALFDENE RX, possibly to be identified with the Halfdan killed at Tettenhall in 910, although the name is not unusual, and the coins may represent an otherwise unknown ruler.[106] Like the coinage of Æthelstan/Guthrum, all three of these imitate Alfred's coinage, but the extensive coinage that followed from the late 890s is more innovative. Issued in York in the names of the kings Cnut and Sievert/Siefredus (Sigeferth), this coinage is both explicitly regal and explicitly Christian, giving the rulers their royal titles, but prominently displaying a variety of forms of the Christian cross, and in some cases carrying biblical quotations such as MIRABILIA FECIT and D[omi]N[u] S D[eu]S O[mnipotens] REX, again clearly showing a conscious identification with Christian kingship. In the case of some of the coins of Cnut, the Christian message is reinforced by the form of the inscription, since rather than a continuous circumscription, the name CNVT REX is arranged sequentially around the points of the cross, reflecting the act of signation.[107]

One important detail of this coinage which apparently sets it apart from Anglo-Saxon issues is that while it is regal, it reflects a pattern of multiple kingship, rather than a single king. This is paralleled in several references in the *Anglo-Saxon Chronicle* to Viking forces being led by several rulers at once, and reflects the fact that titles such as 'king' and 'earl' were seen in a Viking context as reflecting personal status and bloodlines rather than necessarily being linked to the more institutionalised rule of a specific people or

Guthrum's coins imitate earlier East Anglian types, themselves derived from Frankish prototypes. It is unclear exactly how these relate chronologically to the main series imitating Alfred's Two-line type. One could hypothesise that he had already converted and assimilated in the period between the settlement of East Anglia and the Treaty of Wedmore, or that he shifted to a more East Anglian pattern after his Alfredian coinage, perhaps reflecting a conscious attempt to revive a distinct East Anglian identity rather than perpetuating his role as a client king of Alfred.
[105] Mark A. S. Blackburn, 'The Ashdon (Essex) hoard and the currency of the southern Danelaw in the late ninth century', *BNJ* 59 (1989), 13–38, at 18-20.
[106] Blackburn, 'Guthrum', p. 21; *Idem*, 'The coinage of Scandinavian York', in *Aspects of Anglo-Scandinavian York*, ed. Richard Hall, *et al.*, The Archaeology of York: Anglo-Scandinavian York 8.4 (York, 2004), pp. 325-49; Williams, 'Chapter 3: The Cuerdale Coins', with a contribution by Marion M. Archibald, in *The Cuerdale Hoard and Related Viking-Age Silver and Gold, from Britain and Ireland, in The British Museum*, ed. James Graham-Campbell, *et al*, British Museum Research Publication no. 185 (British Museum Press, 2011), pp. 39-71.
[107] Colin S. S. Lyon and Bernard H. I. H. Stewart, 'The Northumbrian Viking coins in the Cuerdale hoard', in Dolley, *Anglo-Saxon Coins*, pp. 96-121; Blackburn, 'Scandinavian York', pp. 331-3; *Idem*, 'Crosses and conversion: the iconography of the coinage of Viking York *c.* 900', in *Cross and Culture in Anglo-Saxon England: studies in honor of George Hardin Brown*, ed. Karen L. Jolly, Catherine E. Karkov and Sarah L. Keefer, Medieval European Studies IX (Morgantown, WV, 2007), pp. 172–200; Williams, 'Kingship, Christianity and coinage', pp. 197-9; *Idem*, 'The Cuerdale coins', pp. 43-9.

[101] *ASC* [A and E], *sub anno* 878; Keynes and Lapidge 'Alfred the Great', pp. 171-2.
[102] Blackburn, 'Guthrum', *passim*.
[103] Mark A. S. Blackburn, 'Presidential Address 2005. Currency under the Vikings. Part 2: The two Scandinavian kingdoms of the Danelaw, *c.* 895-954', *BNJ* 76 (2006), 204-26.
[104] As noted by Blackburn ('Guthrum', pp. 23-30), some of Æthelstan/

territory. The wide variety of permutations of inscriptions in this series includes coins in the names of both Sievert and Cnut, which must indicate a joint issue rather than a monetary alliance of the type earlier seen between Mercia and Wessex. The series also includes coins in the name of ALVVALDVS, generally taken to be Æthelwold, nephew of Alfred, who fled to the Northumbrian Vikings after unsuccessfully contesting the West Saxon kingship with his cousin Edward following Alfred's death in 899, and whom the *Anglo-Saxon Chronicle* tells us the Vikings accepted as a king. A recently discovered unique coin which also fits within the same series carries the inscription AIRDECONVT, combined with an explicitly Christian DNS REX reverse design. This may represent the name Harthacnut, which would probably mean yet another king within the same series, although it is conceivable that AIREDECONVT could represent another form, perhaps including a by-name, of the name normally represented as CNVT REX.[108]

The same period also saw one explicitly non-regal coinage, a small coinage in the name of 'Sihtric Comes', or Earl Sihtric, struck at 'Sceldfor', probably to be identified with Great Shelford in Cambridgeshire rather than Shelford in Nottinghamshire.[109] The *Anglo-Saxon Chronicle* shows Viking forces being led by both kings and earls, and within Scandinavian society in the Viking Age there was not necessarily much difference in the relative power of kings and earls, the distinction being more one of bloodline than authority. That being so, one might expect more coins from the Danelaw to carry the name of earls, and the fact that this is confined to the rare coinage of Sihtric suggests that the Anglo-Saxon custom of regarding coinage as a royal prerogative was quickly recognised and adopted.[110]

Not all of the coinage was explicitly regal. The 'St Edmund' coinage continued into the early tenth century, and was joined *c.* 905-10 by a York issue in the name of St Peter, struck in several phases across the first quarter of the century, although the exact chronology of the Northumbrian coinage in this period is still not fully understood. The St Peter coinage was probably interrupted by a regal coinage in the name of Ragnald (*c.* 919-21), while the 920s saw a revival of the St Peter type, now incorporating a Viking sword into the design, together with four other Sword types, one in the name of St Martin of Lincoln, one in the name of Sihtric Rex (with several examples with blundered inscriptions), a circumscription type normally referred to as the Anonymous Sword type, but now also clearly linked with Sihtric, and a newly discovered issue, also anonymous, from the mint

of 'Rorivacastr', but stylistically linked with both the St Peter issues and some of the Sihtric issues. This last came from a hoard found in North Yorkshire in January 2007, which also contained St Peter, Sihtric and St Martin issues, amongst other things.[111] Immediately prior to this, Mark Blackburn had argued that all of the Sword types were issued under the authority of Sihtric, with the St Peter coins issued in York, and the remainder at different mints in the area often referred to as the Five Boroughs.[112] There are certainly strong similarities between the sub-types of the Sihtric and St Peter coins which support the view that all of these types were issued under the same authority, suggesting that even coins which were not explicitly regal might still be royal issues, and David Rollason's view that the coins demonstrate that the archbishops of York were the real authority in this period does not seem to have a firm basis in the numismatic evidence.[113] Whether or not all of the coins in the name of Sihtric were minted south of the Humber, as Blackburn suggests, remains a matter of debate since one of the coins in his corpus carries a York mint signature, and there are now three hoards north of the Humber containing Sihtric coins, whereas there were none at the time that Blackburn was writing.[114] The important thing, however, is that the coinage as a whole reflects a polity which extended on both sides of the Humber, in a period in which the north Midlands is otherwise extremely poorly documented.

The Anglo-Scandinavian coins of this period carry a variety of designs, and Ragnald's coins imitate both Anglo-Saxon and Frankish designs, reflecting the apparent use of imported Frankish moneyers to strike the coinage of

[111] Ian Stewart and S. Lyon, 'Chronology of the St Peter coinage', *Yorkshire Numismatist* 2 (1990), 45-73; Blackburn, 'Scandinavian York', pp. 331-3; David Rollason, *Northumbria, 500–1100: creation and destruction of a kingdom* (Cambridge, 2003), pp. 224-8; Gareth Williams, 'RORIVA CASTR: a new Danelaw mint of the 920s', in *Scripta varia numismatico Tuukka Talvio sexagenario dedicate. Suomen Numismaattisen Yhdistyksen julkaisuja*, no. 6, Finnish Numismatic Society (Helsinki, 2008), 41-7; Gareth Williams, 'The coins from the Vale of York Viking hoard: preliminary report', *BNJ* 78 (2008), 227-34: Idem, 'Coinage and monetary circulation in the Northern Danelaw in the 920s in the light of the Vale of York Hoard'; Megan Gooch, 'Viking kings, political power and monetisation', in Abramson, *Studies in Early Medieval Coinage 2*, pp. 111-20.

[112] Blackburn, 'The two Scandinavian kingdoms', pp. 210-12. If it is accepted that the coins in the names of Sihtric and St Peter were contemporary rather than consecutive, it is also possible that the coins of Ragnald were also issued in parallel with one or other of the St Peter types, rather than interrupting them, This idea has been considered in the past, but the interpretation of the Regnald coins as an interruption in the St Peter coinage currently represents the orthodox view (Stewart and Lyon, 'Chronology of the St Peter coinage', pp. 58-61; Blackburn, 'Scandinavian York', p. 333). On the concept of the Five Boroughs, and specifically for the suggestion that this is a modern construction which distorts our understanding of the tenth century, see Gareth Williams, 'Towns and Identities in Viking England', in *Everyday Life in Viking Towns: social approaches to towns in England and Ireland c. 800-1100*, ed. Dawn Hadley and Aleida ten Harkel (Oxford, forthcoming). Williams, 'Viking towns'.

[113] Rollason, *Northumbria*, pp. 227-30; Gooch, 'Viking kings', pp. 116-20.

[114] Williams, 'Vale of York'; Idem, 'The northern hoards revisited: hoards and silver economy in the northern Danelaw in the early tenth century', in *Early Medieval Art and Archaeology in the Northern World*, ed. Andrew Reynolds and Leslie Webster (Leiden and New York, forthcoming).

[108] Christopher E. Blunt, 'Northumbrian coins in the name of Alwaldus', *BNJ* 55 (1985), 192-4; Williams, 'The Cuerdale coins', p. 45; Idem, 'A new coin type (and a new king?) from Viking Northumbria', *Yorkshire Numismatist* 4 (2012), 261-76.

[109] Cyril Hart, 'The *Aldewerke* and Minster at Shelford, Cambridgeshire', *Anglo-Saxon Studies in Archaeology and History* 8 (1995), 43-68; Blackburn, 'Aspects of Anglo-Scandinavian minting south of the Humber', p. 132.

[110] Williams, 'Kingship, Christianity and coinage', pp. 200-01; Idem, 'The Cuerdale coins', p. 48.

the northern Danelaw.[115] In addition, there is a design with a bow and arrow which may possibly have derived from a Carolingian ship type, but which may be completely original.[116] Ragnald also introduced a symbol generally identified as Thor's hammer, the most widespread symbol of the Scandinavian religion, and one which also appears on coins of Sihtric, 'Rorivacastr', and on the St Peter coinage. In the last, even the final I of PETRI becomes the handle of the hammer, as well as two different forms of hammer appearing as reverse designs.[117] While this could be taken to undermine the link between coinage and Christianity, none of the coins carry pagan symbols alone, as even the coins of Ragnald have an initial cross in the legend, while the presence of the hammer on coins in the name of St Peter can clearly not be entirely pagan. It is also unlikely that Athelstan would have given his sister in marriage to Sihtric[118] unless Sihtric was at least nominally Christian, and the issue of coins in the names of both St Peter and St Martin also points to a Christian identity for Sihtric. It is therefore unclear exactly what the hammer signifies. It may indicate personal religious ambivalence on the part of Ragnald and Sihtric, or it has been suggested that the combination of Christian and pagan imagery may indicate an atmosphere of religious toleration in early tenth-century Northumbria. It is also possible, as I have suggested elsewhere, that the combination of Thor and St Peter may have some role in conversion, perhaps with an element of religious syncretism, with possible parallels in the use of images from Scandinavian mythology on stone crosses.[119]

Whatever the symbolism of this coinage, it came to an abrupt end following Sihtric's death, and the defeat and the expulsion of his successor Guthfrith by Athelstan in 926/7. While it is unclear exactly how Northumbria was administered under Athelstan's rule, it lost its independent kingship, and with it apparently its coinage.

Phase 5: Transition to national coinage

Athelstan's conquest of the Danelaw meant that this area joined a phase which had begun somewhat earlier in the areas under the control of the West Saxon dynasty. To some extent this is a continuation of the phase of Alfred's sole coinage, but the steady expansion under Edward the Elder and his sister Æthelflæd, lady of the Mercians, saw the

West Saxon dynasty extend its authority over further areas not historically part of the West Saxon kingdom, a process which continued under Athelstan. While this process of expansion saw a temporary reversal following the death of Athelstan, with the re-establishment of an independent kingdom in Northumbria and the north Midlands, the lands south of the Humber were quickly recovered by Eadmund, who was also able to exercise some influence north of the Humber, if only intermittently, while lasting control of Northumbria was established by Eadred in 954.

Thus the tenth century saw West Saxon authority extended over all of the pre-Viking Anglo-Saxon kingdoms. By the time that this phase came to an end in the unified kingdom of Eadgar (959-75), it had been a century since the fall of the Anglo-Saxon kingdoms of Northumbria and East Anglia, and nearly as long since the Viking conquest and division of Mercia. Nevertheless, Viking rulers in East Anglia and Northumbria had helped to preserve the distinct identities of these kingdoms, while Mercia continued to have partial autonomy until the death of Æthelflæd in 919. East Anglia also retained an element of independence when it returned to Anglo-Saxon rule, and the nickname Athelstan Half-King indicates the difficulty of defining the new situation in terms of traditional kingship. With hindsight, it is possible to see this as a transitional period before full unification, but at the time it was probably seen more in terms of the established tradition of over-kingship, if now in a slightly different form. The coinage in this phase reflects the tension between 'national' unity and regional identity, as well as the growing authority of the West Saxon kings. The broad characteristics of this phase are as follows:

- Explicitly regal inscriptions, sometimes with regal imagery

- Mixture of regional/national styles

- Mixture of regional/national circulation

- Extension of burghal structure

- Administration of coinage underpinned by legislation

The strong association between the coinage and kingship, not surprisingly, continues. As before, the coinage was explicitly regal, and across this period there were coin issues symbolising kingship by a crowned bust quite distinct from the Roman diademed bust that had been so common in the eighth and ninth centuries, although these were never apparently the only issues in circulation. The regulation of coinage now also appears in written law, beginning with the Grateley Code of *c.* 926-30.[120] Coinage must have been regulated by law before this, although it does not appear in the few earlier surviving law codes,

[115] Blackburn, 'Expansion and Control', p. 128; *Idem*, 'Guthrum', pp. 26-7; V. Smart, 'The moneyers of St Edmund', *Hikuin* 11 (1985), 83-100; *Idem*, 'Scandinavians, Celts and Germans in Anglo-Saxon England: the evidence of moneyers' names' in *Anglo-Saxon Monetary History*, ed. Mark A. S. Blackburn (Leicester, 1986), pp. 171-84; *Idem*, 'Economic migrants? Continental moneyers' names on the tenth-century English coinage', *Nomina* 32 (2009), 113-156.
[116] Christopher E. Blunt and Bernard H. I. H. Stewart, 'The coinage of Regnald I of York and the Bossall Hoard', *Numismatic Chronicle* (1983), pp. 146-63; Christopher E. Blunt, Bernard H. I. H. Stewart and Colin S. S. Lyon, *Coinage in Tenth-Century England* (Oxford, 1989), p.105.
[117] Reginald H. M. Dolley, 'The post-Brunanburh Viking coinage of York', *Nordisk Numismatisk Årsskrift* [no vol number](1957-8), pp. 13-88, at 42-3; Stewart and Lyon, 'Chronology'; Blackburn, 'The two Scandinavian kingdoms', pp. 209-10.
[118] *ASC* [D], *sub anno* 926.
[119] Williams, 'Kingship, Christianity and coinage', p. 198.

[120] Blackburn, 'Mints, burhs and the Grately code', pp. 160-75; Williams, 'Civil defence or royal powerbase?'.

but from this period on it appears regularly,[121] providing documentary evidence for some of the interpretations which for earlier periods can only be inferred. Firstly, the fact that episcopal coinage was issued as a legally defined right, with the consent of the king, is confirmed by the Grately code, which notes the continued minting rights of the archbishop of Canterbury, as well as the abbot of Canterbury and the bishop of Rochester. It is unclear whether the rights of the latter two were new at this time, as no coins were issued in their names.[122]

It is also at this period that the coins of the archbishops of Canterbury ceased to carry their own names and the distinctive tonsured busts, although the right of minting continued. This thus became a right with purely financial benefits, while the royal monopoly on representation on coins became complete. Recognised sub-rulers such as Æthelred and Æthelflæd in Mercia, and Æthelstan Half-King in East Anglia, were not permitted to issue coins in their own names, although it is possible that they may have enjoyed some of the revenue derived from minting. Two other issues which are clarified by the Grately code are the royal regulation of moneyers, and the relationship between minting and burhs, with specified numbers of moneyers defined for each *burh,* although the number of moneyers visible on the coins appears to have spread beyond the numbers specified in the Grately code fairly quickly. Both the Grately code and later law codes now defined the legal restrictions under which moneyers operated. They do not indicate the financial terms under which minting took place, although it is likely that it was a farmed franchise, but indicate that minting, along with a range of other activities relating both to trade and justice, was limited to *burhs,* thus simultaneously strengthening the role of *burhs* as devolved regional centres of royal authority, while making it easier for *burh* reeves to monitor and regulate activities which took place within the *burhs.* The link with *burhs* is reinforced by the addition of *VRBS* or *CIV* to the names of various *burhs* on the coinage. At the same time, the listing of minting rights within the Grately code is a clear indication of centralised control and authority, as well as perhaps an ideological statement about Athelstan's imperial aspirations, reflecting the wider link with Romanised Christian kingship discussed throughout this paper.[123]

Coinage continued to carry the names of moneyers, and some issues are mint-signed. This allows us to identify certain moneyers with particular towns, so that when the same moneyers appear on coins without mint signatures, these can be attributed to the same mints, or at least to the same regions, and the combination of mint signatures, stylistic analysis and finds distribution has enabled numismatists to identify certain issues firmly with particular regions, as in the pictorial issues in the names of Edward the Elder, which can be attributed with reasonable

certainty to north-western Mercia. Other types were minted on a more national basis, but show regional variation in the style of die-cutting.[124] This clearly demonstrates a regional aspect in the administration of the coinage, which may reflect wider issues of the continued importance of regional identities in the terminology of kinship, and possibly of sub-authorities in royal administration.

Within this general framework, there are indications of the unification that was to come. A short-lived issue in the name of Athelstan carrying an image of a building (probably a church), appears to celebrate Athelstan's (re-)conquest of Northumbria and the Midlands in 926-7, following the death of Sihtric of Northumbria, although York is the only mint specifically identified on the coins.[125] This assumption of authority in the north effectively unified England (excluding Cumbria and parts of Lancashire) for the first time. However, it was two final issues, which carry the names of individual mints as well as moneyers on the reverse, that pre-figure the network of mints seen in the next and final phase of the coinage, indicating standardisation of appearance and quality across the kingdom, but with recognised devolved centres for day-to-day administration and coin-issue. The two types, one with a bust, the other with a circumscription around a cross on the obverse, both issued on a large scale from a large number of mints, must be seen as a move towards a single national coin type. Furthermore, Athelstan's use of the title REX TO[TIUS] BRIT[ANNIAE] on this national coinage, probably issued following the submission of various less powerful rulers at Eamont Bridge in 927,[126] indicates an aspiration towards a single unified over-kingship, although the title probably overstated the extent of Athelstan's authority in the various kingdoms outside his own direct control. One may also note that Athelstan's authority even in England was not unqualified, to judge from the coinage. Some mints in the Midlands, such as Lincoln, appear not to have struck within this national coinage at all, while others such as Derby and Nottingham appear rather pointedly to reject Athelstan's new title, describing him simply as REX SAXONVM.[127]

Whatever degree of over-kingship Athelstan enjoyed at this period it was only temporary. Although Athelstan was victorious at Brunanburh in 937, the alliance against him indicates the rejection of his overkingship by various of the less powerful kings within Britain and Ireland, and the benefits of the victory at Brunanburh also fell apart quickly on Athelstan's death in 939. Even within England both political unity and the unity of the coinage collapsed, with the reassertion of Northumbrian independence, and the minting of new Anglo-Scandinavian issues at York

[121] Screen, 'Anglo-Saxon law and numismatics'.
[122] Naismith, 'Money of the saints'.
[123] Blackburn, 'Mints, burhs and the Grately code', pp. 168-72; Screen, 'Anglo-Saxon law and numismatics', pp. 155-7; Williams, 'Civil defence or royal powerbase?'.

[124] Blunt, Stewart and Lyon, *Coinage in Tenth-Century England, passim.*
[125] Gareth Williams, 'Coinage and monetary circulation in the Northern Danelaw in the 920s in the light of the Vale of York Hoard', in Abramson, *Studies in Early Medieval Coinage 2*, pp. 146-55.
[126] C. E. Blunt, 'The coinage of Athelstan', *BNJ* 42 (1974), 35–158, at 55; Williams, 'Coinage and monetary circulation', p. 150.
[127] Blunt, 'Coinage of Athelstan', pp. 93-6.

and Derby, while mint-signed coins ceased to be the norm in the English coinage.[128]

However, coinage does provide one insight into the relationship of the West Saxon dynasty with the smaller kings under their domination. A unique coin in the name of HOWÆL REX indicates the spread, however short-lived, of Anglo-Saxon practice to Wales.[129] The coin imitates the HT1 variety of the Two-line type, which was the most common Anglo-Saxon type throughout this period, and uses a reverse die in the name of Gillys, who issued coins of this type in the names of both Eadred and Edgar, and the coinage has every appearance of an official issue produced with the sanction of both the moneyer and either Eadred or Edgar. The obverse design is well cut, although minor flaws may indicate that an Anglo-Saxon die had been re-cut to create the HOWÆL inscription. Christopher Blunt argued in 1986 that this could be attributed with some certainty to Eadred's contemporary Hywel Dda (d. 950),[130] but the numismatic evidence is far more ambiguous than Blunt suggested, and there seems no good reason at present to attribute the coin to Hywel Dda rather than the slightly later Hywel ap Ieuaf (d. 985), since the numismatic parallels are as strong or stronger for Edgar's coinage as for that of Eadred.[131] Both kings had close diplomatic links with the English court, especially the later Hywel, who was one of the six kings who reportedly rowed Edgar on the Dee in 873.[132] In either case, the lack of an obvious economic environment within which the coin could function, coupled with the rarity of the type, suggests that the coin was issued as much for the symbolic value of issuing coins as for any other reason. In other words, it appears to reflect the transfer of the model of Anglo-Saxon kingship discussed throughout this paper into a Welsh client kingdom. In this context, it is interesting to note that medieval Welsh tradition credited Hywel Dda with the introduction of written law in Wales, and while the surviving laws attributed to Hywel Dda are unlikely to be anything like so early, the tradition of Hywel as lawmaker may well be genuine, and would also be consistent with the model of kingship discussed here.

Returning to England itself, the characteristic of this period emerges as increasing royal control of the coinage, but with minting spread over a growing number of mints as the burghal structure itself expanded. At the same time, there was some challenge to this unified control from a continued sense of regional identity. In one instance this was enough to disrupt the process of unification, with the resurgence of independent coinage in the northern Danelaw, following the death of Athelstan in 939. The

Viking kingdom of Northumbria was re-established, and temporarily exercised some authority south of the Humber, reflecting the area which coinage suggests had been under the control of Sihtric in the 920s.[133] Not only did these issues break the monopoly of the West Saxon dynasty over coinage, but it challenged the identification with Anglo-Saxon kingship which earlier Anglo-Scandinavian rulers had apparently embraced. Although some of the coin types follow Anglo-Saxon designs, there is a series of coins under several members of Uí Ímair (the Viking dynasty which ruled Dublin) including Olaf and Regnald Guthfrithsson, Olaf Sihtricsson and an otherwise unrecorded member of the dynasty named Sihtric, with designs without parallel in the Anglo-Saxon coinage, coupled with a clear statement of a distinct Scandinavian identity. The coins are still explicitly regal, but no longer used the Latin title REX, although it is clear that the moneyers themselves (with a mixture of Anglo-Saxon and Scandinavian names) remained in post under both Anglo-Saxon and Viking rulers, and must therefore have been familiar with Anglo-Saxon style. Instead, the coins carry variants of the inscription CVNVNC, after the ruler's name, representing *konungr,* the principal Old Norse word for king. Some of the coins also give the moneyers what appears to be an Old Norse equivalent to the Latin title of *moneta[rius]*.

The interpretation of the images on this coinage is problematic. One series attributed to Olaf Guthfrithsson shows a stylised bird with a curved beak.[134] This has often been interpreted as a raven, a bird which is closely associated with the god Oðinn, and has therefore been taken to indicate a consciously non-Christian identity. However, the reverse design is an unambiguous cross, and there is also a cross at the beginning of the inscription on each side. Furthermore, the bird itself is not unequivocally pagan. The raven also has an association with the cult of the Northumbrian Saint Oswald, but the bird might equally well be regarded as an eagle. This bird also has Oðinnic associations, but is also one of the four Evangelist symbols in Christian iconography, as well as a fairly widespread symbol of authority and power.[135] Both ravens and eagles are also closely associated with war and battle in Old Norse poetry. The use of such a distinctive symbol coupled with the Old Norse title must surely indicate the deliberate expression of a royal identity in opposition to the 'national' over-kingship of the West Saxon dynasty, but the exact nature of that identity is unclear, and likely to remain so. Two other distinctive designs appear on this series of coinage. One is a triquetra, which is a common symbol in Viking-Age art. Various interpretations of this have been offered, again including the suggestion that it could be an Oðinnic symbol. However, it has also been

[128] Blunt, Stewart and Lyon, *Coinage in Tenth-Century England,* pp. 117, 212-4.
[129] C. E. Blunt, 'The cabinet of the Marquess of Ailesbury and the penny of Hywel Dda', *BNJ* 52 (1982), 117–22.
[130] Blunt, 'Hywel Dda'.
[131] Gareth Williams, unpublished lecture to Early Medieval Wales Archaeological Research Group, Cardiff 2006.
[132] Blunt, 'Hywel Dda'; David E. Thornton, 'Edgar and the eight kings, AD 973: textus et dramatis personae', *Early Medieval Europe* 10.1 (2001), 49–79.

[133] Blunt, Stewart and Lyon, *Coinage in Tenth-Century England,* pp. 211-19; Blackburn, 'The Coinage of Scandinavian York'; *Idem,* 'The two Scandinavian kingdoms', pp. 218-21.
[134] Dolley, 'The post-Brunanburh Viking coinage of York', pp. 67-8; Blunt, Stewart and Lyon, *Coinage in Tenth-Century England,* pp. 215-6, 219-21.
[135] Rollason, *Northumbria,* p. 226; Blackburn, 'Scandinavian York', p. 336; Williams, 'Coinage, Christianity and kingship', p. 198.

suggested that it might represent the Trinity.[136] On the Northumbrian coinage, it is always found coupled with a reverse design showing a standard or wind-vane. This is again unambiguously Christian, since it is topped with a cross, and another cross is shown in the centre of the standard/vane. If any of the symbols on this coinage carried specifically pagan connotations, they were clearly being represented in a heavily Christianised context, and must be interpreted in this light.

The final group of coins from late Viking Northumbria tell a slightly different story. These are the coins in the name of a documented king Eric, son of Harald, usually associated with Eric Bloodaxe, although this association has been challenged by Clare Downham, who has suggested that he was a member of Ui Imharr, the ruling dynasty of Dublin.[137] There is no use of Old Norse, or of any of the symbols associated with the Dublin dynasty at this time, suggesting that Eric had a distinct royal identity. One of the Eric types is a straightforward copy of an Anglo-Saxon Two-line type, while the other reverts to the sword design seen on Anglo-Scandinavian coins in the 920s. An intriguing possibility here is that the change in the design represents a change in the nature of Eric's kingship. According to Scandinavian tradition, Eric first became king of Northumbria as a recognised sub-king under Athelstan, but was later expelled under Edmund, returning as an independent ruler before eventually being killed at Stainmore in 954.[138] While this version does not receive active support from Anglo-Saxon sources, it equally does not conflict with them, as Anglo-Saxon sources for this period are far from comprehensive, and give no indication of how Northumbria was administered under Athelstan.

Although the general pattern of this phase was for Anglo-Saxon sub-kings and regional rulers to be denied the right to issue coins, the HOWÆL REX coin does seem to indicate that coins might on occasion be permitted in the name of a client king outside the main Anglo-Saxon kingdom, and it is possible that this first type in the name of Eric represents the same thing. In this context, the reversion in the second type to the sword design which had preceded the West-Saxon over-kingship of Northumbria can be interpreted as a rejection of that over-kingship, as well as of the identity of the Dublin dynasty. This would be consistent with the Scandinavian tradition, and does not conflict directly with anything in Anglo-Saxon or Irish sources. However, with such limited evidence available, the interpretation is necessarily speculative. At the same time, it must be noted that several issues of the Dublin dynasty also imitate Anglo-Saxon types, and any interpretation of the coinage must take this into account. While the coinage of this period has been studied intensively from a numismatic perspective, it would repay further study in its historical context. Olaf Sihtricsson and Regnald Guthfrithsson seem to have submitted (at least temporarily) to the overlordship of Edmund,[139] and perhaps other kings of the dynasty made temporary accommodations with West Saxon rulers, but the imitative coinages may also simply represent a general pattern of transitional imitations before the introduction of more distinctive local types. Nevertheless, however the imitative coinages are interpreted, Eric's second type, like those of Anlaf Guthfrithsson and his cousins, must surely be interpreted as a reaction against the aspirations towards national kingship of the West Saxon dynasty.

Phase 6: National coinage, c. 973-1066

Those aspirations were finally realised in the reign of Edgar, and were reflected in a major reform of his coinage, which marks the beginning of the final phase of the Anglo-Saxon coinage. This can be characterised as follows:

- Local issues, national design

- Complete standardisation

- Strong regal and Christian imagery

- Visible delegated local authority

- Fiscal manipulation

- Underpinned by legislation and extensive bureaucracy

Edgar was not immediately in a position to push the 'national' agenda, since the unified kingship of Eadred was divided in 957 between his nephews Eadwig and Edgar, and it was only in 959 that Edgar became sole king at the age of sixteen. Thereafter it took some time to consolidate his position, but by 973 he had not only succeeded in unifying the Anglo-Saxon kingdom, he had also restored a version of the British over-kingship formerly held by Athelstan, as symbolised by the famous incident in which he was rowed by six sub-kings on the River Dee.[140] He chose to have a second coronation to symbolise his authority, and it is likely that he maintained or even extended the West Saxon system of military organisation. Although it has been suggested that this fell into decline in this period,[141] it is notable that England was not prey to recorded Viking attacks under Edgar, despite

[136] Kolbjorn Skaare, *Coins and Coinage in Viking-age Norway* (Oslo, Bergen and Tromsö, 1976), pp. 68-70, 94-5; Blunt, Stewart and Lyon, *Coinage in Tenth-Century England*, pp. 221-2; Blackburn, 'Scandinavian York', p. 336.

[137] Clare E. Downham, 'Eric Bloodaxe – axed? The mystery of the last Viking king of York', *Medieval Scandinavia* 14 (2004), 51-77; *Idem, Viking Kings of Britain and Ireland: the dynasty of Ívarr to AD 1014* (Edinburgh, 2007).

[138] Alfred P. Smyth, *York and Dublin: the history and archaeology of two related Viking Kingdoms*, 2 vols ([Atlantic Highlands], NJ and Dublin, 1975-9), pp. ; Alex Woolf, 'Eric Bloodaxe revisited', *Northern History* 34 (1998), 189-93; Gareth Williams, *Eirik Bloodaxe* (Kernavik, 2010).

[139] *ASC* A, *sub anno* 942 [943]; D, *sub anno* 943; Williams, *Eirik Bloodaxe*, pp. 90-101, 109.

[140] *ASC* A, *sub anno* 973; E, *sub anno* 972; Thornton, 'Edgar and the eight kings'.

[141] Richard Abels, 'English logistics and military organisation, 871-1066: the impact of the Viking wars', in *Military Aspects of Scandinavian Society in a European Perspective, AD 1-1300*, ed. Anne Nørgård Jørgensen and Birthe L. Clausen (Copenhagen, 1997), pp. 257-65; Williams, 'Civil defence or royal powerbase?'.

extensive Viking activity in Ireland, Scotland and Wales, and the *Anglo-Saxon Chronicle* records that God helped him moreover to subdue kings and earls,

> Who cheerfully submitted to his will.
> So that without opposition
> He was able to subdue
> All to his wishes and that
> No fleet however proud,
> No host however strong,
> Was able to win booty for itself[142]

both implying strong military power. Thus by the last years of his reign, the general picture of Edgar's kingship is of strong, confident, unified rule.

This is reflected in his coinage reform. This introduced a standardised (and exclusive) style, with Edgar's name and the title *Rex Anglorum* around a Roman imperial bust on the obverse, and both a moneyer's name and a mint name around a cross on the reverse, indicating a substantial network of mints across England, although York remained the only mint town north of the Humber. The reform cannot be precisely dated, but the comparative rarity of the Reform type suggests that it took place late in the reign, and the symbolism of the integrated national coinage would certainly be consistent with the recorded events of 973.[143]

This coinage reform set a lasting pattern for the remainder of the Anglo-Saxon period and well beyond. Although the details of the designs on the coinage changed frequently, the combination of king's name and title with stylised bust on one side and mint and moneyer with some form of cross on the other remained constant. Some variation took place in the location of mints although, as new finds repeatedly demonstrate, some of the apparent differences in the distribution of mints between different types and reigns represent chance discovery rather than genuine difference. Some short term mints are known from the reign of Æthelred II, which appear to be emergency mints replacing established mints at exposed centres with mints in more easily defended areas, such as the temporary mint at Cadbury in Somerset, but the general pattern is for a mint in each shire town, with several additional small mints in ports and other larger mints in major burhs which were not shire centres, such as Stamford and Thetford.[144]

The network of burghal mints reflects royal authority over the burhs, while the mints in ports reflect the legal prohibitions on the circulation of any coin other than the king's coinage, a prohibition which meets with some support from the archaeological record.[145] Such mints thus effectively served as *bureaux de changes* in addition to domestic minting duties.

The minting rights of a number of bishops and abbots continued but, as in the previous phase, this appears to have been limited to a grant of the profits of minting, and there were no issues which carried the names or images of churchmen, nor was there apparently any differentiation in the appearance of coins struck for kings and coins struck for bishops, with the possible exception of a small group of coins minted at Stamford which have been linked with the Abbot of Peterborough,[146] and even these are only differentiated by the addition of an annulet in one quarter of the field on the reverse. This is in marked contrast with continental coinage in the same period. Although royal coinage continued in the emerging kingdoms of France and Germany in the tenth and eleventh centuries, the right to issue coinage was granted to both ecclesiastical and secular magnates, many of whom issued coins in their own names, and to their own design, providing clear symbols of the fragmentation of royal authority.[147] That the English coinage saw no such devolution of authority is a tribute to the strength of Anglo-Saxon royal power, and of the administrative system which underpinned this. This is all the more remarkable in that the system survived through the reigns of kings such as Æthelred II and Edward the Confessor who have traditionally been regarded as 'weak' kings, and through the conquest of England by both Cnut and William.

It is in the reign of Æthelred II that another remarkable feature of the late Anglo-Saxon coinage becomes apparent. As mentioned above, the specific designs of the obverse bust and reverse cross vary considerably throughout the period. The majority of the busts, predictably, are derived from Roman coinage, but Cnut's first coinage shows him wearing the same type of crown shown in contemporary Anglo-Saxon manuscripts, perhaps demonstrating his desire to be seen as an Anglo-Saxon king rather than a Danish conqueror. Both Cnut and Edward the Confessor issued coins portraying them in contemporary conical helmets, while the latter adopted a number of designs apparently derived from German coinage, including one with a seated regal figure instead of a bust.[148] This variation

[142] *ASC* E, *sub anno* 959, 975.

[143] Reginald H. M. Dolley, 'Roger of Wendover's date for Eadgar's coinage reform', *BNJ* 49 (1979), 1-11; Kenneth Jonsson, 'The New Era: the reformation of the late Anglo-Saxon coinage', *Commentationes de nummis saeculorum IX–XI in Suecia repertis*, n.s. 1 (Stockholm, 1987); Ian Stewart, 'Coinage and recoinage after Edgar's reform', in *Studies in Late Anglo-Saxon Coinage in Memory of Bror Emil Hildebrand*, ed. Kenneth Jonsson, *Svenska Numismatiska Meddelanden* 35 (Stockholm, 1990), pp. 455-86.

[144] For the relative output of different mints in this period, see David M. Metcalf, *An Atlas of Anglo-Saxon and Norman Coin Finds, 973-1086* (London, 1998); Martin R. Allen, 'The volume of the English currency, c. 973-1158', in Cook and Williams, *Coinage and History in the North Sea World*, pp. 487-523; *Idem, Mints and Moneyers in Medieval England* (Cambridge, 2012). For more detailed discussion of the geographical

distribution of minting and burhs, see Metcalf, *Atlas, passim*; Allen, *Mints and Money*, pp. 15-23; Williams, 'Civil defence or royal powerbase?'.

[145] Barrie J. Cook, 'Foreign coins in medieval England', in *Local coins, foreign coins: Italy and Europe, 11th-15th centuries, The Second Cambridge Numismatic Symposium*, ed. Lucia Travaini, Società Numismatica Italiana: collana di numismatica e scienze affini 2 (Milan, 1999), pp. 231-84.

[146] Ian H. Stewart, 'The Stamford mint and the connexion with the Abbot of Peterborough under Ethelred II', *BNJ* 28 (1955-57), 106-10.

[147] Grierson, *Coinage in Medieval Europe*.

[148] Kenneth Jonsson, 'The Coinage of Cnut', in *The Reign of Cnut*, ed. Alexander R. Rumble (Leicester, 1994), pp. 193–230; Tuukka Talvio, 'The design of Edward the Confessor's coins', in Jonsson, *Studies in*

in design was not simply random, but a facilitated fiscal manipulation of the coinage, known as *renovatio monatae,* since every few years the coinage was called in and replaced with a new type, which was sufficiently different from the previous type that it was difficult for coins of the previous type to pass unnoticed. Mint records from this period are lacking, and the process of re-coinage (as well as the sequence of the different types) is inferred from the contents of hoards, combined with the evidence of later and better documented periods. The exact process(es) remains the subject of debate, but the assumption is that with the introduction of each new type, only the new type could legally be used in monetary transactions and that older types could only be exchanged for new on payment of a premium, which generated profit both for the moneyers and the king. It was, in effect, a form of hidden taxation.[149]

The paucity of evidence did not prevent the numismatist Michael Dolley from developing an over-rigid and complicated theory of periodic re-coinage, based on sexennial, and later triennial cycles, and initiating with Edgar's reform.[150] Many aspects of Dolley's arguments were flawed, while others lacked any foundation whatsoever, but they have largely been repeated uncritically by historians, while Dolley's pre-eminence in Anglo-Saxon numismatics and combative attitude effectively stifled debate within the numismatic community, and it was not until after his death that numismatists questioned his theories in print.[151] These articles have yet to make a wider impact on Anglo-Saxon studies. More recent numismatic thinking accepts that re-coinage took place every few years, but notes that there is no evidence for the fixed cycles proposed by Dolley, and quite a body of counter-evidence. Furthermore, it is unclear whether this system of re-coinage was planned from the beginning of Edgar's reform, or whether it was actually introduced in the reign of Æthelred II. The sole type of Eadward the Martyr and the first type of Æthelred were identical to Edgar's Reform type, and Dolley, taking

the dating of 973 for the reform as fact, regarded this as the first of his six-year types, spreading across all three reigns. As mentioned above, the reform certainly took place towards the end of Edgar's reign, and any attempt to interpret his long-term plans can be nothing more than guesswork. It is equally possible, and perhaps more likely, that Edward and Æthelred (or their advisors) in turn chose to imitate their father's national type as a way of stressing their claims as the legitimate successors to the national kingship which he had established, and to emphasise the continuity of kingship. Under this interpretation, the introduction of re-coinage for fiscal purposes (which may or may not have occurred on a regular cycle) should be attributed to the reign of Æthelred, in contrast to his reputation as an ineffective ruler.

Leaving that question aside, however, there is no doubt that Edgar introduced a successful system of national coinage which outlasted the Anglo-Saxon kingdom, and little doubt that a system of comparatively frequent deliberate re-coinage for fiscal purposes was introduced at least as early as the reign of Æthelred II, while the extent of royal control of the coinage is in sharp contrast with other coin-issuing kingdoms in northern Europe. The combination of wealth and power demonstrated by the coinage reflects the wealth and power of the kingdom, which made it such an attractive target for invaders such as Swein, Cnut and William, and also partially explains the desire of the latter two to retain as much as possible of the *status quo* once they had taken the kingdom. The structures of minting were largely unchanged throughout the eleventh century, although William does seem to have experimented with replacing the fees paid by moneyers before the Conquest with a more widespread tax on minting.[152] Both Cnut and William used coin imagery to stress the legitimacy of their kingship, following their respective conquests, and Harold II did the same in the context of the disputed succession to Edward the Confessor in 1066. It is interesting that despite his short reign and the difficulties of controlling the northern earls, he nevertheless seems to have had no difficulty in establishing control of a fully national coinage, with a bust derived from the final bust of Edward the Confessor.[153] It is also interesting that in the brief interim between Harold's death at Hastings and the submission of the Witan to William, the link between coins and kingship was apparently maintained through a short-lived and hastily organised posthumous coinage in the name of Harold minted at Wilton.[154]

Late Anglo-Saxon Coinage in Memory of Bror Emil Hildebrand, pp. 487-500; Marion M. Archibald, 'The German connection: German influences on the later Anglo-Saxon and Norman coinages in their English context; (tenth and eleventh centuries)', in *Fundamenta Historiae. Geschichte im Spiegel der Numismatik und ihrer Nachbarwissenschaften. Festschrift für Niklot Klüssendorf zum 60. Geburtstag am 10. Februar 2004*, ed. Reiner Cunz, Veröffentlichungen der urgeschichtlichen Sammlungen des Landesmuseums zu Hannover 51 (Hanover, 2004), pp. 131-50.

[149] George C. Brooke, 'Quando moneta vertebatur: the change of coin-types in the eleventh century; its bearing on mules and overstrikes', *BNJ* 20 (1929-30), 105-16; David M. Metcalf, 'The taxation of moneyers under Edward the Confessor and in 1086', in *Domesday Studies. Papers read at the Novocentenary Conference of the Royal Historical Society and the Institute of British Geographers, Winchester, 1986*, ed. James C. Holt (Woodbridge, 1987), pp. 279-93; Allen, *Mints and Money*, pp. 8-9, 182-3; Gareth Williams, 'Monetary contacts between England and Normandy, c. 973-1180: a numismatic perspective', in *Circulations monétaires et réseaux d'échanges en Normandie et dans le Nord-Ouest européen (Antiquité-Moyen Âge)*, ed. J. Chameroy and Pierre-Marie Guilhard, Tables rondes du CRAHM 8 (Caen, 2012), pp. 173-84.

[150] Reginald H. M. Dolley and David M. Metcalf, 'The reform of the English coinage under Eadgar', in Dolley, *Anglo-Saxon Coins*, pp. 136-68; Dolley, 'Eadgar's coinage reform'.

[151] John D. Brand, *Periodic Change of Type in the Anglo-Saxon and Norman Periods* (Rochester, 1984); Ian Stewart, 'Coinage and recoinage'; Allen, *Mints and Money*, pp. 35-40; Gareth Williams, 'Monetary contacts', pp. 174-5.

[152] Reginald H. M. Dolley, *The Norman Conquest and the English Coinage* (London, 1966); Brooke, 'Quando moneta vertebatur', *passim*; Philip Grierson, 'Domesday Book, the geld *de moneta* and *monetagium*: a forgotten minting reform', *BNJ* 55 (1985), 84-94; Metcalf, 'Taxation of moneyers', *passim*; Jens C. Moesgaard, 'La Monnaie au temps de Guillaume le Conquérant', in *La Tapisserie de Bayeux: une chronique des temps Vikings?*, ed. Sylvette Lemagnen (Bonsecours, 2009), pp. 88-99; Allen, *Mints and Money*, pp. 183-5; Gareth Williams, 'Monetary contacts', pp. 180-81.

[153] Hugh E. Pagan, 'The coinage of Harold II', in Jonsson, *Studies in Late Anglo-Saxon Coinage in Memory of Bror Emil Hildebrand*, pp. 179-205.

[154] Gareth Williams, 'Was the last Anglo-Saxon king of England a queen? A possible posthumous coinage of Harold II', *Yorkshire Numismatist* 4 (2012), 159-70.

Cnut's first issue shows a crowned bust, similar to the representations of kings in Anglo-Saxon manuscripts, although he later shifted to a type showing a bust with a contemporary conical helmet before reverting to a traditional Roman imperial bust.[155] For a Danish invader, it was initially more important to appear as an Anglo-Saxon king than as a Roman emperor. For William, it was possible to do both at the same time, since he imitated the last coinage of Edward the Confessor, as a way of emphasising his claim to be a legitimate successor rather than simply a conqueror. Like all of Edward's later types, this was derived from German imperial issues,[156] and this may be seen as reflecting a new 'imperial' style of kingship which Edward sought to impose after Godwine's death. This is also reflected in the introduction of a great seal showing Edward as a seated sovereign with orb and sceptre, a design shared with the first of Edward's continental issues.[157] The German coinage was in turn influenced by Byzantine designs, so William can be seen as a Norman interloper imitating an Anglo-Saxon king imitating a German emperor imitating a Byzantine emperor who saw himself as the continuation (rather than the heir) of the Roman imperial tradition which underpinned the fundamental concept of kingship that runs through most of the period covered by this paper.

Conclusion

Coinage is closely linked to kingship from the beginning of locally issued coinage at the end of the sixth century through to the Norman Conquest and beyond. This reflects a broadly similar ideological view of Romanised Christian kingship throughout, but the scale and sophistication of both the late Anglo-Saxon kingdom and its coinage would probably have been unimaginable in Kent at the end of the sixth century, and the process of expanding royal authority was a long and gradual one. Furthermore, this was not always a smooth progression. For example, the Northumbrian styca coinage, produced in base metal but in large quantities, can be seen in some ways as the most developed Anglo-Saxon monetary economy of the early ninth century, but it was brought to a complete stop by the collapse of the kingdom, and coin-production had to start again after a gap, once the new Anglo-Scandinavian rulers of Northumbria had gone through a process of religious, political and cultural conversion comparable to that which had occurred in Kent three hundred years before. The inspiration behind much of Anglo-Saxon kingship, and the coinage in particular, was an awareness of the heritage of the Roman imperial past, but it was really only in the late Anglo-Saxon period, in the last of the phases that I have proposed, that anything approaching a comparable degree of sophistication existed, or the sense of a nation state that allowed such sophistication. Even then, in terms of a developed and functioning monetary economy, the Anglo-Saxons never matched the achievements of their Roman predecessors. However, as a highly visible symbol of kingship, and as evidence for firm royal control over the production and circulation of coinage, the final national phase of Anglo-Saxon coinage is at least as potent as the late Roman coinage which preceded the Anglo-Saxon invasions.

[155] Marion M. Archibald, 'Anglo-Saxon coinage, Alfred to the Conquest', in *The Golden Age of Anglo-Saxon Art, 966-1066*, ed. Janet Backhouse, Derek H. Turner and Leslie Webster (London, 1984), pp. 170- 189, at 180; Jonsson, 'The coinage of Cnut', pp. 199-202.
[156] Talvio, 'The design of Edward the Confessor's coins', *passim*; Archibald, 'The German connection', *passim*.
[157] Archibald, 'Alfred to the Conquest', p. 185.

Chapter 6 Coins, Merchants and the Reeve: Royal Authority in the Anonymous Old English *Legend of the Seven Sleepers*

Mark Atherton

In the second half of the tenth century, an anonymous author working on the margins of the Benedictine reform composed an Old English version of *The Legend of the Seven Sleepers of Ephesus*.[1] As Dorothy Whitelock briefly noted, this Old English story is an adaptation of the traditional Latin source, with a number of additions reflecting contemporary tenth-century conditions such as legal procedures and coinage.[2] It is also skilfully written, as Hugh Magennis has shown, in a vivid rhetorical style with a good deal of psychological interest.[3] In effect, the Old English writer produced an imaginative reworking of the story, which elaborates considerably on the sparsely narrated Latin original.[4] But *The Seven Sleepers* has remained a little-used window on late Anglo-Saxon culture, and the foundational work of Whitelock and Magennis can still be built on, as this paper seeks to show. The following discussion will focus chiefly on the Malchus narrative, the longest episode of the story, and for convenience, since there is no recent modern English translation,[5] this section of the tale is translated in an appendix below.

The depiction of royal authority

The basic plot of The Seven Sleepers

Written in the form of a saint's life, *The Seven Sleepers* goes back to the fifth-century Greek theological world during the reign of the emperor Theodosius II. But the first half of the story is set much earlier, in the pagan Roman past, and the plot relates how seven men escape from Ephesus to avoid the terrible anti-Christian persecution by the pagan emperor Decius. Taking refuge in a cave outside the town, they are overcome with grief and fatigue and fall into a deep and wondrous sleep, a kind of death even, which lasts for no less than 372 years.

In the morning of their awakening, they are unaware of any change in their circumstances and naturally very anxious to hear news about the persecution in Ephesus; so they give their steward Malchus some money and send

him out disguised as a beggar to buy bread. But on his arrival at the marketplace, Malchus is accused of trying to pass off coins from an ancient treasure hoard. Baffled and confused, Malchus causes a stir, but the traders seize him: soon he is arrested by the authorities and interrogated by a sceptical city proconsul. Eventually he is released by the more discerning bishop, who goes out to meet the other saintly sleepers and then summons the emperor Theodosius to come and view this sign of divine power. Hastening to Ephesus in his chariot and hurrying to the cave, the Christian emperor rejoices at this tangible proof of the doctrine of the resurrection of the dead – the main theological theme of the story.

The theme of kingship

From the perspective of royal power, however, the Old English *Seven Sleepers* is a story of kingship and loyalty, a tale of two kings: the pagan emperor Decius, who in the first half of the story exiles his seven loyal followers, and the Christian emperor Theodosius who (372 years later) finally reinstates them. A key to the relationship of king and retainer in *The Seven Sleepers* is a strong emotional bond which is tested and broken: what begins as an affectionate relationship turns drastically to disappointment and then hatred as Decius first admonishes, then reluctantly demotes and finally condemns the seven men.

Terms of affection

The emotional tone is prominent in the vocabulary of the text, in a series of running motifs. Frequently met is the word *dyrling* 'favourite' (cf. modern English 'darling'), often connected with a set of terms denoting the courtly bonds of affection between a king and his men. A case in point is the episode where Theodorus and Rufinus, two of the pagan emperor Decius's retainers who are secretly Christian, write an account of the seven men and leave it in the walled-up cave. The Latin description of the two men is fairly neutral in tone: they are simply *Christianos et fideles imperatoris* 'Christians and followers of the emperor' (line 154), with the word *fideles* connoting 'faithful followers'. The Old English discourse is rather different in its insistence that these men are the emperor's *dyrlingas* 'favourite followers' who are, it is said explicitly, *him swiðe leofe* 'very dear to him'. In Old English terms, a king or emperor, whether good or bad, evidently inspires great affection and respect among his men (lines 301-3).

This is not the only passage where terms such as *leof* and *dyrlingas* collocate. Another instance occurs early in the first half of the story. Here, as the emperor Decius begins his terrible persecution, it is discovered that the

---

[1] *The Anonymous Old English Legend of the Seven Sleepers*, ed. Hugh Magennis (Durham, 1994).

[2] Dorothy Whitelock, 'The numismatic interest of an Old English version of the Legend of the Seven Sleepers', in *Anglo-Saxon Coins: studies presented to F. M. Stenton*, ed. R. H. M. Dolley (London, 1961), pp. 188-94.

[3] Hugh Magennis, 'Style and method in the Old English version of the Legend of the Seven Sleepers', *English Studies* 66 (1985), 285-95.

[4] Hugh Magennis, 'The anonymous Old English *Legend of the Seven Sleepers* and its Latin source', *Leeds Studies in English*, New Series 22 (1991), 43-56.

[5] There is a parallel translation in *Ælfric's Lives of the Saints*, ed. and trans. W. W. Skeat, 2 vols, EETS os 76, 82, 94 and 114 (London, 1881-1900; reprinted as two vols, 1966), xxiii, 'De Septem Dormientibus', I.488-541.

seven young men are worshipping in secret as Christians. The informers, described by the hagiographer as God's enemies, hurry to Decius to report what they have seen (words of interest are highlighted in italics):

> And these enemies of God without delay went in to the *king* and said to him: 'Lord of nations, *our most cared for*, may it come to pass that you live long in the joy and glory of your kingship. *Beloved*, you command nations far and wide to order every man to sacrifice to the great god. And here at hand are those who are said to be your *favourites*. But they flee you and ignore your wishes, and they make offerings every day in the Christian manner. The oldest is Maximianus, and his six companions are regarded as prominent in the city (lines 127-35)

Note here the affectionate terms of address by the thegns to their king. In the Old English text the emperor is referred to as a *ciningc* 'king'; he is addressed as *leof* 'dear' or 'beloved' and 'our most cared for' (*us se besorgesta*), while his seven retainers are described as the king's *dyrlingas* 'favourites'. By contrast in the Latin version of this passage, the courtiers address their ruler in more distant formal terms as *auguste imperator* 'august emperor' and the seven retainers are less affectionately and more neutrally referred to as *proximi tui* 'those nearest to you' (76-7).

When, to take another example, the emperor summons the seven men and confronts them with their refusal to serve the gods he receives a sturdy Christian rebuke from Maximianus, the leader of the seven. The emperor responds by commanding their ritual demotion: their sword belts are removed and they are thrown into irons. In his bitter disappointment he says that the men are no longer as *leofe* 'dear' to him as once they were and he orders them out of his royal presence (lines 162-6). As Hugh Magennis notes on this passage, 'the Old English writer makes use of the traditional theme of lordship and loyalty to give a sense of depth to the relationship between Decius and the seven: Decius feels he is punishing them by cutting them off from his friendship and *comitatus*'.[6]

Parallels in Old English lawcodes

The Old English lawcodes too express a personal bond between ruler and subject in some of their clauses, and historians have emphasised that this was a deliberate policy of tenth-century West Saxon kings in their laws (e.g. II Edward 5-5.2, II Æthelstan 1-1.5): that they actively promoted personal lordship.[7] The clearest early example is

the third lawcode of Edmund, enacted *c.* 943 at Colyton-on-Axe in Devonshire, where all the men swore oaths on relics to be loyal to their king, in just the same way as a man would swear to be loyal to his lord:

> In the first place, all shall swear in the name of the Lord, before whom that holy thing is holy, that they will be faithful to king Edmund, even as it behoves a man to be faithful to his lord, without any dispute or dissension, openly or in secret, favouring what he favours and discountenancing what he discountenances.[8]

The old lordship bond between an ealdorman and his thegns was, so the historian Richard Abels argues, 'undergoing a transformation in the Anglo-Saxon lawcodes' since the hold-oath between a man and his lord is partly appropriated here by the king for securing the direct loyalty of all his subjects.[9]

Oath-swearing became commonplace as a way not only of ensuring loyalty to the king but also of securing the king's peace. The second lawcode of Cnut provides a conveniently worded example in the clause concerning thieves, and here it is clear that theft was regarded as equivalent to disloyalty (and punishable by forfeiture of a man's property):

> *We wyllað þæt ælc man ofer twelfwintre sylle þone að, þæt he nyle ðeof beon ne ðeofes gewita.*

> 'We desire that everyone over twelve years of age must give an oath that he will not become a thief or a thief's accomplice'.[10]

The clause on thieves is followed by the stipulation that any trustworthy man has the right to clear himself of an accusation at the regional court of the hundred, by a 'simple oath of exculpation':

> *And sy ælc getreowe man ðe tihtbysi nære and naðer ne burste ne að ne ordal innan hundrede anfealde lade wyrðe.*

> 'And every trustworthy man, who has never earned a bad reputation and who has never failed either in oath or in ordeal, shall be entitled to clear himself within the hundred by the simple oath of exculpation'.[11]

A similar process of exculpating oneself by oath can be observed in the first half of *The Seven Sleepers* when the emperor Decius summons the kinsmen of the seven men

[6] Magennis, *Seven Sleepers*, p. 25.
[7] Richard Abels, *Lordship and Military Obligation in Anglo-Saxon England* (London, 1988), pp. 81-8.
[8] From III Edmund 1. All citations of the later Old English laws are taken from *The Laws of England from Edmund to Henry I*, ed. and trans. A. J. Robertson (Cambridge, 1925).
[9] Abels, *Lordship and Military Obligation*, p. 88.
[10] II Cnut 21. Author's translation.
[11] II Cnut 22; cf. *The Laws of England*, ed. Robertson, pp. 184-5.

and accuses them of being in league with their apostate relatives.[12] Here the source states simply that the parents *respondentes ... dixerunt* 'replying ... said'; there is no mention of them swearing oaths in the Latin. Their plea is for mercy from their lord emperor: *Oramus te, domine imperator, nos preceptum tuum non sumus transgressi, et deorum timorem non deseruimus* 'we entreat you, lord emperor, we have not transgressed against your command and we have not forsaken our fear of the gods.' In the Old English, by contrast, the author makes a clear addition to the details of the story; the oaths are sworn to their *leof hlaford* 'dear lord':

> Then the kinsmen replied and swore great oaths [*sealdon micele aðas*], and entreated the emperor and spoke to him fearfully, 'We entreat you, dear lord [*leof hlaford*], that you will be willing to hear our words. We have nowhere neglected your royal command [*þin cynelice gebod*], nor did we ever despise the worshipful gods' (lines 273-8).

To clear themselves, the kinsmen swear an oath to the king that they in no way neglected the 'royal command', and in keeping with the theme of personal rulership which this text promotes, the oath is couched in the familiar terms of loyalty and affection to their personal lord.

The coins

Descriptions of coin inspections

The Seven Sleepers contains the only (non-biblical) descriptions in Old English of a person closely scrutinising a coin and examining the image and superscription written on it. The first of these descriptions occurs at the market just before Malchus attempts to flee the strange city. When he offers his ancient pennies in return for some loaves of bread the traders are amazed. The text states that the merchants *looked* eagerly at the pennies (Old English *penegas*), they *wondered at* money of this sort, they *held up* the coins for all to see as a spectacle and *passed* them round from bench to bench. The rapid series of dynamic actions expressed here is characteristic of this writer's style[13] and typical of the many minor additions that he makes to his text. It serves to highlight the spectacle of the unusual coin, the key artefact in the story.

The second coin inspection occurs at the hearing before the proconsul, the *portgerefa* or town-reeve, as he is called in the Old English version of the story. The two officials examine the *peningas* 'pennies' marvelling at the royal image and superscription engraved on them:

> *And se biscop and se portgerefa namon þa his peningas and hi beforan þam folce sceawodon and heora þearle wundrodon, for þi hi næfre*

ær ne gesawon swilc feoh mid heora eagan, þe wæs on ealdum dagum geslagen, on Decius caseres timan, and wæs his anlicnys on agrafen and his naman þær eall onbutan awriten (lines 601-5; see appendix for a translation).

The coins depict the image of the ruler and his name, and naturally the conclusion is that these coins are out of circulation, part of an old treasure-trove, despite Malchus's protests that he has the money from his kinsmen. At the end of the trial the reeve scorns Malchus mercilessly for these (apparent) lies and deceit, since 'anyone with any knowledge of arithmetic can see, and the superscription on these pennies openly declares, that it is even more than three hundred years and seventy-two winters since such money was in circulation on the earth' (lines 642-6).

Tenth-century coinage regulations

The references to coinage in the text make best sense when understood against the tenth-century background of royal control of currency and trade, particularly important from the reign of King Edgar. It was Edgar who reformed the currency in 973; thereafter it was no longer possible for coins to remain in circulation once a new coinage had been issued, and all coins of previous mints had to be delivered to the authorities and replaced (for a fee) with coinage of the new issue. Following Edgar's Reform coinage, there were five successive re-coinages under Æthelred, and then forty-five between 1016 and 1135, and as James Campbell has noted, a feature of the system was that 'a new type might be lighter, or heavier, than its predecessor, sometimes markedly so'.[14] One of many remarkable additions to the *Seven Sleepers* is a description of this very process of demonetization, the four reissues of coinage that take place during the reign of the emperor Decius, each new type being lighter than its predecessor.[15]

Edgar's lawcode issued at Andover in Hampshire probably marked the beginning of this reform. It decrees:

> *And gange an mynet ofer ealne þæs cyninges anweald, and þone nan man ne forsace*

> 'And one coinage shall be current throughout all the king's realm, and no-one shall refuse it'.[16]

The new decree went hand in hand with trading regulations: that there should be one system of measurement and standard of weights; that the price of a measure of wool

---

[12] Noted by Whitelock, 'Numismatic interest', p. 189.
[13] Magennis, 'Style and method', p. 291.

[14] Ann Williams, *Kingship and Government in Pre-Conquest England, c. 500-1066* (Basingstoke, 1999), p. 96. James Campbell, 'Observations on English government from the tenth to the twelfth century', *Essays in Anglo-Saxon History* (London and Ronceverte, 1986), pp. 155-70, at 155; the essay was originally published in *Transactions of the Royal Society*, 5th Series 25 (1975), 255-70.
[15] For the passages see Magennis, *Seven Sleepers*, Old English text, lines 434-45; Latin text, lines 216-21. A detailed discussion of these passages is given by Whitelock, 'Numismatic interest', pp. 190-4.
[16] III Edgar 8; trans. Robertson, *The Laws of England*, p. 28.

should be fixed at 120 pence, and 'if anyone sells it at a cheaper rate, either openly or secretly, both he who sells it and he who buys it shall pay 60 shillings to the king'.[17] After Edgar, the concern of all English kings of the period was to promote a single uniform currency throughout the kingdom; it facilitated control over trade and helped to maintain the royal peace and authority.

The Latin lawcode known as IV Æthelred contains much material of relevance to *The Seven Sleepers*, especially the clauses on trade and on coinage. Its lists of merchants' tolls demonstrate the concern of royal government to regulate trade and to profit from it. As IV Æthelred 3-3.3 shows, the role of the *portireva* (a phonetic Latin rendering of Old English *portgerefa* 'town-reeve') is to ensure the payment of such tolls and prosecute those who attempt to evade them. Particularly harsh are the clauses on coinage, designed to prevent counterfeit (IV Æthelred 5-5.5). No distinction is to be made between actual counterfeiters and traders who employ counterfeiters or who sell counterfeit moneyer's dies. Anyone accused 'whether he be an Englishman or a foreigner' must clear himself by judicial ordeal; convicted coiners will lose a hand, while 'moneyers who carry on their business in woods or work in other such places shall forfeit their lives, unless the king is willing to pardon them'.

As we shall see shortly, the subsequent clauses on merchants are strikingly relevant to Malchus's precarious position at the town assembly:

> 7. *Et diximus de mercatoribus qui falsum et lacum afferunt...* And we have decreed with regard to traders who bring money which is defective in quality and weight to the town, that they shall name a warrantor if they can.

> 7.1 If they cannot do so they shall forfeit their wergeld or their life, as the king shall decide, or they shall clear themselves by the same method as we have specified above, [asserting] that they were unaware that there was anything counterfeit about the money with which they were carrying on their business.

> 7.2 And afterwards such a trader shall pay the penalty of his carelessness by having to change [his base money] for pure money of the proper weight obtained from the authorised moneyers.[18]

As in the case of men accused of possession of stolen goods, the laws make careful provision for vouching to warranty. This process of summoning the vendor in order to prove the lawful origin of the goods is illustrated also by lawsuits recorded in various 'declarations' or administrative documents of the period.

The Merchants

Cypemen, 'merchants'

A key to understanding the accusation levelled against Malchus is the behaviour of the merchants. On his way in and out of the new city, Malchus passes through the market area, *into cypinge þær gehwilce men heora ceap beceapodan* 'into the market place where various men were selling their wares' (lines 481-2). The *cypemen* (cf. the now archaic term 'chapmen') are traders or merchants, by the tenth century a small but growing social class in Anglo-Saxon society, whose business was closely watched and controlled by the king and his officials to prevent unwitnessed trading out-of-town *up on lande*.[19] Vividly depicted in *The Seven Sleepers*, the merchants are Christian in their speech (lines 481-9), but suspicious of the coins which they assume are treasure trove (520-2) and cautious towards the stranger (529-30). They become physically rough when he returns their loaves and asks them to keep both the bread and the money; for them this is a 'pitiful' way of doing business (Old English *ceap drifan*, line 535). Their attitude is robust, even dishonest, and since they would rather make some profit from the hidden treasure, they offer to keep quiet about its whereabouts (lines 539-42).

In response to their offer, Malchus is 'amazed at their talk' and insists that he had the money from his parents; he laments his lot in an elaborate rhetorical speech, complaining that the merchants have taken the money from him as though he had stolen it (549). The canny merchants, however, are bluntly unimpressed. 'No, no, dear sir!' they cry, 'You cannot deceive us with your smooth words!' The Old English has an ironic, colloquial ring:

> *Nese, nese, leofa man, ne miht þu us na swa bepæcan mid þinan smeðan wordan* (lines 551-6).

It is not hard to guess at the motivation of the Old English merchants. Realizing that this young man is unwilling to share his hoard with them, and deciding that discretion is the better part of valour, they decide to abide by the law; securing the stranger with a rope, they haul him off to the justice of the reeve.

Midspreca, 'advocate' (i.e. 'warrantor'?)

In the passage where the merchants make their illegal offer (lines 539-42), they promise Malchus that they will be his *geholan* 'companions' and *midsprecan* 'advocates'. The use of the term *midspreca* is a significant addition here. The Latin simply has *nuntia nobis, et erimus communes tecum et cooperiemus te* ('tell us, and we will be in league with you and will conceal you'). But *midspreca*, meaning literally 'with-speaker' i.e. 'advocate', could imply some kind of legal context, since (as we shall see below) words

[17] Robertson, *The Laws of England*, p. 29.
[18] IV Æthelred 7-7.2.
[19] II Cnut 24; Henry Loyn, *Anglo-Saxon England and the Norman Conquest* (London, 1962), pp. 95-6.

from the lexical field of 'speaking, telling' often also have legal connotations of making a 'claim' or 'defence'.

If the merchants are offering to speak on Malchus's behalf in court, this may mean that they are even willing to perjure themselves for financial gain. Indeed, on the evidence of IV Æthelred 5, it looks as though merchants were notorious for taking money to counterfeiters in order to produce defective coin from it. And traders who were found in possession of defective money had to name a warrantor who would testify on their behalf.[20] Are the merchants in the *Seven Sleepers* offering to act as warrantors for Malchus?

A parallel case

The Wynflæd-Leofwine case, heard at the shire-court in Berkshire in the 990s, concerns some land seized by Leofwine because it once belonged to his father.[21] The text, a brief one-page *swutelung* or 'declaration', is of interest to our discussion of *The Seven Sleepers* for three reasons. First, there is a rigid legalistic attention to procedure: the disputant Leofwine insists that his case should be heard before the shire-court, and the king grants him his request. Secondly, there is an impressive array of witnesses summoned by the lady Wynflæd to prove her ownership of the disputed estate. Thirdly there is a dispute about gold and silver, which allows for some comparison with the Malchus episode in *The Seven Sleepers*. Unfortunately this part of the declaration is expressed very briefly and the circumstances are obscure. The obscurity is no doubt caused by the lack of space on the one-page document, coupled with the fact that all parties involved must already have been acquainted with the details of the case.

Apparently the situation involves a large quantity of silver and gold that is on the property, and presumably this money has been found there, perhaps as a treasure hoard hidden by Leofwine's father (this aspect is of course relevant to the Malchus case since no one seems able to establish how much money there is and who it belongs to). The serious function of oaths and the potentially dire consequences of improper oath-swearing are seen in the fact that both disputants decline to swear at crucial stages in the proceedings. Leofwine dispenses with the oath when he realises that Wynflæd's array of witnesses are bound to prove her ownership of the land convincingly, and he promises 'that he will make no further claim to it' *þæt he þanon forð syþþan þæron ne spræce* (note the verb phrase *sprecan on* literally 'to speak on' i.e. 'to sue for, make a claim for'). But Leofwine also wants reassurance that Wynflæd has returned all his father's silver and gold. He demands an oath, which Wynflæd says she is unwilling to give, just as he was unwilling to give his oath. Here the case ends.[22]

The role of the reeve

As well as regulating the behaviour of merchants, and their abuse of the national coinage, the Latin lawcode IV Æthelred also gives clear guidance on the role of the reeve in such matters:

> 7.3 *Et portirevae qui falsi huius consentanei fuerint* ... And town-reeves who have been accessories to such a fraud shall be liable to the same punishment as coiners, unless the king pardon them, or they can clear themselves by a similar oath of nominated jurors, or by the ordeal specified above.

The liability of the town-reeves to the same punishment as the false moneyers must have been a sharp incentive for them to be particularly vigilant and scrupulously clean in the fulfilment of their duties. It may help to explain something of the harshness of the reeve as he is portrayed in the Old English version of the *Seven Sleepers*.

The summoning of an 'assembly'

In royal government the *witena gemot* literally 'assembly of the counsellors' signifies the royal council; in regional and local government the *gemot* is the court of shire, borough, or hundred at which legal decisions were taken and disputes resolved; in II Cnut 18, for instance, it is stipulated that the *burh-gemot* or 'city-assembly' be held in the presence of bishop and reeve. At the end of the *Seven Sleepers*, despite the fact that the word *burhgemot* does not occur, it is possible that this is how the anonymous author has reconceived the whole episode of the interrogation by the proconsul. The following verbal hints and indicators should be noted:

(1) During his questioning of Malchus, the reeve refers to the presence there of *þysre byrig ealde witan* (line 653) 'the venerable counsellors of this city' and accuses Malchus of trying to deceive them.

(2) When the reeve finally loses patience with Malchus, he threatens to have him whipped *eall swa seo domboc be swilcum mannum tæcð* 'as the lawbook stipulates for such people' (line 656).

(3) After the intervention by the bishop and the decision to go to the cave, the meeting adjourns and 'rises': *se bisceop aras, and mid him se portgerefa and þa yldostan portmen*, literally 'the bishop rose, and with him the town-reeve and the most senior townsmen'.

In addition to these verbal hints, as we shall see, the text contains a number of established legal terms suggestive of the procedures of a *gemot* or assembly and thus providing

[20] IV Æthelred 7, 7.1. and 7.2.
[21] S 1454. The standard edition is *Anglo-Saxon Charters*, ed. and trans. A. J. Robertson (Cambridge, 1939), no. 66.
[22] The text is printed and its language analysed in Mark Atherton, *Teach Yourself Old English* (London, 2006), pp. 220-9. As a legal dispute, the

Wynflæd-Leofwine case is discussed by Ann Williams, *Kingship and Government in Pre-Conquest England c. 500-1066* (London: Macmillan, 1999), pp. 11-12.

further evidence of a conceptual reworking of the Malchus trial in the *Seven Sleepers* story.

The cross-examination of the accused

As we have seen, the trial of Malchus is preceded by the inspection of the coins and the consequent amazement of the bishop and reeve. In the Latin text the proconsul then begins his questions by asking about the concealed treasure. In the Old English text, this first question has become more of a cross-examination before a court. The town-reeve first asks where the treasure is hidden, then (in an added sentence) reminds Malchus of the presence of one of the merchants, a witness who can verify the accusation, should Malchus attempt to deny it:

> *Þy læs þe þu his ætsace, her is se man full gehende þe sum þæt feoh hæfð on handa þe þu hider brohtest, and þu hit him of þinum handum sealdest* (lines 607-9).

> 'In case you deny it, here is the man close by who has some of the money which you brought here in his hand. And you gave it to him with your own hands.'

Malchus is in a similar position to a trader who has brought defective coinage to the town in IV Æthelred 7, and the reeve, perhaps anxious not to be accused of condoning such actions, is a stickler for legal procedure.

Similarly, after Malchus has claimed that the money comes from his parents, rather than from a treasure trove, and after he has affirmed that he was born in Ephesus, the official makes the obvious objection that his parents are not here to confirm this. But where the Latin proconsul simply says *veniant et adtestantur de te* 'let them come and bear witness concerning you' (lines 296-7), the Old English town-reeve calls on Malchus to summon (*gelangigan*) and bring forth (*forð gan*) his kinsmen *þæt hi for þe sprecon, and gif hi on ænige wisan magon þe betellan* 'so that they can represent you, and [we will see] whether they can defend you in any way' (lines 625-6). Even on their own the two verbs *gelangigan* and *gan forð are* suggestive of a court context; in another dispute recorded in *The Fonthill Letter*, for instance, *gan forð* is used of the production before the court of some title deeds.[23] More significantly for this passage, however, the verbs *sprecan for* (literally 'speak for') and *betellan* ('to speak about') both have connotations of 'to defend against a charge'. A classic example of the legal meaning of *betellan* occurs in the E version of the *Anglo-Saxon Chronicle* in the entry recorded for the year 1048, where earl Godwine is accused of treason and wishes to have a guarantee of his safety if he attends the *witena gemot* in London in order to *clear himself* of the charges:

> *Þa geornde se eorl eft griðes and gisla þet he moste hine betellan æt ælc þæra þinga þe him man on lede.*

> 'Then the earl again requested truce and hostages so that he could defend himself against each of the charges with which he had been accused.'[24]

The usage is part of Old English legal register: *betellan* is a term that would have been in current use at court-cases heard before the assembly.

Malchus names his witnesses

In the Malchus trial, the moment of truth finally arrives, and Malchus names his parents, but the official does not recognise them. In the Latin this is told very briefly:

> *Et non cognouit proconsul eos, sed dixit ei, 'Nunc scio quia mendax es et non uerax'* (298-9).

> 'And the proconsul did not recognize them, but said to him, "Now I know that you are a liar and not telling the truth."'

Typically, the Old English author expands this brief rebuke, adding further legal detail to the dialogue; in some four lines of text note the use of the words *gelignian* 'to charge', *edwit* 'scorn', and the collocations: *þinre leasan tale* 'your deceitful claim', *leas man* 'deceitful person', and *lease tale findan* 'to invent a deceitful claim':

> *Ða ne gecneow se portgerefa þara namena nan ðing þe he þær namode, ac he sona gelignode hine, and cwæð him to edwite, 'Nu þurh þinre leasan tale ic her ongyten hæbbe þæt þu eart an forswiðe leas man, and wel canst, gif þu neade scealt, lease tale findan'*

> '[But] when the town-reeve did not recognise any of the names that he named he immediately charged him, and said to him in scorn, "I have now realized through this deceitful claim that you are one very deceitful man, and you know well, if you need to, how to invent a deceitful claim"' (lines 628-32).

The use of *talu* is unmistakable; the word belongs to the same area of discourse and carries the same connotations as it does in legal disputes.

---

[23] *The Cambridge Old English Reader*, ed. Richard Marsden (Cambridge, 2004), pp. 96-102, at p. 99, line 14.

[24] *MS E*, ed. Susan Irvine, *The Anglo-Saxon Chronicle: a collaborative edition*, ed. David Dumville and Simon Keynes 7 (Cambridge, 2004), 82.

Parallels in the Herefordshire lawsuit

A good analogous case is the Herefordshire dispute heard before the 'shire-assembly', *scirgemot*, in the reign of Cnut.[25] It was presided over by the local bishop and attended by both the *scir-gerefa* ('shire-reeve') and a royal representative of the king. As reported in a declaration, the case concerned one Ælfwine, who sued his own mother for an estate which had presumably once belonged to his father and which now he felt should rightly be his. Since no women were present at the meeting the bishop's first task was to find an advocate for the mother's side of the dispute. From the point of view of the legal vocabulary, it should be noted once again how the lexical field of 'telling, speaking' is adapted to the required legal register:

Ða acsode þe bisceop hwa sceolde andswerian for his moder.

'Then the bishop asked who would represent [the man's] mother.'

Here *andswerian for* 'to answer for' serves as the verb phrase meaning 'to represent'. The reply to the bishop's question comes from a minor nobleman present at the meeting called Thorkell the White. It turns out later that Thorkell has a vested interest, since his wife is related to the disputant mother, but at this stage Thorkell admits that he does not actually know the details of her claim:

Ða andsweorode Ðurcil Hwita and sæde þæt he sceolde, gif he þa talu cuðe.

'Then Thorkell the White answered and said that he would [have represented her] if he had known the claim.'

The important lexical point here is that the legal term for the 'claim' is *talu* (literally 'telling, story', related of course to the verb *betellan* discussed above and to *tellan* 'to count, account, tell, speak, claim'). Since Thorkell does not know the *talu*, the Herefordshire court sends three men to Fawley to question the mother about her claim (again the word *talu* is repeated). In her anger at her son's behaviour, the mother formally bequeaths the land and property to her kinswoman (Thorkell's wife) and the account of the case ends with Thorkell riding to Hereford to record this decision for posterity in the gospel book in which the document is still preserved.[26]

The evidence of the swutelung, *'declaration'*

On the material evidence of the coins and the failure of Malchus to summon any reliable witnesses, the reeve effectively declares Malchus guilty and formally insults him for the foolish conduct of his case, before condemning him to a whipping as the lawbook prescribes (lines 638-58). Malchus is saved by the bishop, who has ultimate jurisdiction, and his claim is finally upheld on the basis of a document which turns out to prove the actual truth of his assertions.

The document in question is the account of the martyrdom that had been written by Theodorus and Rufinus – the two favourite courtiers of Decius who are secretly Christians – and hidden in a chest inside the walled-up cave of the seven martyred young men. This document is described in the first half of the story, shortly after Decius has condemned the seven men (lines 301-16). Referred to as a *gewrit* (in lines 305, 308, and 313) the purpose of the document is to declare the facts of 'who these saints were' (line 309). Sealed in a chest, the writ is placed in the cave *þæt hit mid him þærinne læge to swutelunge oð ðone byre þe hi God ælmihtig awehte and hi mancynne swutelian wolde* 'so that it will lie there with them as a declaration until the time when almighty God will declare them to mankind' (lines 307-8). The key term here is 'declaration' or *swutelung*.

In the second half of the story, the document is described again; for it is discovered by the bishop and the townsmen as they go into the cave to meet the other sleepers (lines 693-715). Once more the Old English narrator elaborates on the purpose of the sealed chest *þæt þa insægla wæron eft to swutelunge hwæt man þærinne funde* 'that the seals were there as a declaration of what would be found inside' (line 697). After this momentous discovery, and for full judicial effect, the reeve waits for all the citizens to be summoned before he breaks the seals of the chest and reads out the document. And unlike the Latin which baldly states: 'reading it he found the following names' (line 328: *legens inuenit sic*), the Old English narrator stresses that the reeve *openlice rædde*, that he 'read it openly', i.e. that he read it out loud. This is a dramatic moment, and the narrator expands accordingly, slowing down the pace and highlighting the details of the very process of reading: *þa com he to þære stæfræwe þær he þæt word funde awriten, and he hit þa rædde eall swa* 'then he came to the row of letters where he found the words written, and he read it all thus'. Here we follow the perspective of the reeve as his eyes scan the text and his voice reads the words: in this way the names of the saints are revealed and declared to the assembly and consequently the *talu* – the story, the claim – of Malchus is openly vindicated.

From the language used in the Old English it is fair to interpret this document as being, in Anglo-Saxon terms, the kind of writing known as a *swutelung*. Literally *swutelung* means a 'clarification, a making clear', by extension it can signify a religious revelation or epiphany (as in the feast of Epiphany), while in more everyday terms

[25] Robertson, *Anglo-Saxon Charters*, no. 78; Atherton, *Teach Yourself Old English*, pp. 234-41, 264.
[26] For a literary approach to the text see Daniel Donoghue, *Old English Literature: a short introduction* (Oxford: Blackwell, 2004), pp. 1-5, with a photograph of the actual document at p. 3. The case is also discussed in Clare A. Lees and Gillian Overing, *Double Agents: women and clerical culture in Anglo-Saxon England* (Philadelphia, 2001), pp. 72-89.

it means a 'declaration'. Declarations, as we have seen, were documents used to record the results of disputes and lawsuits; the name stems from the opening formula *her swutelaþ on þisum gewrite* 'here it is declared in this document'. In one notorious case the *swutelunga* were stolen from a cathedral archive and sold to a rival claimant; obviously they were highly valued as legal proof and evidence.[27] Otherwise known as notifications or notices, such documents could also be used to convey instructions from a higher authority to the assembly or court that was hearing a particular case or dispute. Frequently they were read out to the assembly and their contents usually attested by a host of witnesses: *be ealles þæs folces leafe and gewitnesse* 'by the leave and with cognizance of all the people', as the Herefordshire document puts it, a phrase echoed in *The Seven Sleepers* when the declaration is read out *on gewitnysse ealles folces* 'with the cognizance of all the people' (line 703). In *The Seven Sleepers*, then, the final *swutelung* serves both political and theological ends; on the one hand it ensures that royal justice is seen to be done according to standard Old English legal procedures, on the other hand it serves as a proof and *declaration* of the bodily resurrection, thus also vindicating the doctrinal purpose of this unusual saint's life.

Conclusions

The present study has focussed on the coins, merchants and reeve in *The Seven Sleepers* and considered the extent to which we have in this tale a literary depiction of the workings of royal authority and urban government, and their regulation of currency and trade, in late tenth- or early eleventh-century England. The idea that *The Seven Sleepers* is 'merely' a translation of a Latin original needs to be seriously questioned, for the text is clearly a paraphrase or retelling and must be seen as essentially a document of its time. It will be clear from the above discussion that the author makes two kinds of addition to the story:

(1) added phrases and sentences that enrich and develop the plot

(2) anglicised and modernised concepts, made relevant to the contemporary English audience.

Through a study of these additions, various new features of the text come to light. The story highlights a marked (and late-Anglo-Saxon) sense of personal loyalty to the king, coupled with an emphasis on the swearing of oaths. The merchants in the text assume a lively, if not outright dishonest character, which chimes well with regulations in contemporary lawcodes. Above all, the *portgerefa* or town-reeve becomes prominent, an irritable man anxious to preserve the dignity of his position, seen here in the act of presiding over a hearing before the borough assembly. In keeping with this new presentation, the terms *talu*, *betellan* and *swutelung* – the legal terminology of lawsuit and administrative document – are used appropriately and significantly by the Old English author. In short, scholars interested in depictions of late Anglo-Saxon cultural conditions – including the activities of reeves and merchants – would do well to take new notice of this text as a revealing and informative social document of the period.[28]

---

[27] S 1456 and S 1457; see A. G. Kennedy, 'Disputes about "Bocland": the forum for their adjudication', *Anglo-Saxon England* 14 (1985), 175-95, at 182.

[28] Since this paper was first presented the following article has appeared: Catherine Cubitt '"As the lawbook teaches": reeves, lawbooks and urban life in the anonymous Old English *Legend of the Seven Sleepers*', *English Historical Review* 124 (510), (2009) 1021-1149.

Appendix

A translation of the Malchus episode from the anonymous Old English
Legend of the Seven Sleepers

[The following is a translation of the Malchus episode from the anonymous Old English *Legend of the Seven Sleepers*. Line numbers in square brackets following each paragraph refer to the edition by Hugh Magennis.]

And Malchus their steward rose in the early morning and did everything as was his custom: he took with him a portion of the money, as much as could be, though it was sixty-two pennyweight, and the superscription for this money was of the same minting when the coinage was struck in the first year that Decius succeeded to the kingdom. Four times they changed the dies in his day when the saints lived among other men; and in the first issue there was sixty-two pennyweight of silver in one penny and in the second just sixty, and in the third forty-four, and in the fourth even less, so they believed there. The money that Malchus had then was from the first minting in Decius's name. Then between the days of Decius's first coinage, when the saints went into the cave, and Theodosius's time, when Malchus took the money to the city, by the old-style of reckoning three hundred and seventy-two winters had passed from the day that the saints slept to the day they woke again. [430-45]

Malchus set off at daybreak out of the cave, and when he was outside he saw where the dressed stones lay scattered about, and half wondered at this, but did not think too much of it. Fearfully and with great dread he descended the hill, whence he hurried very timidly to the city, continually worried that someone would recognise him and make him known to the emperor; the saintly man did not realise that the latter – poor wretch – was dead: not one bone remained with the other, for they lay everywhere, broken and scattered throughout the wide world. [446-53]

As Malchus was approaching close to the city gate he looked towards it and saw the holy sign of Christ's rood where it stood fixed with great honour above the gate. He was seized with strange wonder and stopped at the sight of it in wondrous amazement, and he stood and looked, and it seemed wondrous to him, and he looked everywhere on all sides and gazed on the cross, and it all seemed wondrous to him. And he considered in his mind what it could mean. [454-60]

He moved on to the next gate of the city and again looked upon the holy rood and was amazed, and he went to all the gates of the city, and on each one he saw the holy rood standing and was filled with wonder and amazement. The city too he saw was all changed in a different way to what it once was, with the buildings throughout the city all built in a different way to what they once were. He could recognise no more of the city than a man who had never set eyes on it before [461-8].

Wondering if this was a dream in the night, he returned again to the same city-gate that he had first come to, and he pondered in his heart and said to himself, 'How is it that all of a sudden I see such wonders here, when yesterday evening the cross was nowhere to be seen in all of this city, and it now is fully revealed and today is fixed above every gate in the city?' [469-74]

Again he pondered in his mind, and raised his hand and crossed himself and said, 'O God almighty, bless me! And tell me whether this sudden wondrous thing that I see here is true, or whether I am dreaming it all in my sleep?' With this thought he drew some comfort, at least in part, and covering his head with a garment, he entered the city wretchedly, taking care to be on his guard. [475-80]

When he came into the market place where various men were selling their wares he heard the people talking among themselves; again and again they swore by their allegiance to Christ, and they did not engage in any transactions except always in Christ's name. [481-4]

When he heard such talk, Malchus was very worried, he was frightened by it all and said in his mind, 'What can it mean that I hear such a wondrous thing as this? Before this I *saw* a great marvel, and now I *hear* a greater one. Yesterday evening no one could name Christ's name in joy, but today Christ's name is foremost on every man's tongue!' [484-9]

Then again he said to himself, 'Truly it does not seem to me that this could ever be the city of Ephesus, because it is built in a completely different way, and constructed with completely different buildings. Nor does any man here speak in the manner of heathen men, but all according to the ways of Christian people.' [490-3]

Once again he rejected his own thought and replied to himself, 'But again I don't know, nor ever did know, of any other city close by, apart from Ephesus, here on the Caelian Hill.' And there he stood still for a short while pondering within himself what his truth was. [494-7]

Then he noticed a young man, and went up to him and asked, 'Good man, may you prosper. I would dearly like to know of you the name of this city, if you were willing to inform me.' [498-500]

The young man replied, 'I will gladly tell you. This city is called Ephesus, and it was given its name a long time ago.' [501-2]

Then he pondered in his mind and said to himself, 'So I was on the right track in my thoughts. But it is better if I leave this town now before I stray too far and so cannot get back to my companions who sent me here. I have certainly come to realise now that my mind is stretched beyond its capacity, so that I do not know very well how I am behaving.' [503-8]

(Malchus later told his companions how it had been for him in all these things when he eventually returned to the cave we spoke of before, and when their wondrous resurrection was revealed to all men and their holy life fully declared.) [508-11]

And Malchus, as it all seemed too wonderful what he saw and heard, and as he was leaving the town, approached in beggar's disguise close to where they were selling bread. When he reached the place, he drew some pennies from his bosom and gave them to the merchants for bread. The merchants looked eagerly at the pennies and wondered at them exceedingly; and they held them up for a spectacle, and passed them from bench to bench, and displayed them for others to see, and spoke among themselves, 'There is no doubt about what we all see here. This unknown young lad has found an ancient treasure from long ago, and has hidden it secretly for many years.' [512-22]

When Malchus saw them examining his pennies so eagerly he became terribly afraid and right where he stood he began to shake and tremble, his only thought being that one of the men would recognise him. He said to himself in his mind, 'O my Lord, how pitiful is my lot. What more can I expect but that they will take me to Decius. Then I certainly won't be able to bring any news to my companions!' [523-8]

Now the merchants looked hard at him and considered in their thoughts what manner of man he might be. Then Malchus spoke to them all in fearful words, 'Good men, I entreat you to grant me my wish: there you have the pennies in your hands, use them as you will. I don't want any bread from you, good men. Enjoy both the pennies and the bread.' [529-34]

As he was speaking to them, driving his pitiful bargain, they suddenly stood up and laid hands on him, and said to him, 'Tell us what kind of man you are or where you have come from; you who have discovered some old money and brought here these old coins that were struck in ancient times long ago! Tell us the truth without any deception, and we will be your companions and advocates all the way.

We won't betray you; we'll just keep it all quiet, so that no one else will discover it except us.' [535-42]

Malchus then was amazed at their talk, and painful thoughts were in his mind, and he appealed to the merchants, 'Strange is my lot for me alone, and I have had wretched experiences above all other men throughout this wide earth. All other men who are born in this life are allowed to feed themselves from their parents' earnings, while I alone, a miserable wretch, cannot be helped. Now my own money has been taken from me as though I had stolen it! Now they want to take from me by force what I acquired by lawful means.' [543-50]

The merchants replied and said to him, 'No, no, young man! You cannot deceive us with your smooth words! The treasure you found and hid for so long cannot be concealed now that it has come to light!' [551-4]

He didn't know what answer he should give them, for the great terror that was in his heart. When they saw that he stood still and gave them no answer, they seized him, tied a rope around his neck and dragged him to the middle of the marketplace, and so he was held within the city, bound with a rope. The news travelled around and was soon widely known, and all the people throughout the city hurried there, and in the clamour each told the other that an unknown young man had been caught in the city who was rumoured to have found an ancient treasure-hoard and brought in antique coins that had been minted in ancient times and used in the time of the emperors of old. A great crowd gathered in amazement and gazed on the spectacle of the solitary man standing bound in their midst. And in all the shouting each person said to the other, 'This is a traveller from another country. We know nothing about him, and no one has ever set eyes on him before.' [555-68]

Malchus listened to all these words, and his unease was ever increasing, and he kept wanting to appease the people with his humility, so that he could arouse their sympathy with his full humility, because he did not know and could not find a plausible claim, nor did he know with whom he should speak. Then everyone looked at him carefully, but no one recognised him. And as he stood there silent and weary in great amazement of mind, a sudden thought came to him that he had great confidence that his kinsmen still lived in the city, and his family that he had in the city was a well-known name to all people. It seemed to him that he could only be certain of this: that just as the evening before he knew everyone and everyone knew him, so in the morning he knew no one and none knew him; otherwise he would allow of no third possibility save that he might be out of his mind. [569-81]

And with that thought he looked upon the crowd from every side in the eager hope of recognising someone: whether a brother or kinsman or someone that he had previously known in the city. It was no better at all, even though he looked eagerly: he could see no one who might recognise him. [581-5]

But as he stood there so wretchedly alone in the midst of the crowd, more and more people came to hear of it throughout the city, until it was known in the holy church at the bishop's throne, and bishop Marinus was informed, as also was the town reeve. The two men ordered Malchus to be guarded carefully lest he escape, but that he should be delivered to them with great haste along with the coins that he had brought with him. And the men who held Malchus at the marketplace took him away at once and set out for the church, with Malchus expecting nothing else but that they were taking him to the emperor Decius. When he came to the church, he looked on either side to where he was going and to the crowd all around staring at the spectacle. Eagerly he looked on either side to where he was going, and the crowd regarded him evilly as though he were guilty of some crime; and the men all dragged him from place to place, and mistreated him as a wonder; he had a bad time of it among them; his eyes fluttered, and he shed bitter tears. [586-600]

And the bishop and the town reeve took the pennies and examined them before the people and were amazed at them, for never before had they set eyes on such coins, minted as they were in ancient times, in the days of the emperor Decius, with his likeness engraved upon them and his name written round about them. [601-5]

Then the town-reeve said to Malchus, 'Tell us now where the ancient gold-hoard is that you have secretly found and completely concealed until now. In case you deny it, here is the man close by who has some of the money that you brought here in his hand. And you gave it to him with your own hands.' [606-9]

Then Malchus answered and said to them all, 'Everything I say before you all is the public truth, and if it is your will you can believe me that I have never yet found a gold-hoard as you accuse me. But I know for certain truth that this money came into my hands from my parents' earnings. From trade in this very town I acquired the money, and I didn't find it anywhere else. But I cannot understand in any way how this has happened to me that I am behaving in this way.' [610-16]

The town-reeve then said to him, 'Tell me now openly in which town you were born, or to which town you belong.' [617-18]

Then he said in reply, 'Sir, this I believe in my thoughts that I do not belong to any town as rightly as I belong to this city, or so it seems to me. Sir, this is the city of Ephesus in which I was born and brought up.' [619-21]

Then again the town-reeve spoke to Malchus, 'If you were born and brought up in the town, where then are your kinsmen who brought you up and can recognize you? Have them brought here to the bishop, and have them come here before us, so that they can represent you, and [we will see] whether they can defend you in any way.' [622-6]

And Malchus replied and named his parents' names, what was the name of the one and what was the name of the other. But when the town-reeve did not recognise any of the names that he named he immediately charged him, and said to him in scorn, 'I have now realized through this deceitful claim that you are one very deceitful man, and you know well, if you need to, how to invent a deceitful claim.' [627-32]

Malchus didn't know what to say then, but stood there and hung his head, and was silent for so long that some men who were standing there said, 'His claim is not true, this is nothing but public fraud; he is pretending to people and concealing his parentage so that he can find a way to escape from here.' [633-7]

And with these words the town-reeve directed all his anger at Malchus, and rebuked him with all hatred, and asked him thus, 'You stupid man, and the greatest fool that ever there was in this city! In what way are we to believe you and your doubtful words that we can know that you got your money from your parents' earnings? Here anyone with any knowledge of arithmetic can see, and the superscription on these pennies openly declares that it is even more than three hundred years and seventy-two winters since such money was in circulation on the earth and all the people traded with it, and that was in the first period when the emperor Decius began his reign. And now no part of this money is among the money that we use nowadays to pay for our needs. And by what you said before when you named them, your relatives lived so long ago in the old days that there isn't a single old man who can think of them or can remember as far back as when your parents lived so many years ago. Now you stand here, a young man, and want to deceive the venerable counsellors of this city with your fraud. But you will be shown otherwise, that you cannot feed us any longer with your lies. I will have you tightly bound both hand and foot, as the law-book stipulates for such people, and [I will have you] whipped again and again and painfully tortured: then you will inform us against your will of the hoard which you stubbornly refused to reveal.' [638-58]

When Malchus heard the town-reeve speaking these words aggressively to him, he immediately threw himself down in fear and prostrated himself before all the people, and then spoke to them all with a tearful voice, 'Sir, I implore you to grant me this, that I might ask one question, and I will tell you at once what I think in my thoughts: I would ask you whether you would tell me where the emperor Decius is who was here in this city? [659-65]

Then Marinus the bishop answered him and said to Malchus, 'My dear boy, there is no emperor alive on earth by the name of Decius. The emperor you ask about was from a distant age, and many years have now passed since he departed this life.' [666-9]

Malchus said to the bishop in reply, 'This is the one thing, my lord, that I have been dreading all day, the one fear that afflicts me so terribly in my mind, and no man will believe what I say. But I humbly entreat you now to walk with me for a short time. I have a few companions very near – they are over here in the cave on the Caelian Hill. You can believe the account of all this without any doubt. Furthermore, I know to be true facts that we all fled together from the emperor Decius, and we endured his persecution for a long time. And this very night I saw with my own eyes how that same Decius arrived in the city of Ephesus, and I and my companions were resident in the city of Ephesus, but because of his great persecution we fled the place and came to this hill and lay all night in the cave hidden from Decius. But today such strange things have happened to me that I cannot recognise at all whether this is Ephesus or another city altogether.' [670-83]

When Malchus had finished speaking, the bishop was amazed and pondered in his mind, and he said to all the people, 'This truly is a marvellous vision that almighty God has revealed to this young man. But let us all now rise quickly and walk there with him.' [684-7]

And bishop Marinus rose, and with him the town-reeve and the most senior townsmen, and a great crowd of all the citizens went forth with them, and they all proceeded there with great reverence and approached the cave. Malchus went in ahead to his saintly companions, and bishop Marinus followed, and then after him some of the most senior and respected men went into the cave. And as they were going in, they found on their right a chest which was sealed with two silver seals – that the two faithful men had placed inside when the emperor Decius had ordered the cave to be blocked – as we reported earlier that the seals were there as a declaration of what would be found inside when the time came, just as had God willed it that the time would come. And they carried out the chest

and ordered all the citizens to be summoned, and showed it to all the people, and no one unsealed it before everybody had arrived there. [688-701]

After they all had gathered before the bishop, the town-reeve took hold of the chest and with the cognizance of all the people he unsealed it and immediately unfastened it, and inside he found a lead tablet covered in writing, and then he read it out loud. Then he came to the row of letters where he found the words written, and he read it all thus, that they had fled from the emperor Decius and suffered his persecution: 'Maximianus, who was the son of the city-reeve, Malchus, Martinianus, Dionisius, Iohannes, Seraphion and Constantinus. These are the saints who on the orders of the emperor Decius were walled up inside this cave with blocks of stone; and we two, Theodorus and Rufinus, have written the account of their martyrdom and laid it here inside with the saints on a stone.' [702-12]

When they had read the document they were all amazed, and they praised and glorified almighty God with one mind for the great wonders that he had declared there and granted to everyone; and they all praised God's holy martyrs with one voice as they sat there all in a row in the cave: and their faces were all like the rose and the lily. And the bishop and the whole multitude fell prostrate to the ground, and they prayed to the saints; and all the people blessed and worshipped God almighty for his great mercy, that he had wished to reveal such great wonders to them. And the holy martyrs sat in the cave and gave an account to bishop Marinus and the senior townsmen of what they had done in the time of the emperor Decius, and how they had experienced great hardships under him; and they revealed many other things to them there that had taken place in his day, and how other martyrs endured under his persecution, just as we have reported in the earlier part of this narrative. [713-26]

Chapter 7 Books and kings – some thoughts on the economic demands on the medieval economy made by the provision of parchment for scriptoria in the Anglo-Saxon world.[1]

C. W. Grocock

The importance of books *qua* books in early medieval Northumbrian monasticism is well known and widely appreciated, particularly through the evidence provided by the Venerable Bede, an edition of whose lesser historical works is currently being prepared for the Oxford Medieval Texts series by the author in partnership with Prof. Ian Wood (University of Leeds). Information from Bede's own writings provide a good indication about the process of book composition and production; for example, in the prologue to his prose *Vita Cuthberti* he indicates that his initial composition was kept *in schedulis* or 'notes' until they could be checked with eye-witnesses, and only then written down *membranulis*, 'on parchment', and even then were submitted to the brethren at Lindisfarne for final approval.[2]

Books as objects

However, less emphasis has hitherto been placed on investigating the pressure on the monastic economy by the physical processes of book production.[3] Surviving codices are evidence of the pressure on monastic estates in terms of both labour and materials, the *Codex Amiatinus* being the prime specimen for consideration. The presence of numerous volumes in the Wearmouth-Jarrow monastery, and their continued manufacture, was dependent on a number of factors, not least of which was royal patronage. This was expressed in a number of ways, beginning with the endowment of lands to support the monasteries (and which supplied the raw materials for book production, at least in part), and also involving continued support for the activity of the monasteries, as can be demonstrated by two comments Bede makes in his *Epistola ad Ecgbertum*

Episcopum 10 and 11: *commodum duxerim habito maiori concilio et consensu pontificali simul et regali edicto prospiciatur locus aliquis monasteriorum ubi sedes fiat episcopalis;* 'I had thought it advisable that with the agreement of a great council and by a decree of both bishop and king, some monastic location should be identified as a likely episcopal see' and *tuam quoque sanctitatem decet cum religioso rege nostrae gentis irreligiosa et iniqua priorum gesta atque scripta conuellere;* 'it behoves your holiness with the pious king of our people to rip up the impious and evil deeds and assignations of our earlier leaders …'.[4]

This information can be correlated with data obtainable through experimental archaeology, carried out in part while the author was Project Manager of Bede's World, Jarrow, from 1993-1996, and further supported by information obtained from the Agricultural Sciences. The results indicate the possible extent of the monastic estates of Wearmouth and Jarrow, recorded in terms of hideage by the surviving literature. The *Codex Amiatinus* referred to above, and the number of skins required for its production, is but one surviving indication of the scale of the demands which book production placed on the local economy: it must have been 'a scriptorium with excellent human and material resources'.[5] This information in turn can be used to shed light on the level of support and the extent of generosity given by royal sources, and may provide a context for the continued close royal involvement in the activities of Wearmouth-Jarrow, with kings acting both as benefactors and as recipients of gifts (for example, the Cosmography given to Aldfrith, in *History of the Abbots* 15). The role of kings in providing for Anglo-Saxon minsters[6] by making grants of land for them is well-known, not least from Wearmouth-Jarrow, the best documented example of all, thanks to the writings of the Venerable Bede. Some of these are cited later; for the moment, I would like to make the point that for supplying the material wants of a minster, even if 600 brethren were members of it,[7] the grants of land seem quite large; if the brothers were following anything like the rule of Benedict, their immediate needs in terms of food and clothing ought

[1] The paper which follows began life as a lecture given to the Mayo Historical Society and (in part) to the Northumbrian scribes in 1996, and the author is indebted to the members of those societies and to associates of Bede's World, Jarrow, and Mayo Abbey, Ireland, for their helpful comments. Particular thanks are due to Miriam Mandelbaum and Anne Hillam of the New York Academy of Medicine, and to Dan Shadrake for his generosity in supplying line drawings to replace the Powerpoint illustrations used when the paper was delivered.

[2] See *Two Lives of St Cuthbert,* ed. and trans. B. Colgrave (Cambridge, 1940), pp. 144-5; the Latin diminutive *membranulis* is simply rendered 'on parchment' by Colgrave, but I wonder if the diminutive is deliberate and may indicate 'scraps of parchment', which would have been readily available as a by-product of the process of making a book, as will be seen later. See note 25, below. George Hardin Brown says that 'he circulated drafts in booklet form for vetting by respected authorities (*Bede The Educator,* Jarrow Lecture 1996, p. 3 and n. 14), but does not refer to this passage. See n. 26 below, and Figs 7.7-9.

[3] Cf. R. L. S. Bruce-Mitford, *The Art of the* Codex Amiatinus (Jarrow, 1967); A. I. Doyle, 'Book production by the monastic orders in England (c. 1375-1530): assessing the evidence', in *Medieval Book Production: assessing the evidence,* ed., L. L. Brownrigg, (Los Altos Hills, CA, 1990), pp. 1-19, a study which focus entirely on scribal activity; the same slant is found throughout *Making the Medieval Book: techniques of production* ed., L. L. Brownrigg, (Los Altos Hills, CA, 1995).

[4] Bede, *Epistola ad Ecgbertum Episcopum* 10,11: text and translations from C. W. Grocock and I. N. Wood, ed., *Abbots of Wearmouth and Jarrow* (Oxford, forthcoming 2013).

[5] Richard Marsden, *The Text of the Old Testament in Anglo-Saxon England,* Cambridge Studies in Anglo-Saxon England 15 (Cambridge, 1995), p. 80, cited in Brown, *Bede the Educator,* n.14.

[6] I use the term 'minster' following John Blair, *The Church in Anglo-Saxon Society* (Oxford, 2005), pp. 3-5.

[7] Bede, *Historia Abbatum* 17; S. Foot, 'Church and monastery in Bede's Northumbria', in *The Cambridge Companion to Bede,* ed. S. DeGregorio, (Cambridge, 2010), pp. 54-68, at 62.

to have been frugal by any modern standards.[8] But it is possible to explore one respect in which the minsters *were* voracious consumers, in keeping with the monastic traditions on which they were founded, and this is as producers – I am tempted to say as manufacturers – of books. Michael Lapidge comments that 'it is possible to ascertain the existence of a significant number of libraries in England during the centuries between the seventh and the eleventh'.[9]

Books as evidence

Artefacts which survive from the Anglo-Saxon world can be studied from a variety of viewpoints in order to evaluate their value and importance in their day and the impact they had socially. In the case of manuscripts, the focus of study has concentrated firstly, on the intellectual value of the surviving evidence – which texts are preserved and transmitted, and which valued, pointing to intellectual trends in the early medieval world; and secondly, on artistic, cultural and palaeographical aspects, examining the volumes which are still accessible to us as evidence of artistic and cultural development and their role in the development of graphic arts.10 The types of study devoted to the oft-referred-to Codex Amiatinus give a good idea of this, and I do not wish to deny the importance of such studies in any way. However, the aim of this paper is much more mundane, artisanal and banausic. I wish to look at a more basic aspect of the very important monastic activity which underpinned all monastic book production, namely the production of one of the raw materials without which it would have been impossible – parchment – and to explore some questions raised by the apparent demands it made on the economy of early medieval England. The aim of doing this is to explore a different dimension of the importance of land to early medieval minsters, one which may have been overlooked or under-estimated in the past. This in turn may further explain the importance of the relations between Anglo-Saxon minsters' connections with royal households and the value of the land-grants made to them. In the space of a few pages I can do no more than provide a brief indication as to the impact of book-production, and to clarify some suggestions made several years ago. In exploring this question it will be useful first of all to give an over-view of the processes involved in parchment manufacture, as it were, from sheep to scribe.

Definition and production

Among other authorities, Bernhard Bischoff provides a brief description of the nature of parchment, together with an outline of how parchment is made, but there is little attention paid in any of these authorities to the demands the process imposed by parchment production must have made on a monastic community.[11] In this regard, more detail is found in the websites, which (as is outlined below) provide useful illustrative material and are largely convergent in their descriptions of production processes involved, though they diverge to quite a degree in the estimated times taken to achieve these processes.[12] In academic studies in particular there have been attempts to distinguish between calfskin and sheepskin – as will be shown later, practical considerations would indicate a vast differential in the likely availability of these two types of material and the impact of providing them on a landscape. In a fascinating study which made use of stereomicroscopic analysis, di Majo, Frederici and Palma noted that various scholars have offered divergent conclusions about the likely use of sheep, goat and calf skins: E. A Lowe changed his mind from time to time but finally concluded that sheep were always the source of parchment, Bernhard Bischoff on the other hand asserted that calf skin constituted first-quality parchment, sheep second-quality, while N. R. Ker could not tell them apart, and Julian Brown thought they could be distinguished by the way the material absorbed ink.[13] Their own conclusion was that calf, sheep and goat skins can be distinguished by the remaining hair follicles, seen through stereomicroscopic analysis. Such intricacies are beyond the scope of this paper, but the distinction between sheep/goat on the one hand and calf on the other is extremely significant in the amount of land required to provide a given number of skins; in the actual production of skins, there is no significant difference, and it is this aspect which will be addressed first.

The steps involved in turning a raw skin into writing material have changed little since medieval times, and according to one present-day manufacturer[14] the process

---

[8] That said, monastic estates in the south of England were often much larger than Wearmouth-Jarrow's total holding: see references in Blair, *Church in Anglo-Saxon England*, p. 87, and discussion in J. Campbell, 'Secular and political contexts', in DeGregorio, *The Cambridge Companion to Bede*, pp. 25-39, at 31-2.

[9] Michael Lapidge, *The Anglo-Saxon Library* (Oxford, 2006), p. 31, introducing chapter 2, 'Vanished libraries of Anglo-Saxon England'.

[10] See for example Lapidge, Anglo-Saxon Library; Bernhard Bischoff, *Latin Palaeography: antiquity and the Middle Ages*, trans. Dáibhí ó Cróinín and David Ganz (Cambridge, 1990); M. B. Parkes, *The Scriptorium of Wearmouth-Jarrow* (Jarrow Lecture, 1982).

[11] Bischoff, *Latin Palaeography*, pp. 8-11. See also R. R. Reed, *Ancient Skins, Parchment and Leathers* (London, 1972), and *An Introduction to Parchment* (Public Record Office Publications, London, 1996).

[12] For example, images from Pergamena Parchment, at http://www.pergamena.net/products-services/how-we-make-parchment and the Central University of Europe, Budapest, at http://web.ceu.hu/medstud/manual/MMM/parchment.html (both accessed 7 August 2012); R. Fuchs, 'The history and biology of parchment', *Karger Gazette* no. 67, at www.karger.com/gazette/67/Fuchs/art_5.htm (accessed 7 August 2012). The sole manufacturer of parchment in England is the Willam Cowley Parchment works, 97 Caldecote Street, Newport Pagnell, Buckinghamshire, MK16 0DB. Contact with this source proved fruitless, but more help was obtained from David and Kate Alexander, of Carbisdale Deerskins & Lambskins, Culrain, Ardgay, Sutherland, Scotland, IV24 3DW.

[13] A. di Majo, C. Frederici, M. Palma, 'La pergamena dei codici altomedievali Italiani', *Scriptorium* 39 (1985) 3-13, at 3-4; includes illustrations of stereomicroscopic analysis to distinguish between calf and sheep.

[14] Information supplied by David and Kate Alexander, of Carbisdale Deerskins & Lambskins; it should be noted that more modern processes can reduce this timescale to a matter of days (e.g. at Pergamena, at Montgomery, NY. I am indebted to Anne Hillam for drawing my attention to this point).

from start to finish it takes about six weeks, 4 of which are for the liming of the pelts in two stages, and two weeks' slow drying time. The practices of liming and drying the skins have in fact changed very little since their employment by the monks of Anglo-Saxon England. Whether in ancient or modern manufacture, the steps involved are as follows:[15]

First comes flaying and preservation – either by salting (for leather) or drying in the case of parchment. This is done within a few hours of slaughter/stripping, and the skins are stored at low temperatures (about 5°C) in the tannery stockroom. At this stage, the skin consists of three layers – epidermis on the outside, dermis below it, and the subcutaneous layer – fat and muscle, in lay terms (Fig. 7.1). This and the process which follows might be carried out on the same day, subject not only to the constraints of time but also of space – the size of the stockroom would be a factor in how many skins could be accepted at any time.

Next, the skins must be limed and de-haired (or de-wooled). They have to be soaked after de-hairing to restore any moisture lost between fleecing and preservation. In medieval times, according to Fuchs,[16] liming involved immersing the fresh animal skin for between two and six weeks in a 5 – 10% solution of slaked lime; this could be done using the

lime-bath that had already been used for de-hairing. The process might take twice as long in winter. The skin could also be dyed at this point. Cleaning the skin was a skilled job which required both speed and great concentration, and was a very dirty and unpleasant one (Fig. 7.2).[17]

It is possible that in the medieval period the skins were then put into a fresh lime bath for a further 8 days – opening the skins up for fresh lime (Reed disagrees, saying that skins were soaked in water for three to ten days).[18] This would add further days to the total manufacturing process. In making parchment the lime was not removed as it is in leather manufacture. As a result of its resulting alkalinity, parchment is less affected by acid; however, the hydroscopic properties of the lime make it prone to damage by water and bacterial growth. 'Scudding' is the term used for cleaning the grain of epidermis remains with a blunt knife (Fig. 7.3). With this process, a total of over 50 days' production could have been involved up to this point.

Next, the skins have to be dried under tension, with more lime applied to remove moisture and grease. The fibres are oriented in sheets as a result of the production process; in particular, the alkalinity of the lime opens up the inner

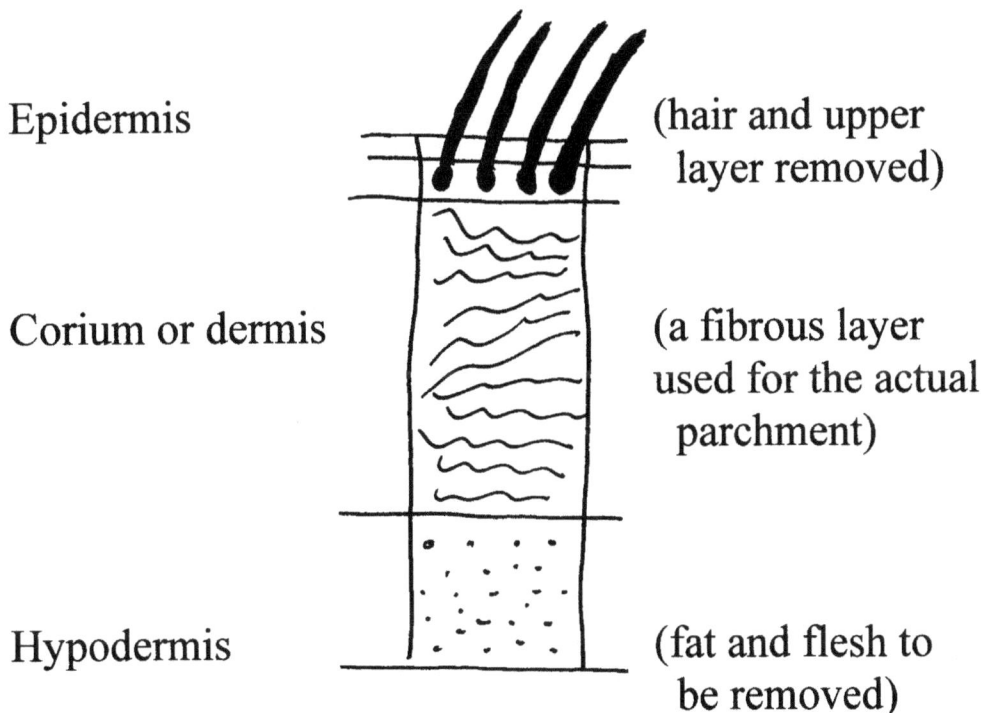

Epidermis ———— (hair and upper layer removed)

Corium or dermis ———— (a fibrous layer used for the actual parchment)

Hypodermis ———— (fat and flesh to be removed)

FIG 7.1 SKIN STRUCTURE IN RELATION TO PARCHMENT (AFTER REED, *ANCIENT SKINS, PARCHMENT AND LEATHERS*, FIG. 3, P.18, AND DIMAJO, FREDERICI AND PALMA, 'LA PERGAMENA . . .', FIG. 1, P.10).

---

[15] Information is drawn from the sources indicated in note 12.
[16] Fuchs, 'History and biology of parchment', under the heading 'The production of parchment'.

[17] Reed, *Ancient Skins, Parchment and Leathers*, p. 139; pers. comm. from Anne Hillam.
[18] Cf. Reed, *Ancient Skins, Parchment and Leathers*, p. 133.

FIG 7.2 'SCUDDING' OR CLEANING OFF THE OUTER LAYER OF THE SKIN AND HAIR

FIG 7.3 'HORSE' AND DRAWKNIVES USED FOR CLEANING THE SKINS

structure of the collagen, allowing the fibres to move; this pulls the fibres into line, and during the air-drying process, air penetrates between the fibres and dries them all through; this results in the parchment becoming opaque and suitable for writing both recto and verso.[19] The skin is scraped on the flesh side straight away, then dried in the shade for two days before being put in the sun. When fully dry, skins are scraped on the flesh side with powdered pumice. The drying process could take anything up to two weeks. In ancient times (pre-medieval) skins were also split, but this was apparently not done after the third century.

The final process, known by the term 'pouncing', involved shaving the skins on the flesh side while they were still taut on the drying frames (Figs. 7.4 and 5) using a semi-circular knife called a *lunelarium*, and then removing any extrameous hair by rubbing the skin with pumice (see Fig. 7.6 – modern producers use an orbital sander!). Adding a further two weeks to the *maximum* time already allowed gives in total about 65 days production time from start to finish; the time needed might have depended on weather conditions and have varied from year to year. The

significant point to arise from this is that if (for arguments' sake) the parchment from 5 skins were being used per day in a minster scriptorium on a continuous basis, and a more modest average production time of 45 days is assumed, there must have been 5 x 45 = 225 skins in the production process at any one time. This would indicate a substantial investment in space and structures which ought to have left some kind of mark in the archaeological record, and raises a further question about the location of this activity.

Lesne made the point that production was probably done away from the scriptorium itself in what he called *ateliers domestiques* nearer to the sheep or cattle pasture.[20] This writer is not aware that there has been any identification of buildings or pits for soaking skins, though parchment manufacture was obviously an important part of monastic activity: Lesne also notes that at Corbie at least there was a *pargaminarius* listed among the *praebendarii*.[21] At the

---

[19] Fuchs, *loc. cit*; M. di Curchi, *The History and Technology of Parchment Making*, at www.sca.org.au/scribe/articles/**parchment**.htm, accessed 18.11.2012; L. G. Gonzalez, J. Hiller, N. J. Terrill, J. Parkinson, K. Thomas and T. J. Wess, 'Effects of isopropanol on collagen fibrils', *Chemistry Central Journal* 2012. 6. 24, at *www.ncbi.nlm.nih.gov* › Journal List › Chem Cent J › v.6; 2012, accessed 18.11.2012.

[20] E. Lesne, *Les livres, 'scriptoria' et bibliothèques du commencement du VIIIe à la fin du XIIe siècle*, Histoire de la propriété ecclésiastique en France 4 (Lille, 1938), p. 326: '*Les membranes utilisées dans le* scriptorium *y sont le plus souvent sans doute apportées toutes préparées. Les peaux étaient vraisemblablement apprêtées d'ordinaire ou recevaient du moins la première préparation dans les ateliers domestiques attenant au cloître*' ('The parchments used in the *scriptorium* are without doubt most often brought there ready prepared. The skins were most likely as a rule got ready or received at least their first preparation in the domestic workshops belonging to the monastic house'. Author's translation).

[21] Ibid.: '*Les Statuts d'Adelhard signalent à Corbie, parmi les diverses catégories de "praebendarii" un "pargaminarius"*' ('The *Statutes*

FIG 7. 4 'POUNCING', FROM FRITZ PYRMENTER, 73RD BROTHER
OF THE NUREMBERG 'MENDELSCHEN ZWÖLFBRÜDERSTIFTUNG',
C. 1425, ILLUSTRATED IN THE HAUSBUCH DER MENDELSCHEN
ZWÖLFBRÜDERSTIFTUNG, BAND 1. NÜRNBERG 1426–1549.
STADTBIBLIOTHEK NÜRNBERG, AMB. 317.2°

FIG 7.5 THE *LUNELARIUM* IN USE (NOTE DOUBLE FRAMES FOR
STRETCHING AND DRYING THE SKIN)

FIG 7.6 A *LUNELARIUM*

same time, it is more than likely that the 'dirty' aspects of production described above took place away from the scriptorium, in outlying areas, possibly the pastures which were located on higher marginal lands; we should also bear in mind that parchment was not the sole aim of sheep herding – cheese, wool, meat, horn and bone were also valuable products which it yielded, and some skins might have been kept for sheepskin then as they are now. Final processes could safely be conducted closer to the centre of book production.[22] Surviving manuscripts occasionally show that gatherings of sheets were made and ruled before writing, like miniature exercise books.[23]

of Adelhard show that at Corbie, among the various categories of *praedebarii* there was a *pargaminarius*'. Author's translation). In addition he notes these lines from a monk of St Gall, *c.* AD 900: *cultro membranas ad libros presulis aptans/ pumice corrodo pellique superflua tollo, /et pressando premens ferrumque per aequora ducens/ linea signatur cum regula recta tenetur* ('shaping the parchment with a knife for the bishop's books/ I remove the detritus from the skin with abrasive pumice/ and lines are marked on it as the rule is held straight'. Author's translation). Unlike Lesne, I think that these activities are all the 'dry' ones of trimming and finishing prepared sheets, not starting with raw skin.
[22] Ibid.: '*À Saint-Pierre-le-Vif, Arnaldus, qui devient abbé en 1096, surveillait lui-même la préparation du parchemin. Sous ses yeux, des moines découpaient et portaient les feuilles prêtes à leurs frères copistes.*' ('At Saint-Pierre-le-Vif, Amaldus, who became abbot in 1096, personally supervised the preparation of parchment. He looked on as the monks cut up and carried the finished pages to their brother copyists.' Author's translation.)
[23] For example London, British Library Harley 3020, or the New York Academy of Medicine no. 1 of *Apicius*.

When comparing a 'raw' parchment skin with a finished book it is immediately obvious how much material has to be discarded when rectangular sheets are cut from the sheep-shaped skin. A skin obtained from Carbisdale Deerskins, Scotland, prepared from a Scottish Blackface lamb (a hill breed that has very little fat in the skin and is therefore suited to being turned into parchment) slaughtered at about seven months old, is said to have shrunk by about 15% during the drying process, resulting in a sheet of parchment 800 mm long and with a maximum width of 460 mm. It is said to be an average size skin from this supplier.[24] We should note that this refers to larger modern breeds of sheep; unimproved breeds such as Manx Loghton or Soay are much smaller in stature and will produce a skin substantially smaller in size, not only in nose-to-tail dimension, but especially in the girth -- perhaps 2 feet 6 inches long and only 2 feet wide as a maximum (that is, about 800 cm x 600 cm), which would produce an 'inner rectangle' of about 30 x 24 inches, 5 square feet (roughly 50 x 30 cm – or 0.35 square metres), with many skins being even smaller. Spring lamb skins produce a sheet approx. 12 x 24 inches (30 cm x 60 cm), in a pale yellow colour.[25] What is immediately striking about any of these skins is their awkward size so far as book production is concerned: cutting it to produce rectangles results in quite a lot of waste. The skin has a maximum 'inner rectangle' measuring about 24 x 16 inches (600 mm by 400 mm), a total of 240 square cm. (fig. 7.7). The largest page size available from such a skin would therefore be 16 inches (400 mm) deep x 12 inches (300 mm) wide. If this were to be adopted as the unfolded size of a page (i.e. a bifolium, or double page), then clearly two sheets are available per skin (Fig. 7.8). By reducing the depth of the page slightly, giving a final page size of about 10 inches (250 mm) deep and about 6 inches (150 mm) wide, it would be possible to cut three rectangular sheets from a single skin (Fig. 7.9).[26]

We should also remember that the manuscripts which have come down to us were, when constructed, made of larger sheets than we have now, possibly left with wany (curving) edges and were trimmed once the gatherings had been copied out. This is shown very often by marginalia which only exist in part (the beginning of a phrase on the left-hand margin of a verso page having been discarded with the trimmings). In addition, the left-over trimmings could have been used as scrap for notes or jottings much as we use scrap paper, or for binding and repair.[27] That said, parchment was clearly precious, and 'defective' pages with holes were frequently used.

The next issue to consider is that of stocking. Although not an exact calculation, it is possible to arrive at some broadly accurate estimates of how many animals land could support in the Anglo-Saxon period.[28] Male stock kept for breeding purposes and losses through sickness are discounted in the calculations which follow.

For bovines, allowing 1 animal per acre would allow the breeding of 1 calf per acre per year, of which there would be a 50-50 division of male and female calves. Assuming only the male calves are taken, 0.5 skins per year per acre would be available for parchment; older animals would produce a skin too thick for parchment, and their hides would become leather instead. For ovines, we can assume a stocking rate of 5 animals per acre. If each ewe produced one lamb per year, again assuming a 50-50 division of males and females, 2.5 skins per year would be available from male lambs; in addition, 2.5 ewes could be culled per year to keep the overall sheep herd size static, and as it is possible to use adult sheep or goat skins for parchment (unlike those of cattle which are suitable only for leathers), a maximum of 5 skins would be available per acre per year. It is possible that some might be kept for sheepskins; so 3.5 skins per year per acre might be a reasonable number to settle on. The significantly larger number of skins for parchment production which sheep pasturing makes available might conceivably have influenced the type of pastoral farming undertaken in areas where minsters were influential: John Blair has commented that 'the great Northumbrian minsters were underpinned by the cattle-rich culture of north Britain'.[29] This should not really be surprising; the suitability of the land in the north east for grazing as opposed to arable farming is well known, and was not confined to that area. Years before the early medieval period, Caesar and Strabo both highlighted this aspect of the economy of Britain, and especially its hinterland, noting the exporting of hides among other products.[30] Archaeology from Catterick and Hartlepool[31] indicates a major amount of activity in processing carcasses in both the Roman and early medieval periods. However, if parchment became a necessary and valuable commodity it might have influenced a move towards farming sheep, to say nothing of the wool and other products which were also required. That said, the *Codex Amiatinus* was written on calf,[32] which indicates that it and its

[24] Pergamena: www.pergamena.net/products.htm (accessed 7th August 2012): '7 square feet from either a calfskin or goatskin'; Carbisdale (at web.ukonline.co.uk/khamblet/ parchment, accessed autumn 2006; no longer available) gave dimensions of 'sheepskins average 3 feet long by 2 feet 6 inches wide, yielding 4 to 5 square feet with some edges left over'.
[25] Reed, *Ancient Skins, Parchment and Leathers*, p. 129.
[26] In *binding* a manuscript the spine in the skin tends to be aligned with the spine of the book, and it is possible that this practice may also have been used in assembling gatherings, as it increases the flexibility of the finished images. I am obliged to Anne Hillam at NYAM for this detail.
[27] Cf. the remarks made by Bede in the preface to the *Vita Cudberti* referred to in note 2; perhaps these are the *membranulis* he refers to.
[28] Data obtained by the author at Gyrwe, Bede's World, and corroborated by information supplied in personal communications by David James, Lecturer at Kirkley Hall Agricultural College, Ponteland, Northumberland, and Louisa Gidney, University of Durham.
[29] Blair, *Church in Anglo-Saxon Society*, p. 151.
[30] Caesar, *De Bello Gallico* 5.14, *The Gallic War / Caesar*, with an English translation by H. J. Edwards. Loeb Classical Library 72 (London and Cambridge, MA, 1994); Strabo 4.5.2-3, in *Literary Sources for Roman Britain*, ed. J. C. Mann, R. G. Penman; *London Association of Classical Teachers, LACTOR 11* (London, 3rd ed. 1996), pp. 12-13).
[31] Cf. P. Wilson, 'Catterick: the end of a Roman town?', in *The Late Roman Transition in the North: papers from the Roman Archaeology Conference, Durham 1999*, BAR, British Series 299, ed. T. Wilmott and P. R. Wilson (Oxford, 2000), pp. 25-31; P. J. Fowler, *Farming in the First Millennium* (Cambridge, 2002), pp. 234-9.
[32] Bruce-Mitford, *Art of the Codex Amiatinus*, p. 2; cf. E. Howie, *Early Insular Illuminated Manuscripts: merging of oral and literate cultures*, at http://www.unc.edu/celtic/catalogue/manuscripts/CoAm.html (accessed 7 August 2012); On the Lindisfarne Gospels cf. D. Ganz, review of M. P. Brown, *The Lindisfarne Gospels: society, spirituality and the scribe*, in *The Library* (7th series) 5 (2) (2004), 202-4; for an earlier and more doubtful view see G. Pollard, 'Notes on the size of the sheet ...' in *The*

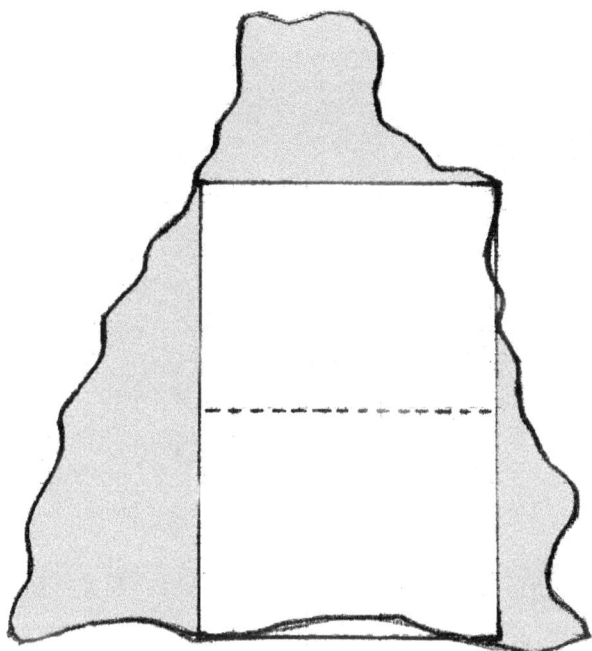

FIG 7.7 A 600MM X 400MM SHEET (APPROX.) USING A
WHOLE SKIN

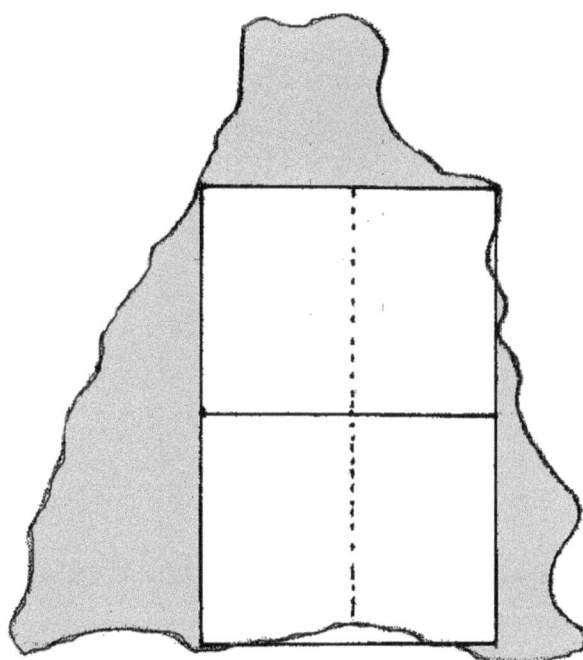

FIG 7.8 TWO SHEETS FROM ONE SKIN: MAX. SHEET SIZE
APPROX. 400 X 300 MM.

two sister pandects were indeed a colossal undertaking, as we shall shortly see.

Table 1 shows a list of manuscripts which I have been able to examine in the course of study of Bede's homilies and the Latin recipe text *Apicius* with some additions to make up the list from Bede's *Historia Ecclesiastica* and the *Codex Amiatinus*. The most obvious point to make is the difference in magnitude from the rest of the *Amiatinus*, which for all its beauty must be considered as decidedly unusual. There is only one manuscript, the New York Academy of Medicine *Apicius*, which might have been made at a smaller size to enable three sheets to be cut from a single skin, though even this is debateable. The finished sizes of the vast bulk of these manuscripts indicate that they were made at two sheets or four pages to the skin (quarto – see Figs. 7.7, 8). No doubt skins of similar size were gathered together (hence *gatherings*) and further collated to produce a book of a given size. It is interesting to note that even books of a given *type* may differ considerably in size: Richard Pfaff notes that in the case of pontificals, 'the page size seems ... to range from 340 x 250 mm. (Corpus-Canterbury) to 180 x 120 (Exeter), with written space proportional (Corpus's 230 x 145 to Exeter's 135 x 85).'[33]

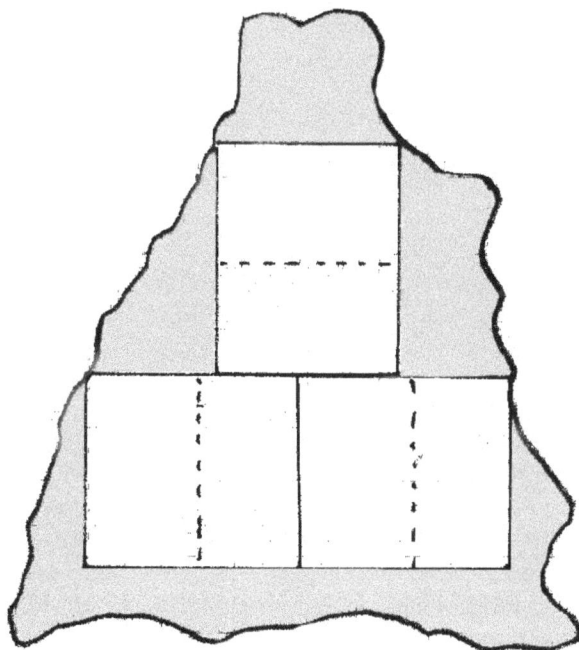

FIG 7.9 THREE SHEETS FROM ONE SKIN: MAX. SHEET SIZE
APPROX. 300 X 250 MM.

Library (4th series) 22 (2-3) (1941), 105-37.
[33] R. W. Pfaff, 'The Anglo-Saxon Bishop and his Book', The Toller Memorial Lecture, *Bulletin of the John Rylands University Library of Manchester*, 91.1 (Spring 1999), 3-24 at 7. This list may be compared with the selection of manuscripts written in the St Amand scriptorium made by R. McKitterick, *The Carolingians and the Written Word* (Cambridge, 1989), p.140.

Table 1

Manuscript page sizes

Manuscript	Depth	Width	Sheet min. size
Codex Amiatinus	660	492	984 x 660
Karlsruhe Aug XIX	402	314	628 x 402
Karlsruhe Aug XXXVII	370	279	558 x 370
Boulogne 75	338	260	520 x 338
Paris BN Lat 2370	335	260	520 x 335
Paris BN Lat 2369	275	255	510 x 275
Paris BN nov. adq.1450	334	245	490 x 334
Lincoln 182	324	235	470 x 324
Moore *Ecclesiastical History*	286	220	440 x 286
Cotton Tiberius *EH*	282	220	440 x 282
Zurich C42	268	205	410 x 268
Vatican *Apicius* Urb L 1146	235	195	390 x 235
NY Academy of Medicine 1, *Apicius*	223	173	246 x 223

To try to put this in context, the total words in Bede's works (using sample pages from the edition in Migne, *PL*) is at least 1,000,000 – nearer 1,250,000! If all of his works were written out as per the Moore MS, at about 400 words per side, this would require some 800 skins, or 228 acres devoted to sheep production to produce an omnibus edition if it were all reproduced at once (see Table 2, below). Put another way, the production from 1,000 acres of pasturage would be needed to produce 100 books of the size of the Moore Bede each year. It is a salutary reminder when handling a manuscript such as this that you have, in the space of a few inches width on a library shelf, the processed outer coverings from a small flock of sheep!

Table 2

Manuscript indications of land requirement

(assuming 0.5 skins per acre per year for calves, and 3.5 skins per acre per year for sheep)

CODEX AMIATINUS 660 x 492 mm 1030 folios – 550 sheets

If made in 1 year, using calves	1100 acres	445 hectares
If made over 5 years, using calves	220 acres	89 hectares
If made over 5 years, using sheep	35 acres	14 hectares

For 3 x codices of this type,

If made in 1 year using calves	3300 acres	1336 hectares
If made in 5 years, using calves	660 acres	267 hectares
If made in 5 years, using sheep	105 acres	42.5 hectares

Cotton Tiberius C. ii (C) of the *Ecclesiastical History*
page size 282 x 220 mm   157 folios, folded from *c.* 80 sheets, say 45 skins inc. some waste

If made in 1 year, using sheep	12.85 acres	5.2 hectares

For comparison, the Moore MS (M) of the *Ecclesiastical History* (page size 286 x 220 mm, with 129 folios from 65 sheets) would require perhaps 35 skins including waste. Using sheep at 3.5 skins per acre, this manuscript would necessitate 10 acres (4.04) hectares of pasture.

These statistics support the accepted view that manuscripts were valuable, some extremely so, because of the labour, time, and facilities needed to produce them. The labour involved in producing them is usually regarded as scribal, while the artisanal aspects described above are not recognised. It is surely the case that both aspects of manuscript production need to be taken into account. The end product was on occasion of great value in terms of land: consider Ceolfrith's astute bargaining (begun by Benedict Biscop) described by Bede in *Historia Abbatum* 15:

> *dato quoque Cosmographiorum codice mirandi operis, quem Romae Benedictus emerat, terram octo familiarum iuxta fluuium Fresca ab Aldfrido rege in scripturis doctissimo in possessionem monasterii beati Pauli apostoli comparauit ... uerum pro hac terra postmodum, Osredo regnante, Ceolfridus, addito pretio digno, terram uiginti familiarum in loco qui incolarum lingua Ad uillam Sambuce uocatur, quia haec uicinior eidem monasterio uidebatur, accepit.*

With the gift of a volume of cosmographies, of marvellous workmanship, which Benedict had purchased at Rome, he also obtained for the possession of the monastery of the blessed apostle Paul eight hides of land along the river Fresca from king Aldfrith, who was very learned in the scriptures … . Later, when Osred was king, Ceolfrith exchanged this land, and a worthy sum of money besides, for twenty hides of land in the place which is called in the local language Elder Farm, because it seemed nearer to that monastery.[34]

As well as Bede's own list of writings, there is a clear witness about the extent of books available to him in a post-Bedan context given by Alcuin – direct descendant in educational terms from Bede, via Aelbert of York, and the most recent summary of books known to Bede has been provided by

---

[34] *HA* 15; text and trans from Grocock and Wood, *Abbots of Wearmouth and Jarrow.*

Michael Lapidge.[35] Studies such as these give an indication of the holdings of the minster libraries, and also I think point to the importance of copying texts, whether in daily use or for reference, in accordance with regular monastic practice. Supporting this was a significant level of economic activity which in turn necessitated land-holdings – and for this, royal sponsorship was surely the key. Blair, citing Rosamund Faith, notes that 'Minsters resembled other major lords in needing to command regular supplies of foodstuffs'.[36] There were different requirements too and parchment surely represents one of the most significant of these, as he comments later: 'Bundles of hidated territories which had hitherto supported the food-circuit must have become subject to different pressures once they were turned into perpetual bookland estates controlled by great royal minsters.'[37] After referring to the acquisition by Ceolfrith already alluded to, he cites 'two dubious texts' S 1782 (twenty hides at Pinswell on top of the Cotswolds for an early eighth-century abbess of Gloucester *ouibus suis illic adhabendas*, 'to keep her sheep there') and S 254 (four hides in the Brendon Hills to Taunton in 737 *ad pecora alenda*, 'to pasture sheep').[38] These are both of interest in the light of the importance we have seen of securing regular supplies of parchment (Fig. 7.10). As Bischoff notes 'The acquisition of parchment must be viewed also as an economic problem. For the production of the *Codex Amiatinus* alone – and it had two sister manuscripts – over 500 (calf)skins were required at Wearmouth or Jarrow. In letters of the Carolingian period (for example, Hrabanus Maurus, Ep. 26) we find instances in which parchment was sent along with a request that it be used for copies of texts. Entries in some manuscripts of the ninth century indicate the portions of parchment supplied by individual monks or canons.[39] The scriptoria of houses in reduced circumstances sometimes had to use marginal pieces; the Codex Toletanus of the *Etymologiae* is an extreme case: for it pieces of parchment from the neck and shoulders (of the animal skin), often irregularly shaped, had to be pressed into service.'[40] In addition, the re-use of parchment as palimpsests is well-known.

Conclusion

The monastic culture which grew up in early medieval England brought with it a need to secure this 'new' form of material ('new' because pre-Christian Anglo-Saxon England

was illiterate) in order to permit the creation of books in the first place. In this, royal patronage was crucial; without their generous donations and grants of land, the monasteries could not have supplied themselves with any of the prerequisites necessary for their survival. Moreover, the finished book began to play a key role in relations between the monasteries, the Church, and the king, as is witnessed most famously by Bede's dedication of his *Ecclesiastical History* 'to the most glorious King Ceolwulf'.[41] He was not the first: Aldfrith was 'an exceptionally learned king' and on his accession 'his two friends Adomnán and Aldhelm both presented him with copies of original works they had composed in Latin'.[42] Ceolfrith took advantage of this interest in books by using a 'volume of cosmographies, of marvellous workmanship' as part-exchange for land along the River Fresca in his negotiations with the royal parties.[43] The book may have functioned equally as an important cult object and a sign of royal authority.[44] The scale of the estates granted by royal patronage is noted by Blair, who notes that 'there are thus three important respects in which minsters may have had the edge on other kinds of proprietor: in the scale of their landholdings and the control over them which charters conferred: in the ability to exploit low-status quasi-monastic personnel, and perhaps a broader range of the peasantry, in ways going beyond the mere extraction of food-rents; and in the ability to invest in new kinds of infrastructure and equipment. It seems likely that the operation of major monastic estates was, by 800, significantly and visibly different from that of territories run in more traditional ways.'[45] One of these 'significant and visibly different' activities was the making of parchment for writing things down. Fig. 7.11, drawn from a wall-painting in the church of St George, Reichenau, showing four devils pulling at a cowhide[46] with two gossips behind, illustrates a German proverb *das geht auf keine Kuhhaut*, meaning 'it won't fit on any size sheet' or 'it's beyond belief". Its location in the church by the pulpit shows that its message was not intended for the congregation, but for the preacher – and while this paper must draw to a close, it is its author's hope that it will stimulate more discussion on the mundane but nevertheless crucial aspects of book production in the medieval context.

[35] Lapidge, *Anglo-Saxon Library*, pp. 191-228.
[36] Blair, *Church in Anglo-Saxon Society*, p. 252.
[37] Blair, *Church in Anglo-Saxon Society*, p. 253.
[38] Blair *Church in Anglo-Saxon Society*, p. 254.
[39] See Bischoff, *Latin Palaeography* p. 10 and n. 17, reading *calf* for *sheep*; most authorities make it clear that the *Codex Amiatinus* was written on calfskin, not sheepskin (see note 31).
[40] Bischoff, *Latin Palaeography* p. 10, referring to E. A.Lowe, *Codices Latini Antiquiores*, 1 – 11 and Suppl. (Oxford, 1934-71), xi. 1638.

[41] *HE* pref.
[42] B. Yorke, *Rex Doctissimus: Bede and King Aldfrith of Northumbria*, Jarrow Lecture (2009), pp. 18, 16.
[43] *HA* 15.
[44] M. P. Brown, *'In the beginning was the Word': books and faith in the age of Bede*, Jarrow Lecture (2000), pp. 1-4.
[45] Blair, *Church in Anglo-Saxon Society*, p. 256.
[46] From *Karger Gazette*, art. cit., p. 1.

FIG 7.10 MAKER AND CLIENT. FROM THE 1255 HAMBURG BIBLE (COPENHAGEN, ROYAL LIBRARY GKS 4. 2°). A TWELFTH-CENTURY ILLUSTRATION

FIG 7.11 ST GEORG REICHENAU: FOUR DEVILS FIGHT OVER A COWHIDE

Chapter 8 Kingship and Prognostication

Marilina Cesario

The *Anglo-Saxon Chronicle*, which was begun during the reign of Alfred the Great (871-899), is a major source for the cultural and political history of the Anglo-Saxons.[1] One of the oldest works in Anglo-Saxon prose, it describes the most important events experienced by the English, by sea and land, from their arrival in this country to the year 1154.[2] Its value resides in its attempt to provide the panoptic survey of a people, described in rapid annual instalments by different writers, through several centuries, and in their own vernacular language.

The present article discusses the *Chronicle(s)*'[3] use of astronomical phenomena, including solar and lunar eclipses and comets, as prognostics announcing momentous events such as the death of kings and popes.[4] Countless classical and medieval works, both scientific and historical, treat these phenomena in this way. In their discussion of the famous description of *reðe forebecna ofer Norðhymbra* 'dire portents over Northumbria', including *ormete þodenas 7 ligrescas 7 fyrenne dracan* 'immense whirlwinds and flashes of lightning and fiery dragons' for the year 793, Rolf Bremmer and L. Sándor Chardonnens argue that:

> To the annalist these extraordinary natural incidents were more than just physical phenomena; excessive whirlwinds and flashes

of lightning and fiery dragons flying through the sky apparently had a deeper significance, portending some major event in the future … . For attributing significance to natural phenomena, particularly with respect to events to come, is the particular domain of prognostics.[5]

Furthermore, Bremmer and Chardonnens draw particular attention to the terms *forebecna* and *tacnum* which appear in the same annal, and they stress the fact that they belong to the same semantic category as *becnan* ('to portend') which occurs prominently in Old English prognostics. Although these linguistic similarities 'may give the impression that the author of this annal was familiar with the genre',[6] Bremmer and Chardonnens are forced to admit that there is no evidence of Old English prognostic texts which predate the Benedictine Reform in order to support this claim. Whether or not the Anglo-Saxon chroniclers were already familiar with the prognostic 'genre' by the ninth century, one cannot deny the fact that in the *ASC*, as in most medieval annals, natural phenomena, in particular comets, became popular with the chroniclers as a way of lending a prognosticatory dimension to particular events. In fact medieval Chronicles use comets abundantly, and they figure continually as portents of war, pestilence, famines, and the fall of kingdoms. Michael Swanton notes:

> The annalist, *strictu sensu*, is not concerned with historical perspective, and will rarely relate one event to another, except that a passing of a comet might be believed to have some relationship with human affairs, whether prognostic or casual.[7]

Beyond this, the *Chronicle* sometimes seems actively to manipulate the timing of phenomena in order to produce a closer combination of the phenomenon with the event that it supposedly portended. Chronicles were often ready to interfere with timing in order to permit the close combination of an eclipse or comet with a death or a change of regime. Solar eclipses tend, in fact, to be seen mostly as signs of change or of the weakening of the power of the established monarch. Comets almost always portend natural disasters generally associated with the death of a king. For later historians the recording of these natural phenomena is of special importance since they can

---

[1] See *Two of the Saxon Chronicles Parallel*, ed. J. Earle and C. Plummer (2nd ed. Oxford, 1952); *Anglo-Saxon Chronicle*, ed. M. J. Swanton (repr., Exeter, 1990). All quotations from the *ASC* are taken from the relevant volumes in Anglo-Saxon Chronicle: a collaborative edition, ed. D. Dumville and S. Keynes, namely: vol. 3, *ASC* MS A, ed. J. M. Bately (Cambridge, 1986); vol. 5, *ASC* MS C, ed. K. O'Brien O'Keeffe (Cambridge, 2001); vol. 6, *ASC* MS D, ed. G. P. Cubbin (Cambridge, 1996); vol. 7, *ASC* MS E, ed. S. Irvine (Cambridge, 2004) and vol. 8 *ASC* MS F, ed. P. S. Baker (Cambridge, 2000). English translations of the *Anglo-Saxon Chronicle* are taken from D. Whitelock's *The Anglo-Saxon Chronicle* (London, 1961).

[2] The *ASC* has come down to us in seven manuscripts and one fragment, known by letters of the alphabet (A-H). These are: Cambridge, Corpus Christi College, 173 (A), often called the 'Parker manuscript'; London, BL, Cotton Tiberius A. vi (B); London, BL, Cotton Tiberius B. i (C); London, BL, Cotton Tiberius B. iv (D); Oxford, Bod., Laud Misc. 636 (E); London, BL, Cotton Domitian viii (F); London, BL, Cotton Otho B. xi (G), and London, BL, Cotton Domitian ix, a twelfth-century single leaf (H).

[3] It is important of course to be aware of the complex compilation and transmission history of the *ASC*. Most scholars agree that there is no such thing as one Anglo-Saxon Chronicle. Charles Plummer, for example, argues that 'the fact that they [MSS A, C, D and E] grow out of a common stock, that even in their later parts they use common material, does not make them one chronicle'; Earle and Plummer, *Two of the Saxon Chronicles*, xlv. A different view is offered by Nicholas Brooks in 'Why is the Anglo-Saxon Chronicle about Kings?' *Anglo-Saxon England* 39 (2010), 43-70.

[4] I am relying here on Sándor Chardonnens' own definition of prognostics as 'a codified means of predicting events in the life-time of an individual or identifiable group of individuals, using observation of signs and times, or mantic divination'; *Anglo-Saxon Prognostics, 900-1100. Study and Texts*, ed. L. S. Chardonnens (Leiden, 2007), p. 8.

[5] R. Bremmer and L. S. Chardonnens, 'Old English prognostics. between the moon and the monstrous', in *Monsters and the Monstrous in Medieval Northwest Europe*, ed. K. E. Olsen and L. A. J. R. Houwen (Leuven, 2001), pp. 153-65 at 154.

[6] Bremmer and Chardonnens, 'Old English prognostics', p. 155.

[7] Swanton, *Anglo-Saxon Chronicle*, xvi.

be independently dated, and thus the political events the *Chronicle* associates them with can be dated in their turn. As D. Justin Schove states:

> The time spectrum of a particular chronicle is a tabulation of the various portents and meteorological events. Often the dates, even in primary sources, are not known or incorrectly computed, and then the different annals are brought into chronological alignment by the recognition of certain 'spectral lines', e.g. great comets, aurorae, meteoric displays, droughts, cold winters, pandemics and other phenomena.[8]

Why did the Anglo-Saxon chroniclers try, sometimes, to match particular phenomena with particular events, showing more concern to describe in detail a natural event than to be accurate about questions of time and place? Most of the information about natural phenomena offered in the *Chronicle* comes from eye-witness reports: the majority of the comets and eclipses, for example, were visible in England and Ireland.[9] A few others, which probably never occurred, were added by the chroniclers only because they could be considered as portents.

The *Anglo-Saxon Chronicle* is consistently interested in astronomical and meteorological phenomena, for various reasons. One is the prominence given to the astronomical entries in the Easter table, since the movements of the sun were of supreme importance in determining the date of Easter in a given year. Another reason is that an association with memorable events in the natural world allowed major political incidents to be fixed more firmly in the historical record. Yet a third reason is that endowing natural events with prophetic suggestiveness assisted the desire of the Church to find evidence of supernatural purpose in the natural world. One may argue that one of the chief functions of the natural phenomena in the *Chronicle* is to portend momentous events in the world of men.[10] Solar and lunar eclipses and comets are frequently

associated with specific historical events in order to give this or that prediction greater force. In the *Chronicle* there are nine references to solar eclipses, about ten to lunar eclipses,[11] eleven to comets, and eleven to celestial signs in general (these include haloes, meteors, blood rains and red moons).[12]

Solar eclipses

Solar eclipses are noted in the following years: 538, 540, 664, 733, 809, 879 [878], 885, 1135 and 1140. Six of these nine eclipses mark bad events (as already stated, generally the death of either a king or a pope).[13] In the case of two dates, those of 538 and 540, the mere fact of an eclipse is noted, and no repercussions or consequences are attached to either phenomenon. According to D. J. Schove, for both of these eclipses the earliest known record is in Bede.[14]

---

[8] D. J. Schove, 'Sunspots, aurorae and blood rain: the spectrum of time', *Isis* 42 (1951), 133-38 at 134.

[9] For example, in MS E for the year 1106 the annalist stresses the importance of eyewitness reports: *Gehwylce sædon þet hig ma on þison timon uncuðra steorra gesawon, ac we hit openlicor ne awriton, forþam þe we hit sylfe ne sawon*, 'Some said that at this time they saw more strange stars. However, we do not write of it more plainly because we did not see it ourselves'.

[10] Floods and earthquakes, apart from being naturally destructive forces, also function as portents. Earthquakes occur four times in the *ASC*, in each case foretelling something calamitous. Similar portents are said to have marked the death of important individuals and many catastrophes. Year 1048 MS C *Her on þisum geare wæs mycel eorðstyrung wide on Engla lande; 7 on þam ylcan geare man gehergode Sandwic. 7 With. 7 ofslohan þa betsta men þe þar wæron*, 'In this year there was a great earthquake far and wide in England, and in the same year Sandwich and the Isle of Wight were ravaged, and the best men who were there were killed'. Year 1060 MS D *On þisan gere wæs micel eorðdyne. on Translatione sancti Martini. 7 Heinric se cyng forðferde. on Francrice. 7 Kynsie arceb on Eoferwic gewat on xi Kl. Ian: 7 he ligeð on Burh*, 'In this year there was a great earthquake on the Translation of St. Martin. And King Henry died in France. And Archbishop Kynsige of York died on 22 December, and he lies at Peterborough'. Year 1119 MS E *On sce Michaeles mæsse æfen wæs mycel eorðbifung on suman steodan her on lande. Þeah swyðost on Glowe ceastrescire. 7 on Wigreceastre scire. 7

on þis ylcan geare forðferde se papa Gelasius on þas halfe þære muntan. 7 wæs on Clunig be byrged, 'On the eve of Michaelmas there was a great earthquake at some places in this country, though most severe in Gloucestershire and Worcestershire. In this same year Pope Gelasius died on this side of the Alps and was buried at Cluny'. Year 1129 MS E *7 ealle þa be þis half þa muntes. Nu wærð swa mycel dwyld on Cristen dom swa it næfre ær ne wæs. Crist sette red for his wrecce folc. Ðis ilces geares on S. Nicholaes messe niht litel ær dæi wæs micel eorðine*, 'There now grew up such heresy as there had never been before. May Christ establish counsel for his wretched people! In the course of this same year on St. Nicholas's eve, a little before day, there was a great earthquake'. Floods occur twice as negative portents. 1099 (MS E) *Ðises geares eac on sce Martines mæsse dæg asprang up to þan swiðe sæ flod 7 swa mycel to hearme ge dyde swan nan man ne ge munet þ hit æfre æror dyde. 7 wæs ðæs ylcan dæges luna prima. And Osmund biscop of Sear byrig innon Aduent forðferde*, 'This year also on St. Martin's Day, the tide rose so much and did so much damage that it could not be remembered to have done so much before, and there was on the same day a new moon. And Osmund, bishop of Salisbury, died in Advent'. 1125 (MS E) *On ðes ilces geares wearð swa micel flod on sce Laurenties messe feola tunes 7 men weorðan adrencte. 7 brigges to brokene. 7 corn 7 mædwe spilt mid ealle. 7 hunger 7 cwealm on men 7 on erue. 7 on ealle westme swa micel un time wearð swa hit ne wæs feola gear ær. 7 þes ilces geares forð ferde se abbot Iohan of Burch on ii Idus Octobris*, 'In the course of the same year there was so great a flood on St. Laurence's Day that many villages were flooded and many people drowned, and bridges broken down, and corn and meadows utterly ruined, and famine and disease among men and cattle; and there was more bad weather for all crops than there had been for many years. And in the course of the same year Abbot John of Peterborough died on 14 October'.

[11] Some descriptions of natural phenomena are rather ambiguous. In some cases, chroniclers confuse aurorae with comets, lunar eclipses and meteors. Umberto Dall'Olmo states that in the early Middle Ages 'there was no science devoted to the study of these phenomena to "freeze" the words into a precise language, and so most astronomical occurrences are described in a variety of ways and this is sometimes confusing'; U. Dall'Olmo, 'Latin terminology relating to aurorae, comets, meteors and novae', *Journal for the History of Astronomy* 11 (1980), 10-22 at 10.

[12] For a discussion on the function of the wind in MSS C, D and E of the *Anglo-Saxon Chronicle*, see M. Cesario, 'Romancing the wind: the role of boreas in the *Anglo-Saxon Chronicle*', *Germanic Philology* 5, forthcoming 2013.

[13] In most cases, the natural phenomenon (in this case a solar eclipse) appears at the beginning of the account.

[14] D. J. Schove suggests that the accounts in the *ASC* are copied directly or indirectly from Bede. The eclipse of 540 was total or almost total (near Rome), and it is likely that the news made its way into England from Rome. One must also remember that Bede constantly received information from correspondents, or it is possible that the record comes from a now lost continental chronicle which Bede used. See D. J. Schove, *Chronology of Eclipses and Comets AD 1-1000* (Woodbridge, 1984) p. 124.

In other dates, such as 664, 733, 879, 885, 1135 and 1140 solar eclipses appear to have been deliberately associated to negative events and seen as omens. Solar eclipses are among those dramatic celestial occurrences which have always evoked, by their immensity and beauty, feelings of *admiratio* and *terror*. In Pliny's words, *defectus solis, rem in tota contemplatione naturae maxime miram et ostento simile, magnitudinum umbraeque exsistere* '... eclipses of the sun, the most marvellous and indeed portentous occurrence in the whole of our observation of nature, serve as an indications of their dimensions and shadow'.[15]

For the year 664, most versions of the *Chronicle* (MSS A, B, C, D) report that:

> Her sunne aþiestrode,[16] ₇Arcenbryht Cantwara cyng forþferde; Colman mid his geferum for to his cyððe. Þy ilcan geare wæs micel man cuealm; ₇Ceadda ₇Wilferþ wæron gehadode, ₇þy ilcan geare Deusdedit forþferde.

> 'In this year there was an eclipse of the sun, and Eorcenberht, king of the people of Kent, died. And Colman went with his companions to his own land. And the same year there was a great pestilence. And Ceadda and Wilfrid were consecrated. And the same year Deusdedit died.'

In addition, MSS E and F give the day on which the eclipse took place (*on .v. nonas Mai*), as Bede does in the *Historia ecclesiastica*. There was a notable solar eclipse in 664,[17] and according to D. J. Schove, 'Bede is the earliest known author to mention this eclipse *quam nostra aetas meminit*. It occurred before he was born, and doubtless he used oral or written Northumbrian evidence'.[18] It is famous as the first solar eclipse recorded from authentic observation in England itself, and conveniently for those who wished to invest it with prophetic significance, it was followed by a terrible plague.[19]

Charles Jones claims that Bede, in both *De temporum ratione* and *De temporibus*, tried to avoid any discussion of eclipses because he knew that the topic was not free from superstitious interpretation, and therefore when Bede talks about the eclipse of 1 May 664 (3 May according to him), he does not call it an eclipse.[20] Jones's claim appears bizarre if we compare *Historia ecclesiastica* III.28 where Bede refers to this same eclipse as *eclipsis solis*. Moreover, Bede treats the eclipse as a sign which predicted both the pestilence that raged through England and the deaths on the day of the eclipse of the King of Kent and the Archbishop of Canterbury. This pestilence was especially calamitous as it carried off Bishops Tuda and Cedd and caused the partial apostasy of the East Saxons. All this information is historically accurate: there was indeed a plague in this year, Eorcerbert, king of Kent, really did die on the same day, and Deusdit, archbishop of Canterbury died on 28 October 663, which Bede would have regarded as falling in 664.[21]

In the year 733, the chronicler does not only connect the eclipse to a negative event, but he gives the impression that he is playing with the dates in order to create a cause-effect relationship between the occurrence of the eclipse and the historical events which is portended.

> MSS A (B, C) *AN. dccxxxiii. Her Eþelbald geode Sumurtun, ₇sunne aþiestrode.*

> 'In this year Æthelbald occupied Somerton, and there was an eclipse of the sun.'

MSS E (D) add that *Acca wæs adrifen of biscopdome*, 'Acca was driven from his bishopric', and MS F provides a more detailed description of the astronomical phenomenon *Hic sol obscuratur quia eclipses facta est, et totus orbis solis quasi nigerrimo et horrendo scuto uidebatur esse coopertus circa tertiam horam diei*, 'there was an eclipse of the sun and all the circle of the sun became like a black shield'. In 733 there was indeed a total solar eclipse: it was visible in central England on 14 August. However, Acca was driven from his bishopric not in 733, but in 731. Of course, this may be a copyist's mistake in reporting the annal (which is not uncommon),[22] but it might also be a

---

[15] *Pliny Natural History*, vol. I. ed. and trans. H. Rackham, The Loeb Classical Library (1938. Repr., Cambridge, 1979), II.6. vii, pp. 196-97.
[16] The Anglo-Saxon chroniclers always use the expression *sunne aþiestrode* ('the sun grew dark') to refer to a solar eclipse. The phenomenon is never called by its name *eclipsis solis* as in Bede's *Historia*, although the Anglo-Saxon annalists use Latin *cometa* to describe comets.
[17] The best record comes from Ireland, noted in *The Annals of Ulster*; see Schove, *Chronology*, p. 126.
[18] Schove, Ibid., pp. 128-9. *Eodem autem anno dominicae incarnationis DCLX quarto, facta erit eclipsis solis die tertio mensis Maii, hora circiter decimal diei; quo etiam anno subita pestilencia lues depopulatis prius australibus Brittaniae plagis, Nordanhymbrorum quoque prouinciam corripiens atque acerna clade diutius longe lateque desaeuiens, magnam hominum multitudinem strauit. Qua plaga praefactus Domini sacerdos Tuda raptus est de mundo, et in monasterio, quod vocatur Paegualaech, honorifice sepultus. Haec autem plaga Hiberniam quoque insulam pari clade premebat.* 'In this year of our Lord 664 there was an eclipse of the sun on 3 May about 4 o'clock in the afternoon. In the same year a sudden pestilence first depopulated the southern parts of Britain and afterwards attacked the Kingdom of Northumbria, raging far and wide with cruel devastation and laying low a vast number of people. Bishop Tuda was carried off by it and honourably buried in the monastery called *Pægnalæch*. The plague did equal destruction in Ireland.' This occurred on 1 May 664, not 3 May as Bede says (*HE* III.27, pp. 310-3). Texts and translations are those of *Bede's Ecclesiastical History of the English People*, ed. B. Colgrave and R. A. B. Mynors (Oxford, 1999).
[19] For a detailed discussion on this epidemic, see J. C. Russell, 'The

earlier medieval plague in the British Isles', *Viator* 7 (1976), 65-78 at 73-4.
[20] See C. W. Jones, *Bedae opera de temporibus* (New York, 1943), pp. 230 and 361.
[21] F. Stenton, *Anglo-Saxon England* (1971, Oxford, repr. 2001), p. 129. In the *Annals of St Neots* Deusdit's year of death is given as 664: *Anno Christi 664 eclipsis facta. Ceadda et Wilfridus Nordanhymbrorum ordinantur episcope et anno eodem Sanctus Deusdedit archiepiscopus transit* 'in the year 664 there was an eclipse, Ceadda and Wilfrid were ordained bishops of Northumbria, and in the same year the archbishop, St. Deusdedit passed away' (author's translation); *Asser's Life of King Alfred and the Annals of Saint Neots*, ed. W. H. Stevenson (Oxford, 1904), p. 123.
[22] As Whitelock points out, 'the chronology of the Chronicle causes many complications. Mechanical dislocations arise easily out of the habit of numbering a series of years in advance, for it was easy to make an entry against a wrong number, or to take too much space for an entry and fail to adjust the numbers of the subsequent annals; or a copyist might fail to notice a blank annal and so pre-date events for a considerable stretch'; Whitelock, *The Anglo-Saxon Chronicle*, xxiii.

deliberate change by the chronicler in order to link the eclipse and Acca's expulsion.

In the year 879 the eclipse is linked to the arrival of the Vikings:

> 879 [878] MSS A, B, [C 880], D, E, F *Her for se here to Cirenceastre of Cippanhamme. 7 sæt þær an gear; 7 þy geare gegadrode on hloþ wicenga, 7 gesæt æt Fullan hamme be Temese; 7 þy ilcan geare aþiestrode sio sunne ane tid dæges*

> 'In this year the army went from Chippenham to Cirencester, and stayed there for one year. And the same year a band of Vikings assembled and encamped at Fulham by the Thames. And the same year there was an eclipse of the sun for one hour of the day.'

The eclipse reported for 879[23] is probably that of 29 October 878.[24] There were actually two total solar eclipses in 878: the first was visible in Ireland and Germany on 15 October, and the second was seen on 29 October in Ireland, England and Germany. D. J. Schove believes that 'all the solar eclipses recorded in the British Isles and Europe between 874 and 880 really refer to the solar eclipse of 878'.[25] The English sources which were more or less contemporary with the eclipse, such as the *Chronicle* and *Asser's Life of Alfred the Great*, do not give the month or the day.[26] Alfred Smyth notes that the fact that the chronicle offers no details must be an indication that the astronomical event was recorded a long time after it occurred:

> A total eclipse, however, was an event of such rarity and loaded with such ominous associations, that had it been observed by strictly contemporary witnesses in any part of Wessex, Berkshire, Surrey or Kent in 878, the month of year, at least might certainly be expected to have been given by a West Saxon chronicler.[27]

The *Chronicle* regards the eclipse as heralding the arrival of the Danish army which remained at Chippenham in 878, moved to Cirencester, and then sailed down the Thames and took winter quarters at Fulham.[28] The same eclipse of 878 is still mentioned in the year 885:

> MSS A, B, [C 886], D, E, F *Þy ilcan geare ær middum wintra. forþferde Carl Francna cyning, 7 hiene ofslog an efor, 7 ane geare ær his broður forþferde, se hæfde eac þæt west rice, 7 hie wæron begen Hloþ wiges suna; se hæfde eac þæt west rice, 7 forþferde þy geare þe sio sunne aþiestrode ...*

> 'That same year before Christmas, Charles, king of the Franks, died. He was killed by a boar, and a year previously his brother, who had also held the western kingdom, had died. They were both sons of Louis, who died in the year [879] of the eclipse of the sun ...'.

The *Annals of Fulda* say that Charles died on 12 December 884,[29] Louis, his brother, on 5 August 882,[30] and Louis the Stammerer, their father, on 10 April 879. Nevertheless, the solar eclipse mentioned is still that of 878. This particular eclipse must have been considered an important and impressive event worthy to be remembered since King Alfred's charter to Denewulf, Bishop of Winchester (AD 979 probably for 878) mentioned it at the beginning of the charter:

> *Abbo ab incarnatione domini nostri Jhesu Christi. Dccccclxxviiii ..... in hunc annum sol obscuratum fuit. Ego Ælfredus Rex hanc donationem meam cum signo sanctæ crucis confirmavi.*[31]

> 'In the year 979 [proably for 878] from the Incarnation of our Lord, Jesus Christ ... in the year in which the sun darkened, I king Alfred have confirmed this gift of mine with the sign of the holy cross'.

In both 1135 and 1140 the scribe voluntarily manipulated information in order to make the appearance of the eclipse coincide with the historical event which it portended:

> 1135: MS E *On þis gære for se king Henri ouer sæ æt te Lammasse. 7 ðat oþer dei þa he lai an slep in scip, þa þestrede þe dæi ouer al landes, 7 uuard þe sunne suilc als it uuare thre niht ald*

---

[23] Numerous English and continental writers note an eclipse in 879; Schove, *Chronology*, p. 200.

[24] The wrong year can be attributed to a copyist's mistake; Whitelock, *The Anglo-Saxon Chronicle*, p. 50.

[25] Schove, *Chronology*, p. 97.

[26] See Stevenson, *The Annals of Saint Neots*, p. 124 and Stevenson, *Asser's Life*, pp. 47-8. In The *Annals of Fulda* the year is correct: 878. 'There was an eclipse of the moon on the ides of the same month (15 October), in the last hour of the night. The sun was also so dimmed for about half an hour after the ninth hour of 29 October that stars appeared in the sky and all thought that night was threatening. There was a terrible cattle plague in Germany, especially around the Rhine, and this was followed by many deaths. There is a certain villa in the county of Worms, not far from the palace of Ingelheim, called Walahesheim, where a remarkable thing happened. The dead animals were dragged daily from their stalls to the fields, where the village dogs, as is their wont, tore them up and devoured them. One day almost all the dogs gathered together in one place and went off, so that none of them could be found afterwards, either alive or dead'; *The Annals of Fulda*, trans. T. Reuter (Manchester, 1992), p. 85.

[27] A. P. Smyth, 'The solar eclipse of Wednesday 29 October AD 878: ninth-century historical records and the findings of modern astronomy',

in *Alfred the Wise. Studies in Honour of Janet Bately on the Occasion of her Sixty-fifth Birthday*, ed. J. Roberts, J. L. Nelson and M. Godden (Woodbridge, 1997), pp. 187-210 at 198.

[28] Stenton, *Anglo-Saxon England*, p. 237.

[29] 884: 'Carloman, the young King of Gaul, is said to have been killed by a boar while hunting; in fact he was unintentionally wounded by one of his vassals while hunting, and died on 12 December'; Reuter, *The Annals of Fulda*, p. 96.

[30] 882: 'A comet appeared on 18 January in the first hour of the night with an exceptionally long tail, which prefigured by its appearance the disaster which quickly followed. For Louis's illness grew worse and on 20 January he died'; Ibid., p. 91.

[31] S 352. London, BL, MS Additional 15350, fol. 113r (s. xii). The authenticity of this charter is questionable.

mone, an sterres abuten him at middæi. Wur\þ/ en men suiðe ofuundred 7 ofdred, 7 sæden ðat micel þing sculde cumen hereafter, sua dide, for þat ilc gær warth þe king ded. ðat oþer dæi efter Sancte Andreas massedæi on Normandi. Þa þestre sona þas landes, for æuric man sone ræuede oþer þe mihte.

'In this year King Henry went overseas at Lammas, and the next day, when he was lying asleep on board ship, the day grew dark over all lands, and the sun became as if it were a three-nights'-old moon, with stars about it at midday. People were very astonished and terrified, and said that something important would be bound to come after this – so it did, for that same year the King died the second day after St. Andrew's Day, in Normandy. Then forthwith these lands grew dark, for everyone who could forthwith robbed another'.

King Henry's sea journey did take place in an eclipse year, but the year was 1133, not 1135 as the *Chronicle* reports.[32] Changing the voyage to 1135 makes the eclipse occur just before the King's death. This appropriation of the eclipse of 1133 is an example of an 'assimilated eclipse', an anachronistic juxtaposition which gives a supernatural dimension to a particular event. All the other details are chronologically correct.

The *Chronicle* stresses the significance of the eclipse as a prognostic: *Wur\þ/en men suiðe ofuundred 7 ofdred, 7 sæden ðat micel þing sculde cumen hereafter, sua dide, for þat ilc gær warth þe king ded. ðat oþer dæi efter Sancte Andreas massedæi on Normandi*, 'People were very astonished and terrified, and said that something important would be bound to come after this – so it did, for that same year the King died the second day after St. Andrew's Day, in Normandy'. In this account the natural phenomenon noted is given intensified emotion-language: people are described as *ofuundred 7 ofdred*. Caroline Walker Bynum notes that 'it is when phenomena such as eclipses or double suns are recounted in conjunction with troubled and human events such as war, crime, or corruption that they are given heightened emotion-language'.[33] Witnesses in the account for the year 1135 wonder at the greatness of the event (*þa þestrede þe dæi ouer al landes, 7 uuard þe sunne suilc als it uuare thre niht ald mone, an sterres abuten him at middæi*, 'the day grew dark over all lands, and the sun became as if it were a three-nights'-old moon, with stars about it at midday'), but I would argue that the fear described here is not merely linked to the actual phenomenon *per se* but rather to the meaning attached to that celestial occurrence

as a portent. Therefore, the feeling of fear (which is also expressed in the year 793 with reference to the celestial portents *þet folc earmlice bregdon*[34] 'that sorely frightened the people') is not necessarily fear of the unknown; on the contrary it can be read as fear of what is bound to happen, and in this sense, to return to Bremmer and Chardonnens' argument, the cognitive process compares to that employed in prognostics texts. One can argue that, for the Anglo-Saxons, *admiratio* and *terror* were to be read in the context of a renewed *scientia*, that is knowledge of the meanings attached to those *tacna* or natural phenomena, and certain feelings such as fear and/or wonder, attached to them, do not derive from what cannot be explained or grasped (*ignorantia*), but rather from renewed interest in the natural world and in light of the prognostic texts which were circulating in the same monastic houses from which the late versions of the *ASC* emanated.

The account for the year 1140 is another example of 'assimilated eclipse':

MS E *On þis gær wolde þe king Stephne tæcen Rodbert eorl of Gloucestre þe kings sune Henries, ac he ne myhte, for he wart it war. Þerefter in þe lengten þestrede þe sunne 7 te dæi. abuton nontid dæies þa men eten, ðat me lihtede candles to æten bi, 7 þat was xiii Kalendas Aprilis; wæron men suythe of wundred. Þerefter fordfeorde Willelm ærcebiscop of Cantwarberi … .*

'In this year King Stephen meant to capture Robert, earl of Gloucester, King Henry's son, but he could not because he became aware of it. After that, in spring, the sun grew dark, during the day, about midday when people were eating, so that they lit candles to eat by. That was 20 March, and people were very much astonished. After that William, Archbishop of Canterbury, died …'.

In the *Chronicle* for 1140 there is a rearrangement of dates which permits the linkage of disparate events. A total solar eclipse on 20 March 1140 is noted, and William, archbishop of Canterbury, is said to have died in the same year. He actually died on 21 November 1136, four years before the eclipse. This seems to be an attempt on the chronicler's part to force a connection between the natural phenomenon and the death of the archbishop.

Lunar eclipses

Lunar eclipses are noted in the following years: 795 [796], 800, 802, 806, 827, 904, 1078, 1117 and 1121. In four of these nine the implications of the eclipse are negative. Whereas the solar eclipse is an evil portent in nearly all of its occurrences, the lunar one does not have one single

---

[32] *Gesta regum Anglorum 1 vol in 2 Parts: History of the English Kings/ William of Malmesbury*, ed. and trans. R. A. B. Mynors (Oxford, 1999), II, pp. 533-6; Simeon of Durham, *A History of the Kings of England*, trans. J. Stevenson (Lampeter, 1987), II, pp. 285 and 295-6. *The Chronicle of John of Worcester* reports King's Henry journey on the right year which is 1133; see *The Chronicle of John of Worcester*, 3 vols., ed. and trans. P. McGurk (Oxford, 1998), III, pp. 209-11.

[33] C. Walker Bynum, 'Wonder', *The American Historical Review* 102.1 (1997), 1-26, at 23.

[34] *Bregdon* from *brégean* also means 'to astonish, to marvel'. See Bosworth-Toller.

symbolic meaning. For instance, in 795, an eclipse of the moon is linked to Eardwulf's succession to the kingdom of the Northumbrians; in 802 the phenomenon precedes Beormod's consecration as Bishop of Rochester, and in 827 King Egbert conquered the kingdom of the Mercians and everything south of the Humber.[35]

In the *Anglo-Saxon Chronicle* in the year 800, the chronicler intervenes to make the date of a lunar eclipse coincide with that of an historical event.

> MSS D, E, F (801) *AN .dccc. Her wæs se mona aðistrad on ðære oðre tid on niht on .xvii. kalendas Februarii; 7 Brihtric cining forðferde 7Wo\r\r ældorman, 7 Ecgberht feng to Wæstseaxna rice. 7 þa ilcan dæg rad Æþælmund ealdorman of Hwiccum of\e/r æt Cynemæresforda; þa gemette hine Weohstan ealdorman mid Wilsætum, 7 þær wæð mycel gefeoht, 7 þær begen ofslagene wæron þe ealdormen, 7 Wilsete na<mo>n sige ...*

> 'In this year there was an eclipse of the moon in the second hour of the eve of 16 January. And King Brihtric and Ealdorman Worr died, and Egbert succeeded to the kingdom of the West Saxons. And that same day Ealdorman Æthelmund rode from the province of the Hwiccians across the border at Kempsford. And Ealdorman Weohstan with the people of Wiltshire met him, and a great battle took place, and both ealdormen were killed and the people of Wiltshire had the victory ...'

In 800 the *Chronicle* notes a lunar eclipse and follows this with the death of King Brihtric. There was indeed an eclipse in this year (it was visible in England on 15 and 16 January), but Brihtric did not die until 802.

In the year 806, the appearance of a lunar eclipse is connected with the expulsion of Eardwulf, king of the Northumbrians, and with the death of Eanberht, bishop of Hexham:

> MSS E (D) *AN .dcccvi. Her se mona aðistrode on kalendas Septembris; 7 Eardwulf Norðanhymbra cining wæs of his rice adrifen, 7 Eanberht Hagusteald biscop forðferde.*

> 'In this year there was an eclipse of the moon on 1 September. And Eardwulf, king of the Northumbrians, was driven from his kingdom. And Eanberht, bishop of Hexham, died.'[36]

MS F adds that: *Eac on ðys ylcan geare, .ii. nonas Iunii, rodetacn wearð ateowed on ðan monan anes Wodnesdæges innan ðare dagende. An eft on ðis geare an kalendas Septembris an wunderlic trendel wearð ateowed abutan ðare sunnan,* 'Also in the same year on 31 May the sign of the cross was revealed in the moon, on a Wednesday at dawn. And again in this year on 30 August a wonderful circle was revealed around the sun'. According to Umberto Dell'Olmo, the sign of the cross may refer to either a lunar halo or to paraselenic features.[37]

Comets

Comets are noted in the following years: 678, 729, 892, 905, 975, 995, 1066, 1097, 1106, 1110 and 1114.[38] Nine times out of eleven they are treated as bad omens marking a death, or anticipating a misfortune befalling a prominent historical figure. In year 678 a comet appears and Bishop Wilfrid is driven from his bishopric;[39] in 729 King Ecgberth dies;[40] in 905 the Danish army slaughter Ealdorman Sigehelm, and Æthelwold's thegn Ealdwold, and many others;[41] in 975 a comet announces Edgar's death

---

ær Candelmæssan. Ægelwig se woruldsnotra abbod on Eofeshamme forðferde on sancta Iuliana mæssedæg, 7 Waltere wæs to abode geset on his stede, 7 Hereman biscop forðferde; se wæs biscop on Bearrucshire 7 on Wiltunscire 7 on Dorsætan. 7 her Malcholom kyngc gewann Mælslæhtan modor 7 ealle his betsan men 7 ealne his gærsuman 7 his orf. 7 he sylf uneaðe ætbærst. 7 her wæs se dria sumor, 7 wilde fyr com on manega scira, 7 forbærnde fela tuna, 7 eac manega burga forbu<r>on; 'This year the moon was eclipsed three nights before Candlemas. And Æthelwig, the abbot of Evesham, who was skilled in secular affairs, died on St. Juliana's Day, and Walter was appointed abbot in his place. And Bishop Hereman died who was bishop of Berkshire and Wiltshire and Dorset. And King Malcolm captured the mother of Mælsnechtan ... and all his best men and all his treasure and his cattle; and he himself escaped with difficulty ... . And this year there was the dry summer; and wildfire came upon many shires and burned down many villages; and also many towns were burned down'.

[37] See Dell'Olmo, 'Latin terminology', p. 13.
[38] Bremmer and Chardonnens believe that the fiery dragons of 793 may refer to a comet. See Bremmer and Chardonnens, 'Old English prognostics', p. 156. I did not include this account in the comet section since 'fiery dragons' may also be interpreted as either aurorae borealis or meteors. See, for example, Dall'Olmo, 'Latin terminology', pp. 12-13.
[39] MSS A, B, C *Her opiewde cometa se steorra. 7 Wilfriþ biscop wæs adrifen of his biscdome from Ecgferþe cyninge* 'In this year the star called "comet" appeared; and Bishop Wilfrid was driven from his bishopric by King Ecgfrith'. This refers to the comet of 676 which is reported under year 677 by *The Chronicle of John of Worcester*.
[40] MSS A, B, C *Her cometa se steorra hiene opiewde, 7 Sanctus Ecgbryht forþferde*; 'In this year the star called "comet" appeared and St. Egbert died'.
[41] *ASC* MS D *Her cometa æt eowde xiii Kl. Nouembris. Her gelædde Apelwold þone here on East Englum to unfriðe þæt hi gehergodon ofer eall Myrcna land oð hi common to Creoccgelade, 7 foron þær ofer Temese, 7 namon ægþær on Brædene ge þæronbutan eall þæt hi gehentan meahton, 7 wendon þa east hamweard. Þa he eft þanon faran wolde, þa het heo beodon ofer ealle þa fyrd þæt hi foron ealle ut ætsomne. Þa ætsæton þa Centiscan þær beæftan ofer his bebod, 7 .vii. ærendracan he him hæfde to asend. 7 her wæs se here hi þær, 7 hi ðær gefuhton, 7 þær <weard> Siulf ealdorman ofslægen, 7 Sihelm ealdorman, 7 Eadwold cynges þeng, 7 Kenulf abbod ...* 'In this year Æthelwold induced the army in East Anglia to break the peace so that they harried over all Mercia until they reached Cricklade. And they went then across the Thames, and carried off all that they could seize both in and round about Braydon, and turned then homeward. Then King Edward went after them as soon as he could collect his army, and harried all their land between the Dykes and the Ouse, all as far north as the fens. When he wished to go back from there he had it announced over the whole army that they were all to set out together. Then the men of Kent lingered behind there against

[35] This lunar eclipse was total in England and Frankia on 25 Dec. 828 (a.m.). According to Schove, 'the eclipse was briefly total, and occurred on the night of Dec. 24-25. It is recorded in England, under 827, in the *ASC* also in Ethelweard and Florence of Worcester. The year 827 is wrong by any reckoning; if a Christmas year-beginning was intended, the year should have read 829'; Schove, *Chronology*, p. 184.
[36] The account of year 1078 in MS D is another instance of *luna eclipsis* being linked to the death of an abbot: *Her mona apystrode þreom nihton*

and a famine;[42] in 995 another comet precedes the death of Archbishop Siric;[43] in 1066 a comet foretells the arrival of the Normans; in 1097 it is followed by an oppressive and severe year; in 1110 a star appears from the north-east and its beam goes out before it in the south-west, and Philip of Briouze, William Malet, and William Bainard are deprived of their lands;[44] and in 1114 a comet is described alongside other natural phenomena, including an ebb-tide and very strong winds in the month of October, but exceptionally violent on the night of 18 November, in that they damaged woods and villages.[45]

---

[42] his command – and he had sent seven messengers to them. Then the Danish army overtook them, and they fought there. And there were killed Ealdorman Sigewulf and Ealdorman Sigehelm, and the king's thegn Ealdwold, and Abbot Cenwulf ...'.

[42] (MSS D, E) From MS D *N. dcccclxxv. .viii. idus Iulii: Her Eadgar gefor, Angla reccend, Westseaxena wine, 7 Myrcna mundbora. Cuð wæs þæt wide geond feola þeoda, þæt afaran Eadmundes ofer ganetes beð cynegas hyne wide wurðodon swiðe, bugon to þam cyninge, swa him wæs gecynde. Næs se flota swa rang, ne se here swa strang, þæt on Angelcynne æs him gefætte, þa hwile þe se æþela cyning cynestol gerehte. Her Eadweard, Eadgares sunu, feng to rice. 7 sona on þam ilcan geare on hærfest æteowde cometa se steorra, 7 com þa on ðam æftran geare swyðe mycel hungor 7 swyðe mænigfealde styrunga geond Angolcynn ...*; 'In this year died Edgar (MS D adds 8 July), ruler of the Angles, friend of the West Saxons and protector of the Mercians. It was widely known throughout many nations across the gannet's bath, that kings honoured Edmund's son far and wide, and paid homage to this king as was his due by birth. Nor was there fleet so proud nor host so strong that it got itself prey in England as long as the noble king held the throne. In this year Edgar's son Edward succeeded to the kingdom. And soon in the same year in harvest time there appeared the star "comet", and in the next year there came a very great famine throughout England'.

[43] MS E *Her on þissum geare æteowde cometa se steorra. 7 Siric arcb. forðferde*; 'In this year the star "comet" appeared, and Archbishop Sigeric died'.

[44] MS E *Ealle þa niht wæs seo lyft swiðe clene 7 þa steorran ofer eall þa heofon swiðe beorhte scinende, 7 treowwæstmas wurdon þære nihte þurh forste swiðe fornumene. Ðæræfter on Iunies monðe ætywde an steorra norðan eastan, 7 his leoma stod toforan him on þet suðwest, 7 þus manega niht wæs gesæwen, 7 furðor nihtes syððan he ufor astah he wæs gesewen on bæc on þet norðwest gangende. Ðises geares wurdon belænde Philippus de Brause 7 Willelm Malet 7 Willelm Bainart. Eac þises geares forðferde Elias eorl þe þa Mannie of þm cynge Heanri geheold 7 oncneow, 7 æfter his forsiðe feng to se eorl of Angeow 7 hi togeanes þam cynge heold. Ðis wæs swið gedeorfsum gear her on lande þurh gyld þe se cyng nam for his dohter gyfte 7 þurh ungewædera, for hwan eorðwestmas wurdon swiðe amyrde 7 treowwæstmas ofereall þis land forneah eall forwurdon*; 'All that night the sky was very clear, and the stars all over the heaven shining very bright, and fruits were badly damaged by frost that night. After that, in the month of June, a star appeared from the north-east and its beam went out in front of it in the south-west, and it was seen like this for many nights, and later on in the night, after it had risen higher, it was seen going backwards to the north-west. In the course of this year, Philip of Briouze, William Malet, and William Bainard were deprived of their lands. Also in the course of this year Count Elias died, who held Maine from King Henry, and acknowledgment for it, and after his decease the count of Anjou succeeded and held it against the king. This was a very severe year in this country because of taxes that the king took for the marriage of his daughter, and because of storms by which the products of the soil were badly damaged and the fruits of trees over all this country nearly all perished. In the course of this year work was begun on the new monastery of Chertsey'.

[45] MS E *... Ðises geares on æfteward Mai wæs gesewen an selcuð steorra mid langan leoman manege niht scinende. Eac on þis ylcan geare wæs swa mycel ebba æghwær anes dæges swan an man æror ne gemunde 7 swa þet man ferde ridende 7 gangende ofer Tæmese be eastan þære brigge on Lunden. Ðises geares wæron mycele swiðe windas on Octobris monðe, ac he wæs ormæte mycel on þa niht octabe Sancti Martini, 7 þet gehwær on wudan 7 on tunan gecydde. Eac on þisum geare se cyng geaf þet arcebiscoprice on Cantwarabyrig Raulfe se wæs æror biscop on Hrofeceastre. And se arcebiscop on Eoferwic Thomas forðferde, 7 feng Turstein þærto se wæs æror þæs cynges capelein ...*; 'In this year,

Bede too treats comets as predicting significant events. In 729, for instance, he associates the comet with the Saracens' invasions of Gaul and the deaths of Ecgberht of Iona and King Osric of Northumbria.

Anno dominicae incarnationis DCCXXVIIII apparuerunt cometae duae circa solem, multum intuentibus terrorem incutientes. Una quippe solem praecedebat mane orientem, altera uespere sequebatur occidentem, quasi Orienti simul et Occidenti dirae cladis praesagae; uel certe una diei, altera noctis praecurrebat exortum, ut utroque tempore mala mortalibus inminere signarent. Portabant autem facem ignis contra aquilonem, quasi ad accendendum adclinem, apparebantque mense Ianuario et duabus ferme septimanis permanebant. Quo tempore grauissima Sarracenorum lues Gallias misera caede uastabat, et ipsi non multo post in eadem prouincia dignas suae perfidiae poenas luebant. Quo anno sanctus uir Domini Ecgberct, ut supra conmemorauimus, ipso die paschae migrauit ad Dominum; et mox, peracto pascha, hoc est septima iduum Maiarum die, Osric rex Nordanhymbrorum uita decessit, cum ipse regni successorem fore Ceoluulfum dcreuisset, fratrem illius qui ante se regnauerat Coenredi regis, cuius regni et principia et processus tot ac tantis redundauere rerum aduersantium motibus ut, quid de his scribi bebeat quemue habitura sint finem singula, necdum sciri ualet

'In the year of our Lord 729 two comets appeared around the sun, striking great terror into all beholders.[46] One of them preceded the sun as it rose in the morning and the other followed it as it set at night, seeming to portend dire disaster to east and west alike. One comet was the forerunner of the day and the other of the night, to indicate that mankind was threatened by calamities both by day and by night. They had fiery torch-like trains which faced northwards as if poised to start a fire. They appeared in the month of January and remained for almost a fortnight. At this time a terrible plague of Saracens ravaged Gaul with cruel bloodshed and not long afterwards they received the due reward of their treachery in

---

towards the end of May, a strange star was seen, shining with a long trail of light for many nights. Also one day in this same year there was an ebb-tide which was everywhere lower than any man remembered before; so people went riding and walking across the Thames to the east of the London Bridge. In this year there were very strong winds in the month of October, but exceptionally violent on the night of 18 November, and left a trail of damage everywhere in woods and villages. Also in this year the king gave the archbishopric of Canterbury to Ralph who had been bishop of Rochester, and Thomas, the archbishop of York, passed away, and Thurstan succeeded him; he had formerly been the king's chaplain ....'.

[46] According to Schove, one comet was first noted in January and was seen for three weeks. It is likely that we are dealing here with the appearance of one comet. Schove, *Chronology*, p. 134.

the same kingdom. In the same year the holy man of God, Ecgberth, went to be with the Lord on Easter Day as has already been described; and soon after Easter, on 9 May, Osric, King of the Northumbrians, departed this life when he had reigned eleven years, after appointing Ceolwulf, brother of his predecessor Cenred, as his successor. Both the beginning and the course of his reign have been filled with so many and such serious commotions and setbacks that it is as yet impossible to know what to say about them or to guess what the outcome will be'.[47]

Despite the length and detail of this entry, there is no independent record of a comet in 729 in any annals. Harrison thinks that the comet, which is called Bede's comet, is actually the one which appeared in 730. The *ASC*'s references to comets in the entries for 678 and 729 derive from Bede's *Historia ecclesiastica*, and are not recorded elsewhere, apart from MSS D, E and F of the *ASC*.[48] Since comets did really appear in 676 and 730, one might suggest that Bede intentionally altered the dates in order to stress their function as *dirae cladis praesagae*, which confirmed the momentous nature of the events following their appearance.

The earliest authentic observation of a comet in the *ASC* is the one recorded in May 891 during the reign of Alfred the Great. The record is peculiar to MS A (CCCC MS 173) where one scribe copied up to the end of 891, and a second continued the annal for 891 on the top of the next page with a description of the appearance of a comet, but failed to delete the year number 892 already written on the previous page:

7 þy ilcan geare ofer Eastron. ymbe 'gang' dagas oþþe ær, æt eowde se steorra þe mon on boc læden hæt cometa, same men cwepaþ on Englisc þæt hit sie feaxede steorra. forþæm þær stent lang leoma of, hwilum on ane healfe, hwilum on ælce healfe.[49]

'And the same year after Easter, after the Rogation days or before, there appeared the star which is called in Latin *cometa*. Some men say that it is in English the long-haired star, for there shines a long ray from it, sometimes on one side, sometimes on every side.'

According to Simon Keynes, the second scribe, aware of the Viking invasion which occurred in 892, intended the comet to be seen as a portent and allowed the connection to remain unchanged.[50] The account shows the annalist's interest in the celestial phenomenon; he provides the name in Latin and its meaning in the vernacular. Alfred Smyth argues that, notwithstanding these details, ' ... there is, even here, a slight vagueness as to the precise time of year that the phenomenon occurred and this may suggest that, yet again, an event of the past – albeit the recent past – is being described. This would fit with a chronicle compiled in 896 or soon after'.[51]

Sometimes phenomena in the *ASC* are seen as portents or as a sort of divine punishment and are used by God to express his own emotions, which are generally negative. A good example is the appearance of a comet in 975:

MS A *7 þa wearð æt ywed uppe on roderum steorra on staðole, þone stiðferhþe, hæleð hige gleawe, hatað wide cometa be naman, cræft gleawe men, wise (S)(w)oðboran. Wæs geond wer ðeode. Waldendes wracu. wide gefrege hungor ofer hrusan.*

'Then was also revealed up in the skies a star in the firmament, which men firm of spirit, wise in mind, skilled in science, wise truth-bearers, far and wide call comet by name. The vengeance of the Ruler was manifested widely through all the people, a famine over the earth.'[52]

All phenomena were generated from the Creator and used according to His own will. Knowledge of natural phenomena was for the Anglo-Saxons a way to understand God's creation. To this end awareness of natural science, astronomy and meteorology became of paramount importance for them.

There were various comets, some visible in England and others visible abroad and reported in other medieval annals, which the Anglo-Saxon chroniclers failed to register (years 451, 530, 607, 684, 760, 837, 912, 989 and 1018).[53] One suspects that they were not mentioned in the *Chronicle* because no negative events were significant enough to be recorded for those years.

[47] *HE* V.22, pp. 556-8. This is generally called Bede's comet; see Harrison, 'The beginning of the year in England c. 500-900', *ASE* 2 (1973), 51-70, at 67.
[48] MSS D, E and F *AN. dccxxix. Her atewoden twegen cometan. 7þi ilcan geare Osric forðferde seo wæs .xi. winter cining, 7 seo halga Ecgbriht in Ii. Þa feng Ceowulf to rice 7 heold .viii. gear*; 'In this year two comets appeared; and the same year Osric, who had been king eleven years, died, and the holy Egbert died in Iona. Then Ceowulf succeeded to the kingdom and held it eight years'.
[49] This comet is also mentioned in the Latin version of MS F.
[50] S. Keynes, 'The comet in the Eadwine Psalter', in *The Eadwine Psalter: text, image and monastic culture in twelfth-century Canterbury*, ed. M. Gibson, T. A. Heslop and R. W. Pfaff (London, 1992), pp. 157-63.
[51] Smyth, 'The solar eclipse', p. 200.
[52] The account in MS F reads: *Her Eadgar cing forþerde, 7 Eadward his sunu feng to rice; 7 ðis ylcan geares on hærfæst atywde cometa se steorra, 7 on ða æftran geare com swyþe mycel hunger 7 swyðe manifealde styrunga geond Angelcynn; 7 Ælfere ealdermann het towyrpon mani numeclif þe Eadgar cing het þone haligan biscop Aðelwold gestaðelian*; 'In this year King Edgar died and his son Edward succeeded to the kingdom. And soon in the same year in harvest time there appeared the star "comet", and in the next year there came a very great famine and very manifold disturbances throughout England. And ealdorman Ælfhere caused to be destroyed many monastic foundations which king Edgar had ordered the holy bishop Æthelwold to institute'.
[53] See Schove, *Chronology*.

The association of a comet with the death of a grand person is a standard idea from classical and Latin literature onwards. The 'scientific' works of many Fathers of the Church contain descriptions of a comet's appearance together with its name and meaning. Its function as a bad omen was known to Bede, Ælfric and Byrhtferth. Bede describes comets in the following way:

> *Cometae sunt stellae flammis crinitae, repente nascentes, regni mutationem aut pestilentiam aut bella, uel uentos eastusue, portendentes. Quarum aliae mouentur errantium modo, aliae immobiles haerent. Omnes ferme sub ipso septentrione, aliqua eius parte non certa sed maxime in candida quae lactei circuli nomen accepit. Breuissimus quo cernerentur spatium septem dierum adnotatum est, longissimus lxxx. Sparguntur aliquando et errantibus stellis ceterisque crines. Sed cometes numquam in occasura parte caeli est.*

'Comets are stars with flames like hair. They are born suddenly, portending a change of royal power or plague or wars or winds or heat. Some of these move in the manner of the planets, others remain immobile. Almost all are found towards the North, not in any particular part of it, but chiefly in the radiant part which takes the name of the Milky Way. The briefest period of time that they have been observed is seven days, the longest is eighty. Hairy tails are sometimes found scattered upon the planets and the other stars. But a comet is never found in the western part of the sky.'[54]

A similar view is expressed by Byrhtferth:

> *An steorra ys genemned cometa; þonne he ætywð, þonne getacnað he hungor oððe cwealm oððe gefeoht oððe tostencednyss þæs eardes oððe egeslice windas*

'A certain star is called a comet; when it appears, it foreshadows famine, pestilence, war, the earth's destruction or terrifying winds'[55]

Bede as well as his predecessors undoubtedly believed in the prognosticative function of a comet. This well established idea of *cometae sunt stellae flammis crinitae, repente nascentes, regni mutationem aut pestilentiam aut bella, uel uentos eastusue, portendentes* is clearly expressed in the *Anglo-Saxon Chronicle* and visual depictions of comets occur in Anglo-Saxon and Anglo-Norman art and poetry. The best-known example is the comet which appears in the 32nd scene in the *Bayeux Tapestry*, where the caption is *Isti mirant stella*, 'they marvelled at the star'. At Easter 1066 a comet, identified as Halley's, terrified the Western world, and in the *Tapestry* the English are seen pointing and marvelling at the star. Someone comes to tell Harold who inclines his head to hear what the comet portends and has a vision of ships.[56] As for the account of Halley's Comet in the *ASC*, Thomas A. Bredehoft notes that:

> In annal 1066 CD, there are great tokens in the heavens (including Halley's Comet) *swylce nam mann ær ne geseh* ('such as no man had seen before'). Here the juxtaposition of natural events (the appearance of a comet) with the political and martial upheavals of 1066 suggests the comet itself (in the Chronicle's use of this trope) takes the greater portion of its significance as a betokening of significant human, political events than from its status as natural phenomenon.[57]

There is a more perplexing illustration of a comet in the *Eadwine Psalter*, in the lower margin of fol. 10, accompanied by a note in Old English which says:

> *Be cometa þam steorran. Ðillicne leoman hæft cometa steorra 7 on englics hine man nemð se feaxeda steorra he hine ætywð ymbe fela wintra 7 þonne for fortacne*

'The star comet has a ray such as this, and in English is called the long-haired star. It appears rarely during the course of the year, and then as a portent'

Simon Keynes says that 'the lore which it contains represents no more (and not much less) than the sum total of the understanding of comets which would have been readily available to an interested person in the late Anglo-Saxon period'.[58] The *Psalter*'s reference to this comet (probably Halley's Comet, which arrived in the spring of 1145) has enabled scholars to date the manuscript to the mid-1140s.[59] Many other Anglo-Saxon illuminated

---

[54] Bede, *De natura rerum*, xxiiii; *Bede On the Nature of Things and on Times*, trans. C. B. Kendall and F. Wallis (Liverpool, 2010), p. 89. Bede is relying here, among other sources, on Isidore's *De natura rerum*. See *De natura rerum: Traité de la nature*, ed. with French trans. J. Fontaine (1960, repr. Paris, 2002), xxvi.13; p. 213. For a discussion on comets as portents, see Bremmer and Chardonnens, 'Old English prognostics', pp. 157-60.

[55] *Byrhtferth's Enchiridion*, ed. M. Lapidge and P. S. Baker, EETS ss 15 (Oxford, 1995), pp. 120-21. See also Ælfric's account of comets: *Comête sind gehatene þa steorra ðe færlice 7 ungewunelice æteowiað. 7 sind geleômode swa þæt him gæð of se leôma swilce oðer sunbeam hi ne beoð na lange hwile gesewene ac swa oft swa hi æteowiað hi gebicniað sum ðing niwes toweard þære leode ðe hi ofer scinað; Ælfric's De temporibus anni*, ed. H. Henel, EETS os 213 (London, 1942), p. 70. 'Comets is the name given to those stars which unexpectedly and strangely appear, and are so radiant that light comes off them like a second sunlight. They are

not seen for long, but whenever they appear they signify something new towards the land over which they shine'; *Ælfric's De temporibus anni*, ed. and trans. M. Blake (Cambridge, 2009), p. 93.

[56] *The Bayeux Tapestry*, ed. D. M. Wilson (London, 2004), Plate 32.

[57] T. A. Bredehoft, 'History and memory in the *Anglo-Saxon Chronicle*', in *Readings in Medieval Texts. Interpreting Old and Middle English Literature*, ed. D. Johnson and E. Treharne (Oxford, 2005), pp. 109-21 at 118.

[58] S. Keynes, 'The comet in the Eadwine Psalter', p. 157.

[59] *Catalogue of Dated and Datable Manuscripts c. 737-1600 in*

manuscripts are rich in representations of comets, especially Psalters and versions of the Psalms.[60]

Biblical terminology used in the Anglo-Saxon Chronicle to refer to 'heavenly' happenings

Solar and lunar eclipses, comets and other astronomical phenomena also occur quite frequently in the Bible and other sacred books. In particular, *The Revelation of St John* mentions most of the astronomical occurrences cited in the *Chronicle*. This final book of the Bible was for Christians a reliable guide to the heavenly signs announcing the Last Judgment, and the chroniclers regularly draw on its phraseology to describe portents in the *ASC*. Some examples follow:

Rev. vi: 12: 'the Sun became black' and 'the Moon became as blood' (*luna facta est sicut sanguinis*).[61]

The *ASC* always has *sunne aþiestrode* (Lat. *oscurari*); the noun *eclipsis* is never used.

Se mona swelce he wære mid blode appears in 734 and in Bede's *Anno DCCXXXIIII luna sanguineo rubore perfusa quasi hora integra*.

Rev. vi: 13: 'The stars fell unto the earth' (*stellae ceciderunt super terram*).

ASC has *steorran foran swyðe cotienda* in 744;

Rev. viii: 10: 'And then a fell a great star from the heaven burning as it was a lamp' (*cecidit de caelo stella magna ardens tamquam facula*).

HE 729: *Anno dominicae incarnationis DCCXXVIIII apparuerunt cometae duae circa solem ... Portabant autem facem ignis contra aquilonem, quasi ad accendendum adclinem*. 'In the year of our Lord 729 two comets appeared around the sun ... They had fiery torch-like trains which faced northwards as if poised to start a fire'.

Rev. ix: 1: 'A star fell from heaven into earth' (*stellam de caelo cecidisse*).

ASC MS E (1095): has *mæni fealdlice steorran of heofenan feollan*. 'very many stars falling from the sky'.

Rev. xii: 3: 'Great Dragon' (*draco magnus*).

ASC MSS E, F (793): *fyrene dracan*.

Rev. xii: 9: 'Serpents'(*serpentes*).

ASC MS A (773): *wunderleca nædran*.

ASC MS E (774): *wundorlice nædran*.[62]

It is thus clear that the chroniclers' prognosticatory interpretation of natural phenomena makes use of the Bible, from which they borrowed some expressions to refer to celestial events, as well as classical scientific tracts on astronomy and *computus* from which they took their knowledge of prognostics.

Conclusion

Natural phenomena are noted in the *ASC* from the ninth to the twelfth centuries, without any interruption, reflecting the sustained interest and knowledge of Anglo-Saxon monks in astronomy. The chroniclers seem to have assumed a level of familiarity in the audience. A striking feature of the Chronicles' description of eclipses, and of natural phenomena, is its 'accuracy'. Long passages are devoted to descriptions of solar and lunar eclipses, comets and marvellous signs in the sky, while the death of a bishop or a king, or a battle against an invading army is generally dealt with in a single line. It is likely that these phenomena were regarded by contemporary observers as portents which were linked to historical events. Bede and the chroniclers of the *ASC* seem to have been ready to adapt the date of some events in order to validate the phenomena as prognostics. This readiness to bring a particular political or historical event into suggestive relation with the appearance of a sign (as it now becomes) in the sky demonstrates that sometimes the prognostic properties of natural phenomena were stronger than the chroniclers' respect for chronological exactitude.

Since some natural phenomena were interpreted as warnings of events in the world of men, the prognostic qualities of the Chronicle demonstrate a morality, a warning of the limitation to the power of rulers: a king can control a whole country and decide about taxes and wars, but cannot avoid mortality.

Cambridge Libraries, ed. P. R. Robinson, 2 vols (Woodbridge, 1988), I, p. 99; Keynes, 'The comet in the Eadwine Psalter', p. 157.
[60] For a detailed list of manuscripts which depict stars, see *Insular and Anglo-Saxon Illuminated Manuscripts: an iconographic catalogue c. A. D. 625 to 1100*, ed. T. H. Ohlgren (New York, 1986).
[61] *The Revelation of St John*, intr. and comm. C. L. Morris (London, 1969), p. 110.

[62] Ibid., pp. 111-56.

Index

Places are located by their current country or, if English or Scottish, by county

www.ingramcontent.com/pod-product-compliance
Lightning Source LLC
Chambersburg PA
CBHW061008030426
42334CB00033B/3412